Taking Stock of Programs to Develop Socioemotional Skills

DIRECTIONS IN DEVELOPMENT
Human Development

Taking Stock of Programs to Develop Socioemotional Skills

A Systematic Review of Program Evidence

Maria Laura Sánchez Puerta, Alexandria Valerio, and
Marcela Gutiérrez Bernal

WORLD BANK GROUP

1 2 3 4 19 18 17 16

ISBN (paper): 978-1-4648-0872-2
ISBN (electronic): 978-1-4648-0873-9
DOI:10.1596/978-1-4648-0872-2

Cover photo: © Susanne Riber Christensen/Getty Images. Used with permission. Further permission required for reuse.
Cover design: Debra Naylor, Naylor Design, Inc.

Library of Congress Cataloging-in-Publication Data has been requested

Contents

http://dx.doi.org/10.1596/978-1-4648-0872-2

Boxes

Figures

Tables

http://dx.doi.org/10.1596/978-1-4648-0872-2

Acknowledgments

This report was prepared by a team composed of Maria Laura Sánchez Puerta, Alexandria Valerio, and Marcela Gutiérrez Bernal from the World Bank. Claire Miller provided technical and research support, and Sergio Guerra prepared a background paper that was instrumental in the creation of the report. The team appreciates the strategic guidance and overall support received from Claudia Costin (senior director, Education Global Practice), Amit Dar (director, Education Global Practice), and Luis Benveniste (practice manager, Global Engagements, and Education Global Practice).

Helpful peer review comments were received from Margo Hoftijzer (senior economist), Ines Kudo (senior education specialist), and Victoria Levin (senior economist) from the World Bank and Laura Ripani (lead economist) from the Inter-American Development Bank. The report also incorporates inputs received from Omar Arias (lead economist, World Bank) and from participants in the technical seminars sponsored by the World Bank's Skills Global Solutions Group held in December 2015.

The team appreciates the overall assistance of Lorelei Lacdao, Fahma Nur, and Marie Madeleine Ndaw from the World Bank. The written pieces contained within this review were edited by Marc DeFrancis.

The report received financial support from the Skills and Information, Communication, and Technology (ICT) Trust Fund of the Government of the Republic of Korea.

http://dx.doi.org/10.1596/978-1-4648-0872-2

About the Authors

Maria Laura Sánchez Puerta is a senior economist in the Jobs Group of the Social Protection and Labor Global Practice at the World Bank, where she specializes in the intersection of labor and development economics. She currently leads the jobs and skills agenda and coleads the global STEP initiative, which includes household and employer surveys measuring adult skills in 17 countries. She prepared one of the first job diagnostics at the country level and contributed to an innovative, multisector work program on jobs in Kenya.

Maria Laura's research includes cognitive and noncognitive skills and labor outcomes; design, implementation, and evaluation of active labor market programs; income mobility in Latin America; informality and labor market segmentation; and the effects of globalization on working conditions. Maria Laura has also supported analytical and operational work in Argentina, Brazil, Cambodia, Colombia, El Salvador, Indonesia, Kenya, Lebanon, Rwanda, and Tunisia.

Maria Laura holds a PhD in economics from Cornell University and joined the Institute for the Study of Labor (IZA) as a research fellow in 2007.

Alexandria Valerio has over 20 years of experience leading and managing large-scale research projects, multidisciplinary teams, and senior-level client relationships, with a policy focus on education reform (early, primary, and tertiary education), entrepreneurship, skills, and training in diverse country contexts. She has led multidisciplinary teams in the analysis, design, implementation, and evaluation of investment operations. Alexandria is currently leading global research agendas focused on measuring adult skills using large-scale household and employer surveys in 17 countries, analyzing the impact of different types of education and skill sets on employment and development outcomes, and identifying the characteristics of effective entrepreneurship education and training programs.

Prior to joining the Global Engagement and Knowledge unit in the Education Global Practice, she was responsible for the World Bank's education policy dialogue and lending portfolios in the Latin America and the Caribbean Region (Argentina, Brazil, Chile, Nicaragua, Paraguay and Panama), as well as in Angola and Mozambique.

Alexandria`s work extends beyond the education sector, covering a wide range of issues including social protection and labor, jobs, growth and competitiveness, child development, and school health. Her published work includes peer-reviewed books and papers on workforce development policy, technical and vocational training, entrepreneurship training, tools to measure skills in adult populations, cost and financing of early childhood education, social impact analysis of school fees, and school health programs to prevent HIV/AIDS in school-age populations. She is currently a global lead for the World Bank's Skills Global Solutions Group and a core member of the global interagency group on Technical Vocational Education and Training/Skills and the technical working group on Human Resource Development for the G-20.

Alexandria holds a PhD in comparative education and economics of education from Columbia University and a master's degree in public administration in economic development policy from the Maxwell School at Syracuse University.

Marcela Gutiérrez Bernal has five years of experience designing, implementing, and evaluating social programs in more than 10 countries in Latin America, Asia, the Middle East, and the Western Balkans. Her areas of work include poverty reduction and social protection systems, conditional and emergency cash transfer programs, financial inclusion initiatives, and early childhood development strategies. She worked with the World Bank Group as a project coordinator of the STEP Skills Measurement Program, the first-ever initiative to measure cognitive and socioemotional skills in more than 16 developing countries. She also worked as a senior adviser to the Ministry of Social Protection and Inclusion in Peru. Previously, she was employed at the Inter-American Development Bank, where she assisted in the ideation, execution, assessment, and continuous improvement of government programs and strategies in Colombia and Panama.

Marcela is currently pursuing a master's degree in public administration and international development at Harvard University. She holds MA and BA degrees in economics from Universidad de los Andes (Bogotá, Colombia) and a BA in business administration.

http://dx.doi.org/10.1596/978-1-4648-0872-2

Executive Summary

Relevance

Possessing a range of cognitive, socioemotional, and technical skills is important for individuals to maximize their chances of success in many aspects of life. In particular, a growing body of research highlights the effects that socioemotional skills have on a variety of outcomes, from wages and academic performance to health. Programs to help participants develop such skills continue to expand in both high-income and lower-income countries, targeting individuals of almost all ages and life stages. Socioemotional skills development is embedded in programs as diverse as early-childhood nutrition programs for adolescent mothers, K–12 academic curricula, and workforce training programs for vulnerable adults.

However, the characteristics that make some programs more successful than others—or even what types of outcomes programs use to measure "success"—are less clear in the literature. This analysis seeks to fill this knowledge gap through a systemic review of socioemotional skills development programs. It uses a new conceptual framework to examine diverse programs that have been rigorously evaluated to answer the following research questions:

- What is the existing landscape of socioemotional skills development programs?
- How do these programs measure success?
- What do we know about programs that work?

Conceptual Framework

To categorize the wide range of socioemotional program objectives, this analysis breaks down programs by where they occur, program characteristics, participant characteristics, and outcomes measured. Only programs with randomized or quasi-randomized evaluations are included. The programs in this review are divided into three categories, on the basis of when they are implemented in the life cycle: (a) before-school programs (infants and young children), (b) school-based programs (preschool to secondary education), and (c) out-of-school programs (usually targeted, vulnerable populations). Next, the review assesses programs by their specific characteristics: objectives, components and complementary elements, setting, and quality. It also classifies programs by participant profiles, including ages of participants and participant-targeting systems. Importantly, the review further assesses programs by their outcomes. Although all programs emphasize socioemotional skills development, they present a wide variety of outcome indicators used to measure success. Reported outcomes are classified into four broad categories: (a) health related, (b) risk factor related, (c) academic/cognitive related, and (d) economic related.

Methodology

Within each of the three life-cycle stages, we identified potential studies and programs from relevant databases, online resources, and experts; screened them in order to include only studies that were written in English after the year 2000, that included randomized or quasi-randomized control trials, that had sufficient sample sizes, and that reported information on standard errors; and determined which papers and follow-ups on the same program were most relevant and were analyzed using the most rigorous approaches.

For programs that targeted children before they entered school, the review includes 21 programs, 42 percent of which were conducted in low- or middle-income countries. They included follow-up periods ranging from three months to 37 years. For school-based programs, the review includes 45 programs, 10 percent of which came from low- and middle-income countries, with follow-up from nine weeks to six years. For out-of-school programs, the review includes 20 programs, 75 percent of which took place in low- and middle-income countries; follow-up periods ranged from less than two weeks to four years (most less than one year).

Key Findings

Before-school programs typically target children younger than age five and tend to focus not only on children but also on their families. Most before-school programs measure outcomes related to academics (such as academic performance and graduation rates) or risk factors (such as criminal activity); smaller percentages measured health and economic outcomes.

School-based programs target a broad range of grades (prekindergarten through 12th grade), often through classroom curricula that usually follow a yearly sequence, that have grade-specific content, and that tend to include all children attending an institution. Of the 45 sample programs, few included curricula for an entire system of prekindergarten through 12th grade, and most focused on lower grades, rather than explicitly targeting adolescents. Most of the school-based programs (59 percent) measured outcomes related to risk factors (such as behavioral variables like aggression toward peers and cooperation); 32 percent measured academic-related outcomes. Few evaluated economic and health outcomes.

Out-of-school programs typically promote skills formation in teenage and adult populations who are not enrolled in, and may not have completed, formal education. Out-of-school programs with socioemotional skills components have a

http://dx.doi.org/10.1596/978-1-4648-0872-2

range of objectives, such as helping individuals find jobs or decreasing gender-based violence. Socioemotional skills development is usually only one part of a larger set of outcomes. The programs surveyed targeted ages ranging from 10 to 55 years, but most focused on working-age teenagers and adults, especially those between ages 16 and 30. Labor market outcomes were the goal of about 75 percent of the programs included in this review.

Most successful programs teach socioemotional skills as an embedded component of a broader curriculum that includes active pedagogical, classroom, and training programs:

- Among before-school programs in particular, programs with multiple components that target health, cognitive development, and emotional development tend to yield greater and longer-term results. In addition, the type of curriculum followed affects the program's effectiveness; most desirable are curricula where children plan, carry out, and review their own activities while engaging in active learning, or where teachers respond to children's self-initiated play in loosely structured, socially supportive settings. Programs that have more qualified staff and that are implemented with greater intensity and fidelity exhibit greater effects.
- Successful school-based programs tend to follow the SAFE approach, that is, they are sequenced, active, focused, and explicit. Programs that take a whole-school approach and prioritize implementation fidelity tend to be more successful. Programs that were integrated into the school day tended to demonstrate more success than after-school programs.
- Such findings stress the value of developing socioemotional skills in coordination with other types of skills, as part of a comprehensive, intertwined curriculum—rather than offering separate, stand-alone socioemotional skills "modules."

Programs are particularly effective when they target vulnerable populations and, in particular, young children:

- Before-school programs appear to have a greater impact than those that take place later in life. However, these early-childhood programs also tend to be more intensive, more targeted toward vulnerable populations, more likely to involve family members, and have longer follow-up periods.
- Most school-based programs tend to be universal and offered to all children; whereas evidence on the impact of these programs is more mixed, the greatest effects appear to be on risk factors (such as externalizing or internalizing behavior or aggression toward peers) among vulnerable populations.
- A number of out-of-school programs observed small but statistically significant impacts on economic outcomes, such as employment, participation in the formal job sector, number of hours worked weekly, and earnings. However, overall evidence on the programs' effect on employment levels and quality is mixed. Most programs appear to work better for younger participants, for females, and when implemented in urban areas.

http://dx.doi.org/10.1596/978-1-4648-0872-2

School-based and out-of-school programs need longer follow-up periods and more clarity on proxies used to evaluate socioemotional skills as outcomes:

- Whereas over one-third of before-school programs included a follow-up period of 10 years or more, only 3 percent of school-based programs and no out-of-school programs did so. Thus, any potential effects of these programs can be observed only over a short time, and the longevity of any positive outcomes is uncertain.
- Although programs explicitly target socioemotional skills development, few explicitly state exactly what socioemotional skills they intend to improve. In addition, most impact evaluations do not measure the skills that the program seeks to alter. Future research should include skills assessment in order to measure these outcomes more directly.

http://dx.doi.org/10.1596/978-1-4648-0872-2

Abbreviations

4Rs	reading, writing, respect, and resolution (program, United States)
ASQ	Ages and Stages Questionnaire
CARE	character actualization requires education (program, United States)
CSE	cognitive-social-emotional
DAS	developmental assessment session
DPII	Developmental Profile II
ECD	early childhood development
ELA	Empowerment and Livelihood for Adolescents (program, Uganda)
EPAG	Economic Empowerment of Adolescent Girls (program, Liberia)
ERIC	Education Resources Information Center
GED	General Educational Development
GPA	grade point average
HIPPY	Home Instruction Program for Preschool Youngsters (program, United States)
HIV/AIDS	human immunodeficiency virus/ acquired immune deficiency syndrome
ICPS	I Can Problem Solve (program, United States)
ICT	information and communication technology
IQ	intelligence quotient
ISFP	Iowa Strengthening Families Program (United States)
KIPP	Knowledge Is Power Program (United States)
LEAD	Leadership Education Through Athletic Development (program, United States)
LIFT	Linking the Interests of Families and Teachers (program, United States)
MAPs	Mindful Awareness Practices (program, United States)
NICHHD	National Institute of Child Health and Human Development Early Child Care Research Network
NOW	New Opportunities for Women (program, Jordon)

OECD	Organisation for Economic Co-operation and Development
PALS	Play and Learning Strategies (program, United States)
PAT	Parents as Teachers (program, United States)
PATHS	Promoting Alternative Thinking Strategies (program, United States)
PDFY	Preparing for the Drug Free Years (program, United States)
PEF	Peace Education Foundation
PIDI	Proyecto Integral de Desarrollo Infantil (program, Bolivia)
PPVT	Peabody Picture Vocabulary Test
RCT	randomized control trial
SAFE	sequenced, active, focused, and explicit; Strategies Aimed at Family Empowerment (program, United States)
SEAL	Social and Emotional Aspects of Learning (program, United Kingdom)
SEL	social and emotional learning
SET	Social and Emotional Training (program, Sweden)
SF	Strengthening Families (program, United States)
STAR	Student/Teacher Achievement Ratio (program, United States)
TEEP	Turkish Early Enrichment Program
UNESCO	United Nations Educational, Scientific, and Cultural Organization
UNICEF	United Nations Children's Fund
WHO	World Health Organization

http://dx.doi.org/10.1596/978-1-4648-0872-2

CHAPTER 1

Motivation and Objectives

Recent literature has shown that a combination of cognitive, socioemotional and technical or job-related skills is a stepping-stone for success. According to the Organisation for Economic Co-operation and Development (OECD 2012), poorly skilled individuals are at higher risk of economic disadvantages, unemployment, and long-term reliance on social benefits. Those findings are consistent with the research of Heckman, Pinto, and Savelyev (2013), who identify cognitive, socioemotional and job-related skills as having an important effect on life outcomes. Similarly, Cunha and others (2005) find that wages, schooling, criminality, and teenage pregnancy are affected by cognitive ability, perseverance, motivation, self-control, self-esteem, and risk and time preferences.

A robust literature documents the effects of cognitive skills on a range of economic and life outcomes, yet comparatively less information is available on the effects of socioemotional skills on similar outcomes. The lack of information has prompted a new line of academic inquiry that examines the role of socioemotional skills in a range of outcomes. Interestingly, recent literature indicates that noncognitive or social skills mediate cognitive performance, educational attainment, behavior, health, and labor market outcomes (Carneiro, Crawford, and Goodman 2007; Heckman, Stixrud, and Urzua 2006).[1] Research from Durlak and others (2011) shows that the lack of socioemotional competencies, together with the lack of connection to the schooling environment, can harm academic performance, behavior, and health.[2] Finally, research has also found that noncognitive or personality skills rival IQ in predicting educational attainment, labor market success, health, and criminality.[3]

From a public policy perspective, socioemotional skills have gained importance as they might offer policy makers an unexplored opportunity to improve individual life outcomes and strengthen workforce productivity. More important, these skills deserve careful attention for several reasons. First, unlike cognition,[4] they may be malleable throughout the life cycle (Almlund and others 2011; Boyatzis 2008; Cherniss and others 1998; Goleman 2000). The exact duration of that malleability is debated. For example, Heckman and Carneiro (2003)

http://dx.doi.org/10.1596/978-1-4648-0872-2

indicate that although cognitive skills are set by age 8, noncognitive skills can be modified until the late teenage years; others contend that personality traits are set by age 30 (Costa and McCrae 1990, 1994, 2006; James 1890; McCrae and Costa 2003). Yet other researchers, including Walsh (2005), indicate that, given the slow development of the prefrontal cortex, socioemotional skills remain malleable even after age 30.

Second, investments in socioemotional skills can foster equity and promote social mobility, economic growth, social cohesion, and general well-being. Research indicates that given the positive associations found between socioemotional skills and labor market outcomes, improving these skills could lead to greater equity (Hartas 2011). Since skill formation promotes employability and employment, skills can pave the way for expanding economic growth. Ultimately, skill formation can promote social cohesion, that is, the capacity of societies to manage collective decision making (World Bank 2012). Finally, as the following chapters will show, socioemotional skills increase the well-being of the population, as individuals increase their optimism levels, improve their self-concepts, and form healthier relationships, among other outcomes.

Despite the increasing importance of the role of socioemotional skills, little systematized and rigorous (experimental) evidence exists documenting the effectiveness of programs that seek to develop these skills throughout the life cycle. The lack of information constrains the policy dialogue with client countries seeking evidence and programs to foster socioemotional skills.

This systematic review[5] aims to fill an important knowledge gap by distilling existing evidence and offering a menu of program approaches to develop key socioemotional skills to influence important life outcomes. This review contributes to the existing literature on socioemotional skills by identifying and organizing programs using a new conceptual framework. The review includes a number of diverse programs that have been rigorously evaluated and that seek to effect different outcomes in multiple contexts, including in developing countries. The inclusion of developing countries is important, as most of the accumulated evidence comes from programs implemented in developed countries where constraints and context may be different from those in developing countries and, thus, could potentially mediate outcomes differently.

In an effort to generate robust policy advice from proven programs, the review casts a narrow net by considering evidence only from programs that had randomized or quasi-randomized evaluations. All of the evaluations analyzed in this review include the information needed to calculate the statistical significance of the effect sizes. The program descriptions (such as components, target populations, objectives, intensity, and costs) were collected from published or publicly available evaluation documents, as an analysis of administrative data was beyond the scope of this review.

The review focuses on programs that are preventive in nature. They include programs that target universal and primarily young populations, as well as programs that aim to prevent negative behaviors largely among at-risk youth. Other important programs, such as those that fight recidivism

http://dx.doi.org/10.1596/978-1-4648-0872-2

among adults with criminal histories, substance dependence, or other clinical conditions, are beyond the scope of this review and are excluded from the analysis even if they have important components of socioemotional skill formation.

Notes

1. Carneiro, Crawford, and Goodman (2007) refer to noncognitive or social skills and measure them using the Bristol Social Adjustment Guides, which capture social maladjustment. Heckman, Stixrud, and Urzua (2006) discuss noncognitive skills and measure them using Rotter's locus of control scale and Rosenberg's self-esteem scale.
2. In their meta-analysis of socioemotional learning programs, the authors include six different outcomes: (a) social and emotional skills, which include "different types of cognitive, affective, and social skills related to such areas as identifying emotions from social cues, goal setting, perspective taking, interpersonal problem solving, conflict resolution and decision making" (Durlak and others 2011, 410); (b) attitudes toward self, school, and social topics; (c) positive social daily behaviors, including getting along with others; (d) conduct problems, such as disruptive class behavior, noncompliance, aggression, bullying, and delinquency, among others; (e) emotional distress, including depression and anxiety; and (f) academic performance.
3. Heckman and Kautz (2012) measure noncognitive skills, including self-reports, teacher reports, or behaviors that relate directly to these skills (externalizing and internalizing behavior, dysregulated aggression, creativity, verbal intelligence, hostility, beliefs and attitudes, impulse control, dependency, self-esteem, and self-efficacy, among others). Almlund and others (2011) measure personality and traits, such as trust, reciprocity, risk aversion, and the Big Five (openness to experience, conscientiousness, extraversion, agreeableness, and neuroticism). Borghans and others (2008) measure personality using the Big Five factors.
4. Almlund and others (2011) state that cognition becomes stable around age 10.
5. We adopt the definition of *systematic review* coined by Waddington and others (2012, 360): "studies which synthesise all the existing high-quality evidence using transparent methods to give the best possible, generalisable statements about what is known. ... [A] systematic review has a clear protocol for systematically searching defined databases over a defined time period, with transparent criteria for the inclusion or exclusion of studies."

References

Almlund, Mathilde, Angela Lee Duckworth, James J. Heckman, and Tim D. Kautz. 2011. "Personality Psychology and Economics." NBER Working Paper 16822, National Bureau of Economic Research, Cambridge, MA.

Borghans, Lex, Angela Lee Duckworth, James J. Heckman, and Bas ter Weel. 2008. "The Economics and Psychology of Personality Traits." *Journal of Human Resources* 43 (4): 972–1059.

Boyatzis, Richard E. 2008. "Leadership Development from a Complexity Perspective." *Consulting Psychology Journal: Practice and Research* 60 (4): 298–313.

http://dx.doi.org/10.1596/978-1-4648-0872-2

Carneiro, Pedro, Claire Crawford, and Alissa Goodman. 2007. "The Impact of Early Cognitive and Non-Cognitive Skills on Later Outcomes." Discussion Paper 0092, Centre for the Economics of Education, London School of Economics.

Cherniss, Cary, Daniel Goleman, Robert Emmerling, Kim Cowan, and Mitchel Adler. 1998. "Bringing Emotional Intelligence to the Workplace." Consortium for Research on Emotional Intelligence in Organizations, Rutgers University, New Brunswick, NJ.

Costa, Paul T. Jr., and Robert R. McCrae. 1990. "Personality Disorders and the Five-Factor Model of Personality." *Journal of Personality Disorders* 4 (4): 362–71.

———. 1994. "Set Like Plaster? Evidence for the Stability of Adult Personality." In *Can Personality Change?*, edited by Todd F. Heatherton and Joel Lee Weinberger, 21–40. Washington, DC: American Psychological Association.

———. 2006. "Age Changes in Personality and Their Origins: Comment on Roberts, Walton, and Viechtbauer." *Psychological Bulletin* 132 (1): 26–28.

Cunha, Flavio, James J. Heckman, Lance Lochner, and Dimitriy V. Masterov. 2005. "Interpreting the Evidence on Life Cycle Skill Formation." In *Handbook of the Economics of Education*, vol. 1, edited by Eric A. Hanushek and Finis Welch, 697–812. Amsterdam and New York: North-Holland.

Durlak, Joseph A., Roger Weissberg, Allison Dymnicki, Rebecca Taylor, and Kriston Schellinger. 2011. "The Impact of Enhancing Students' Social and Emotional Learning: A Meta-Analysis of School-Based Universal Programs." *Child Development* 82 (1): 405–32.

Goleman, Daniel. 2000. "Leadership That Gets Results." *Harvard Business Review* March–April: 78–90.

Hartas, Dimitra. 2011. "Families' Social Backgrounds Matter: Socio-Economic Factors, Home Learning and Young Children's Language, Literacy and Social Outcomes." *British Educational Research Journal* 37 (6): 893–914.

Heckman, James, J., and Pedro Carneiro. 2003. "Human Capital Policy." NBER Working Paper 9495, National Bureau of Economic Research, Cambridge, MA.

Heckman, James J., and Tim Kautz. 2012. "Hard Evidence on Soft Skills." *Labour Economics* 19 (4): 451–64.

Heckman, James J., Rodrigo Pinto, and Peter A. Savelyev. 2013. "Understanding the Mechanisms through Which an Influential Early Childhood Program Boosted Adult Outcomes." *American Economic Review* 103 (6): 1–35.

Heckman, James J., Jora Stixrud, and Sergio Urzua. 2006. "The Effects of Cognitive and Noncognitive Abilities on Labor Market Outcomes and Social Behavior." *Journal of Labor Economics* 24 (3): 411–48.

James, William. 1890. "The Consciousness of Self." Chap. 10 in *The Principles of Psychology*. New York: Henry Holt and Company.

McCrae, Robert R., and Paul T. Costa Jr. 2003. *Personality in Adulthood: A Five-Factor Theory Perspective*. New York: Guilford Press.

OECD (Organisation for Economic Co-operation and Development). 2012. "Better Skills. Better Jobs. Better Lives: The OECD Skills Strategy." Paris, OECD. http://www.oecd.org/general/50452749.pdf.

Waddington, Hugh, Howard White, Birte Snilstveit, Jorge Garcia Hombrados, Martina Vojtkova, Philip Davies, Ami Bhavsar, John Eyers, Tracey Perez Koehlmoos, Mark Petticrew, Jeffrey C. Valentine, and Peter Tugwell. 2012. "How to Do a Good

Systematic Review of Effects in International Development: A Tool Kit." *Journal of Development Effectiveness* 4 (3): 359–87.

Walsh, David. 2005. *Why Do They Act That Way? A Survival Guide to the Adolescent Brain for You and Your Teen*. New York: Free Press.

World Bank. 2012. *World Development Report 2013: Jobs.* Washington, DC: World Bank.

http://dx.doi.org/10.1596/978-1-4648-0872-2

CHAPTER 2

Literature Review

The Relationship between Socioemotional Skills and Life Outcomes

As mentioned previously, growing evidence suggests that socioemotional skills predict a range of important life outcomes. Research from Heckman, Stixrud, and Urzua (2006) uses data from the National Longitudinal Survey of Youth in the United States and indicates that noncognitive skills (measured through Rotter's locus of control scale and Rosenberg's self-esteem scale) have a positive and strong influence on schooling decisions, employment, work experience, occupational choice, and wages, while simultaneously minimizing risky behaviors (such as smoking, participation in illegal activities, and unplanned pregnancy). Carneiro, Crawford, and Goodman (2007) find similar evidence for the United Kingdom using information from the National Child Development Survey. Their analysis shows that noncognitive or social skills (measured using the Bristol Social Adjustment Guides, which capture social maladjustment) are positively associated with important education and labor market outcomes at different follow-up periods (at ages 16, 23, and 42). For instance, individuals with higher social skills experience longer school trajectories (remaining in school beyond age 16), higher graduation rates from tertiary education (obtaining a degree by age 42), better employment opportunities and higher wages (by age 42), a greater number of months of accumulated work experience between ages 23 and 42, lower smoking rates at age 16, lower teenage pregnancy and criminality rates at ages 16 and 42, and better health at age 42.

In particular, studies that focus on the role of socioemotional skills in labor market outcomes report statistically significant effects. Using information on 5,025 graduates from Wisconsin high schools in the United States, Muller and Plug (2006) report that personality (measured using the Big Five scale) in high school had a statistically significant effect on earnings later in life. They also report that the magnitude of the effect was comparable with effects commonly generated by cognitive ability.[1] Also, Kuhn and Weinberger (2002) document that leadership skills produce higher wages for adults in the United States, even when cognitive skills are held constant. For their part, using data from Germany,

http://dx.doi.org/10.1596/978-1-4648-0872-2

Heineck and Anger (2010) find that personality traits, and especially locus of control, have an important effect on wages.[2]

Employers acknowledge the importance of socioemotional skills in the workplace. For example, using the STEP (Skills Toward Employment and Productivity) Survey in Vietnam, Bodewig and Badiani-Magnusson (2014) find that the most important skills that employers seek in blue-collar workers are job-specific technical skills, followed by behavioral and cognitive skills, such as teamwork and problem solving. With regard to white-collar workers, employers seek individuals with critical thinking, problem-solving, and communication skills. Guerra, Modecki, and Cunningham (2014) identify the following eight skill areas that employers demand (summarized as PRACTICE): (a) problem solving, (b) resilience, (c) achievement motivation, (d) control, (e) teamwork, (f) initiative, (g) confidence, and (h) ethics. According to *Job Outlook 2015* (NACE 2015), the five main attributes that employers look for on candidates' résumés are (a) leadership, (b) ability to work in a team, (c) written communication skills, (d) problem-solving skills, and (e) work ethic, all of which can fall under the realm of socioemotional skills. These are followed by analytical and quantitative skills and technical skills, which can be considered cognitive.

Evidence of Programs That Modify Socioemotional Skills

Given the accumulating evidence on the role of socioemotional skills in shaping key life outcomes, there is growing interest in gathering information on the programs that can modify these skills. For instance, Almlund and others (2011) analyze 15 programs in developed countries. Their results show that some programs can modify personality and behavior and, as such, they may be considered promising mechanisms to address poverty and disadvantage.[3] Guerra, Modecki, and Cunningham (2014) distill findings from 53 successful programs; a key finding from their analysis is that the socioemotional skills valued by employers and commonly targeted by programs that aim to improve labor market outcomes can be taught successfully when aligned with the optimal stage for skills development.

Cost-effectiveness and effects tend to be greatest in programs targeting young children. In a systematic review of 84 research reports, mostly from the United States, Lösel and Beelmann (2003) find that socioemotional skills training for individuals under age 18 can help prevent antisocial behavior, especially among at-risk students.[4] In a review of 27 programs, mostly from developed countries and covering primarily programs for young children, Kautz and others (2014) find that although programs aimed at adolescents can work, programs at early stages in life appear to be the most successful.[5] This finding is supported by research from Cunha, Heckman, and Schennach (2010), who find that the optimal stage to invest in noncognitive skills development is during early childhood.[6]

To date, most of the evidence available is for comprehensive programs that aim to develop socioemotional skills along with other types of skills and behaviors, making it sometimes difficult to disentangle results. Since most systematic reviews

http://dx.doi.org/10.1596/978-1-4648-0872-2

and meta-analyses are not limited to stand-alone programs on socioemotional skills, it is important to interpret results carefully. Such caution is especially important for programs that have not been evaluated using rigorous methodologies.

Impacts of Early Childhood Development Programs

Evaluations of early childhood programs to develop socioemotional skills, which are more readily available than programs later in life, show positive effects. For example, Baker-Henningham and López Bóo (2010) aim to identify the effectiveness of early childhood stimulation in developing countries and report that, regardless of nutritional supplementation, early stimulation benefits cognitive development. Their study is not limited to experimental or quasi-experimental evaluations and does not yield conclusive evidence on the effects of early childhood programs in developing countries on schooling, behavior, or maternal outcomes. Finally, after analyzing experimental evidence from 31 home-visiting programs for pregnant women and parents of young children, Olds and Kitzman (1993) find that not all programs work; the programs more likely to succeed are those that are comprehensive in focus, involve frequent visits and well-trained professionals, and serve at-risk families.

Impacts of School-Based Programs

School-based programs can also prove effective. Heckman, Stixrud, and Urzua (2006) and Kautz and others (2014) find that schooling generates cognitive and noncognitive skills even after controlling for reverse causality (the fact that stronger skills may lead to more schooling). Durlak and others (2011) analyze the results from 213 broad school-based learning programs to develop social and emotional skills, mostly in developed countries, and find that such programs improve social and emotional skills, attitudes, behavior, and academic performance.[7]

Lösel and Beelmann (2003) report findings from a meta-analysis of 84 randomized evaluations of skills-training programs to prevent antisocial behaviors in children of all educational levels. Their analysis shows greater effects in studies with smaller samples. They also find that the majority of evaluations reviewed have higher positive effects on social and cognitive outcomes than on antisocial behavior.[8]

Finally, for a study published by the Collaborative for Academic, Social, and Emotional Learning, Payton and others (2008) summarize the results from 317 studies of children in kindergarten through eighth grade and find that programs can be effective whether they are implemented during or after school, whether they target students with or without behavioral problems, whether they are implemented in different grades or locations (urban, rural, or suburban), and whether they include diverse racial and ethnic characteristics.[9] These findings are consistent with a more recent study from Domitrovich and others (2013), which focuses on 11 middle school and high school programs in the United States where preliminary findings show promising effects.

http://dx.doi.org/10.1596/978-1-4648-0872-2

After-school programs, primarily from the United States, can also show promising results. Durlak (1997) studied 69 after-school programs implemented from kindergarten through high school in the United States with the objective of fostering socioemotional learning. The review shows that some programs significantly affected behaviors and academic achievement. Those effects were particularly strong for programs that followed the "SAFE approach," that is, they were appropriately sequenced, active, focused, and explicit.[10] A report from the Afterschool Alliance (2014) analyzes more than 70 evaluations of after-school programs in the United States and concludes that those programs generate important gains for children in improving academic performance, safety, discipline, school attendance, and avoidance of risky behavior.[11]

Impacts of Training Programs

Out-of-school initiatives with socioemotional skills components are usually training programs that seek to improve job-related outcomes. Based on evidence from developed countries, Heckman, Lalonde, and Smith (1999) and Kluve and others (2007) find inconclusive evidence of the effects of training programs on labor market–related outcomes. In contrast, Martin and Grubb (2001) state that formal classroom training and on-the-job training appear to help female reentrants. Dar and Tzannatos (1999) examine nearly 100 evaluations of active labor market programs and find similar results: training for the long-term unemployed can help when the economy is improving, and youth training generally has no positive effect on employment or earnings.

Programs that foster labor market–related outcomes in the developing world are rarely analyzed, but existing evidence appears promising. Urzúa and Puentes (2010) broaden this literature to include studies of programs around the world. In their analysis of 215 job-training programs, they find that effective programs tend to be intensive and integrated, involve the public sector, and start early. However, only 30 of these programs had experimental evaluations (23 of them in the United States), and those showed positive or neutral results. Similarly, Betcherman and others (2007) gather evidence from 289 studies from 84 countries (42 percent of them in member countries of the Organisation for Economic Co-operation and Development) and observe that evidence in developing countries is lacking and that the level of program evaluation is weak (close to 40 percent of all of the programs included had no evaluation information on outcomes or effects). With the existing information, they report that most programs appear to have positive labor market impacts, but just over half of the programs that had cost–benefit analyses were cost-effective (only 25 had such analyses, and 14 were found to be cost-effective). Further, the impact on youth employment appears to be more favorable in developing and transition countries than in developed countries. Card, Kluve, and Weber (2015) analyze 200 studies, finding that effects are significant two to three years after program completion. They also find greater effects for programs that focus on human capital accumulation and for those that are implemented during a recession.

http://dx.doi.org/10.1596/978-1-4648-0872-2

Both developed and developing countries have many programs for out-of-school youth focusing on improving employability and employment prospects. However, only the new wave of employability programs tends to include socioemotional skills as part of their comprehensive packages. For example, Honorati and McArdle (2013) identify successful programs in developing countries as those that are demand driven, have a sound governance structure, and take a comprehensive approach (combining different types of skills training with support services). Ibarrarán and Rosas-Shady (2009) find that in contrast to evidence from developed countries, the results from seven comprehensive programs in Latin America and the Caribbean range from modest to meaningful. González-Velosa, Ripani, and Rosas-Shady (2012) analyze programs in Latin America and point out that, because of low levels of investment, only modest (but sustained) effects could be expected.

Notes

1. "The *Big Five* taxonomy of personality traits is now widely accepted as the organizational structure of personality traits … consists of conscientiousness, openness to experience, neuroticism, agreeableness, and extraversion" (Pierre and others 2014, 28). Refer to page 17 of their article for further details.
2. The authors measure locus of control, reciprocity, and the Five Factor Personality Inventory.
3. Personality is measured using Rotter's locus of control scale, Rosenberg's self-esteem scale, personal behavior (absences and truancies, lying and cheating, stealing, and swearing or use of obscene words), externalizing behavior, the Big Five scale, effort, initiative, disruptive behavior, and so forth.
4. Social skills were measured through reported antisocial behavior; social skills such as social interaction skills and prosocial behavior; or social cognitive skills like self-control and social problem-solving skills.
5. The authors measure noncognitive skills, including externalizing and internalizing behavior, creativity, verbal intelligence, hostility, beliefs and attitudes, impulse control, and self-esteem.
6. The explanation behind this finding is that higher initial levels of skills increase the productivity of future investments in skill generation (investment in socioemotional skills early in life builds the base for subsequent investment).
7. For a list of the outcomes included in this research, please refer to footnote 7 in their article.
8. For more information, refer to footnote 13 in their article.
9. Payton and others (2008) group social and emotional competencies in self-awareness, self-management, social awareness, relationship skills, and responsible decision making.
10. The author measures social and emotional skills, including "identifying emotions from social cues, goal setting, perspective taking, interpersonal problem solving, conflict resolution, and decision making" (Durlak 1997, 410).
11. These variables were measured through school attendance, class participation, homework completion, attitudes toward school, self-concept, and decision making, among others.

http://dx.doi.org/10.1596/978-1-4648-0872-2

References

Afterschool Alliance. 2014. "Taking a Deeper Dive into Afterschool: Positive Outcomes and Promising Practices." Afterschool Alliance, Washington, D.C.

Almlund, Mathilde, Angela Lee Duckworth, James J. Heckman, and Tim D. Kautz. 2011. "Personality Psychology and Economics." NBER Working Paper 16822, National Bureau of Economic Research, Cambridge, MA.

Baker-Henningham, Helen, and Florencia López Bóo. 2010. "Early Childhood Stimulation Programs in Developing Countries: A Comprehensive Literature Review." Inter-American Development Bank, Washington, DC.

Betcherman, Gordon, Martin Godfrey, Susana Puerto, Friederike Rother, and Antoneta Stavreska. 2007. "A Review of Interventions to Support Young Workers: Findings of the Youth Employment Inventory." Social Protection Discussion Paper 715, World Bank, Washington, DC.

Bodewig, Christian, and Reena Badiani-Magnusson, with Kevin Macdonald, David Newhouse, and Jan Rutkowski. 2014. *Skilling Up Vietnam: Preparing the Workforce for a Modern Market Economy*. Washington, DC: World Bank.

Card, David Edward, Jochen Kluve, and Andrea Weber. 2015. "What Works? A Meta-Analysis of Recent Active Labor Market Program Evaluations." NBER Working Paper 21431, National Bureau of Economic Research, Cambridge, MA.

Carneiro, Pedro, Claire Crawford, and Alissa Goodman. 2007. "The Impact of Early Cognitive and Non-Cognitive Skills on Later Outcomes." Discussion Paper 0092, Centre for the Economics of Education, London School of Economics.

Cunha, Flavio, James J. Heckman, and Susanne M. Schennach. 2010. "Estimating the Technology of Cognitive and Noncognitive Skill Formation." *Econometrica* 78 (3): 883–931.

Dar, Amit, and Zafiris Tzannatos. 1999. *Active Labor Market Programs: A Review of the Evidence from Evaluations*. Washington, DC: Social Protection, World Bank.

Domitrovich, Celene, Joseph A. Durlak, Paul Goren, and Roger P. Weissberg. 2013. *2013 CASEL Guide: Effective Social and Emotional Learning Programs—Preschool and Elementary School Edition.* Chicago: Collaborative for Academic,Social, and Emotional Learning.

Durlak, Joseph A. 1997. *Successful Prevention Programs for Children and Adolescents*. New York: Plenum Press.

Durlak, Joseph A., Roger Weissberg, Allison Dymnicki, Rebecca Taylor, and Kriston Schellinger. 2011. "The Impact of Enhancing Students' Social and Emotional Learning: A Meta-Analysis of School-Based Universal Programs." *Child Development* 82 (1): 405–32.

González-Velosa, Carolina, Laura Ripani, and David Rosas-Shady. 2012. "How Can Job Opportunities for Young People in Latin America Be Improved?" Technical Note IDB-TN-345, Inter-American Development Bank, Washington, DC.

Guerra, Nancy, Katherine Modecki, and Wendy Cunningham. 2014. "Developing Social-Emotional Skills for the Labor Market: The PRACTICE Model." Policy Research Working Paper WPS 7123, World Bank, Washington, DC.

Heckman, James J., Robert J. Lalonde, and Jeffrey A. Smith. 1999. "The Economics and Econometrics of Active Labor Market Programs." *In Handbook of Labor Economics,* vol. 3, edited by Orley Ashenfelter and David Card, 1865–2097. Amsterdam and New York: North-Holland.

http://dx.doi.org/10.1596/978-1-4648-0872-2

Heckman, James J., Jora Stixrud, and Sergio Urzua. 2006. "The Effects of Cognitive and Noncognitive Abilities on Labor Market Outcomes and Social Behavior." *Journal of Labor Economics* 24 (3): 411–48.

Heineck, Guido, and Silke Anger. 2010. "The Returns to Cognitive Abilities and Personality Traits in Germany." *Labour Economics* 17 (3): 535–46

Honorati, Maddalina, and Thomas P. McArdle. 2013. "The Nuts and Bolts of Designing and Implementing Training Programs in Developing Countries." Working Paper 78980, World Bank, Washington, DC.

Ibarrarán, Pablo, and David Rosas-Shady. 2009. "Evaluating the Impact of Job Training Programmes in Latin America: Evidence from IDB Funded Operations." *Journal of Development Effectiveness* 1 (2): 195–216.

Kautz, Tim, James J. Heckman, Ron Diris, Bas ter Weel, and Lex Borghans. 2014. "Fostering and Measuring Skills: Improving Cognitive and Non-Cognitive Skills to Promote Lifetime Success." NBER Working Paper 20749, National Bureau of Economic Research, Cambridge, MA.

Kluve, Jochen, David Card, Michael Fertig, Marek Góra, Lena Jacobi, Peter Jensen, Reelika Leetmaa, Leonhard Nima, Eleonora Patacchini, Sandra Schaffner, Christoph M. Schmidt, Bas van der Klaauw, and Andrea Weber. 2007. *Active Labor Market Policies in Europe: Performance and Perspectives*. Berlin and New York: Springer.

Kuhn, Peter, and Catherine Weinberger. 2002. "Leadership Skills and Wages." IZA Discussion Paper 482, Institute for the Study of Labor, Bonn.

Lösel, Friedrich, and Andreas Beelmann. 2003. "Effects of Child Skills Training in Preventing Antisocial Behavior: A Systematic Review of Randomized Evaluations." *Annals of the American Academy of Political and Social Science* 587 (1): 84–109.

Martin, John P., and David Grubb. 2001. "What Works and for Whom: A Review of OECD Countries' Experiences with Active Labour Market Policies." *Swedish Economic Policy Review* 8 (2): 9–56.

Muller, Gerrit, and Erik J. S. Plug. 2006. "Estimating the Effect of Personality on Male and Female Earnings." *Industrial and Labor Relations Review* 60 (1): 3–22.

NACE (National Association of Colleges and Employers). 2015. *Job Outlook 2015*. Bethlehem, PA: NACE.

Olds, David L., and Harriet J. Kitzman. 1993. "Review of Research on Home Visiting for Pregnant Women and Parents of Young Children." *Future of Children* 3 (3): 53–92.

Payton, John, Roger P. Weissberg, Joseph A. Durlak, Allison B. Dymnicki, Rebecca D. Taylor, Kriston B. Schellinger, and Molly Pachan. 2008. "The Positive Impact of Social and Emotional Learning for Kindergarten to Eighth-Grade Students: Findings from Three Scientific Reviews—Technical Report." Collaborative for Academic, Social, and Emotional Learning, Chicago.

Pierre, Gaëlle, Maria Laura Sanchez Puerta, Alexandria Valerio, and Tania Rajadel. 2014. "STEP Skills Measurement Surveys: Innovative Tools for Assessing Skills." Social Protection and Labor Discussion Paper 1421, World Bank, Washington, DC.

Urzúa, Sergio, and Esteban Puentes. 2010. "La evidencia del impacto de los programas de capacitación en el desempeño en el mercado laboral." Inter-American Development Bank, Washington, DC.

CHAPTER 3

Definitions: What Are Socioemotional Skills?

In this chapter we present some of the most cited definitions used to refer to the broad concept of socioemotional skills. In trying to define this concept, most authors make reference to a list of personality traits[1] that have been found useful in many facets of life. Authors explicitly state that socioemotional skills are different from traditional intelligence quotient (IQ) measures or from raw intelligence. At the same time, they recognize that socioemotional skills interact with intelligence, which must be taken into consideration when measuring outcomes and estimating causal relationships.

As illustrated by figure 3.1, there are diverse definitions that refer to the broad concept of socioemotional skills. However, despite their apparent differences, the definitions presented subsequently describe similar underlying concepts. Heckman and Kautz (2013) suggest that all of them refer to the same concept and that they are often used interchangeably. This similarity is observed in several of the papers analyzed here. For example, in the impact evaluation of the program Juventud y Empleo (Youth and Employment Program), Ibarrarán and others (2012) use the terms *socioemotional skills, non-cognitive skills, life skills,* and *soft skills* to describe the intervention and its observed effects. Duckworth and Yeager agree with this position and state that "all of the ... terms refer to the same conceptual space, even if connotations differ" (2015). They further mention that all of the attributes are "(a) conceptually independent from cognitive ability, (b) generally accepted as beneficial to the student and to others in society, (c) relatively rank-order stable over time in the absence of exogenous forces ... (d) potentially responsive to intervention, and (e) dependent on situational factors for their expression" (Duckworth and Yeager 2015).

Although the definitions presented here are drawn from the available literature base of socioemotional abilities, we recognize that some important concepts are beyond the scope of this review and, as such, are not included.

http://dx.doi.org/10.1596/978-1-4648-0872-2

Figure 3.1 Defining Socioemotional Skills

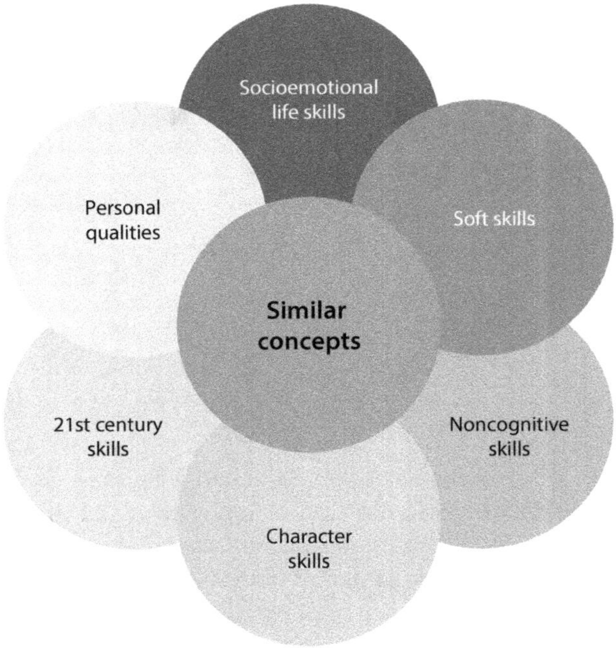

These traits are professional skills, life-coping skills, and performance character, for example.

This section is intended to present the concepts typically associated with programs that seek to instill changes in behavior, personality traits, customs or habits, grit, and others.

Socioemotional Skills

The concept of socioemotional skills is typically found in the psychology literature, particularly in publications by psychologists and psychiatrists whose work is related to education or the learning process.

Authors such as Payton and others (2008) and Durlak and others (2011) define socioemotional competencies as skills that enable individuals to (a) recognize and manage their emotions, (b) cope successfully with conflict, (c) navigate interpersonal problem solving, (d) understand and show empathy for others, (e) establish and maintain positive relationships, (f) make ethical and safe choices, (g) contribute constructively to their community, and (h) set and achieve positive goals. Accordingly, they define socioemotional learning as the process of acquiring and applying this set of competencies effectively.

Pierre and others state that socioemotional skills "relate to traits covering multiple domains (such as social, emotional, personality, behavioral, and attitudinal)"

http://dx.doi.org/10.1596/978-1-4648-0872-2

(2014, 8). The NoVo Foundation, a private foundation that supports initiatives for girls and women, defines social and emotional learning (SEL) as "the process of developing fundamental skills for life success ... SEL's skills include recognizing and managing emotions, developing caring and concern for others, establishing positive relationships and making responsible decisions."[2]

One advantage of the term *skill* in the previous definitions is that it denotes malleability, which opens the possibility for programs that can generate change. However, not everyone agrees. Duckworth and Yeager contend that "referring to them as skills may implicitly exclude beliefs (for example, growth mindset), values (for example, prosocial motivation), and other rational attitudes (for example, trust)" (2015).

Soft Skills

The Oxford Dictionaries website defines soft skills as all "personal attributes that enable someone to interact effectively and harmoniously with other people."[3] Note that the term *soft skills* is typically found in business and management literature. In fact, more than 80 percent of the papers found in the Education Resources Information Center—or ERIC—database that include the specific term *soft skills* present findings from analyses of issues in postsecondary education. For example, those papers often analyze programs that target managers and executives or programs that promote leadership skills in business.

Bancino and Zevalkink define them as "the cluster of personality traits, social graces, facility with language, personal habits, friendliness, and optimism that mark people to varying degrees" (2007, 22). Kaplan, Sorensen, and Klebanov (2007) and Kaplan, Klebanov, and Sorensen (2012) mention similar characteristics as those embraced by Bancino and Zevalkink, including creativity, listening skills, and team skills. Similarly, Heckman and Kautz use the concept of soft skills to describe "personality traits, goals, motivations, and preferences that are valued in the labor market, in school, and in many other domains" (2012, 451).

Although the previous definitions are not entirely overlapping, the concept of soft skills is similar to that of socioemotional skills.

Noncognitive Skills

Another commonly used term is *noncognitive skills*, an expression used primarily by economists. They typically use noncognitive skills to refer to the bundle of skills that are not covered in standard definitions of cognitive skills (numeracy, literacy, and so forth). According to Messick, "once the term cognitive is appropriated to refer to intellective abilities and subject-matter achievement in conventional school areas ... the term non-cognitive comes to the fore by default to describe everything else" (1978, 2).

However, leading scholars outside of economics find the term unfitting. As pointed out by Duckworth and Yeager (2015), using the term noncognitive

http://dx.doi.org/10.1596/978-1-4648-0872-2

has a number of shortcomings. First, because the term is broad, it is "difficult to define with precision, often misinterpreted because of lack of consensual definitions, hard to measure ... and representative of heterogeneous rather than homogenous categories" (Duckworth and Yeager 2015). Heckman and Rubinstein suggest that the term is unhelpful and elusive, given that "no single factor has yet emerged to date in the literature on non-cognitive skills, and it is unlikely that one will ever be found, given the diversity of traits subsumed under this category" (2001, 145).

Another often cited limitation of using the term noncognitive skills is that it indirectly implies that all that is contained under the noncognitive skills category (for example, personality, self-control, grit, perseverance, dependability, persistence, self-esteem, optimism, and time preference) is unrelated to cognition. This implication is inaccurate in psychology, as facets of psychological functioning involve processing information and thus are inherently cognitive (Duckworth and Yeager 2015).[4]

Character Skills

In the psychology literature, Colman defines character skills as "the aggregate or combination of psychological traits that distinguish a person from others" (2009, 125). In the economics literature, Heckman and Kautz refer to the term character skills "to describe the personal attributes not thought to be measured by IQ tests or achievement tests" (2013, 10). They suggest character skills include "perseverance ("grit"), self-control, trust, attentiveness, self-esteem and self-efficacy, resilience to adversity, openness to experience, empathy, humility, tolerance of diverse opinions, and the ability to engage productively in society" (2013, 6). Detractors of this terminology point out that character and virtue are admirable qualities with a positive connotation and that psychological traits or attributes do not necessarily need to be positive or negative.

Personality Traits and Temperament

A number of studies use personality and temperament to define socioemotional skills. Psychologists have a long-established tradition of studying the determinants, characteristics, and instruments to measure with a level of precision an individual's personality traits and temperament. According to the American Psychological Association, "personality refers to individual differences in characteristic patterns of thinking, feeling, and behaving."[5] Sanson, Prior, and Kyrios (1990, 179) state that temperament "refers to early-appearing, intrinsic individual differences in the style of behavior, as distinct from its content or motivation."

Psychologists have made significant advances in personality measurement, and today there is a wide array of taxonomies to measure personality. Some of the most commonly used include the Big Five, the Big Three, the MPQ, and the Big Nine.[6] This diversity of instruments should not be interpreted as a lack of agreement on the measurement of personality and temperament. Rather, the diversity

http://dx.doi.org/10.1596/978-1-4648-0872-2

should be seen as an ability to measure finer grades embedded in the measurement of personality and temperament (Rothbart, Ahadi, and Evans 2000).

Of these measurement instruments, the Big Five is a well-accepted and widely used taxonomy. It measures the following five facets of personality: (a) openness to experience, (b) conscientiousness, (c) extraversion, (d) agreeableness, and (e) neuroticism. The five are usually referred to as OCEAN.

Whereas there is generally agreement on the measurement of personality, there is a lack of consensus on the extent to which personality can be used to denote the presence or absence of socioemotional skills. A key disagreement in the literature relates to the practice of equating "personality traits" to competencies, skills, attitudes, beliefs, or values, given that personality and temperament tend to remain stable over time. However, research has found that personality traits and temperament are mutable and can be altered by experiences (Almlund and others 2011).

Twenty-First Century Skills or Competencies

The term *21st century skills* describes "a comprehensive set of skills that, along with content mastery, are what all sectors can agree are essential for success."[7] The 21st century skills encompass a wide range of competencies, including learning and innovation skills (creativity and innovation, critical thinking and problem solving, and communication and collaboration); information, media, and technology skills (information and media literacy and information and communication technology); and life and career skills (flexibility and adaptability, initiative and self-direction, social and cross-cultural skills, productivity and accountability, and leadership and responsibility). Whereas the 21st century skills are not labeled as socioemotional skills, it could be argued that some of the competencies can fall in the realm of socioemotional skills. Although Duckworth and Yeager (2015) embrace the skills, they contend that referring to the skills as 21st century skills might be misleading. The name implies that such skills have only come to light recently and are a requirement for the needs of this century when, in fact, some of them (for example, self-control and gratitude) have been around and deemed important well before the turn of the 21st century.

Life Skills

A term that has been used for some time to capture socioemotional abilities is *life skills*. The United Nations Educational, Scientific, and Cultural Organization (UNESCO), the United Nations Children's Fund (UNICEF), and the World Health Organization (WHO) have used the term extensively, yet it is interesting that these organizations acknowledge that there is no universally accepted definition of life skills (Singh 2003; WHO 1999). According to UNESCO's working definition, life skills encompass "a mix of *knowledge, behaviour, attitudes, and values* and designate the possession of some skill and know-how to do something or

http://dx.doi.org/10.1596/978-1-4648-0872-2

reach an aim. They include competencies such as critical thinking, creativity, ability to organise, social and communication skills, adaptability, problem solving, and ability to co-operate on a democratic basis to shaping a peaceful future" (Singh 2003, 4; italics in original). UNICEF and WHO define life skills as "psychosocial abilities for adaptive and positive behavior that enable individuals to deal effectively with the demands and challenges of everyday life. They are loosely grouped in three broad categories of skills: cognitive skills for analyzing and using information, personal skills for developing personal agency and managing oneself, and interpersonal skills for communicating effectively with others."[8] These skills are linked to health, peace education, human rights, citizenship education, and other social issues.

This review will subsume the various terminologies described in table 3.1 under the term socioemotional skills. This examination is done with the understanding that these categories include certain levels of overlap and important differences. In fact, 21st century skills include many job-specific skills such as problem solving and critical thinking that are not contained under the socioemotional terminology.

Table 3.1 Examples of the Constructs Measured under Each Concept

Terminology	*Contents*
Socioemotional skills	Cover multiple domains such as social, emotional, personality, behavioral, and attitudinal (Pierre and others 2014)
Soft skills	Creativity, listening skills, problem solving, creative thinking, leadership, teamwork, ability to work independently
Noncognitive skills	Every skill not captured by cognitive tests
Character skills	Performance character: "those qualities needed to realize one's potential for excellence—to develop one's talents, work hard, and achieve goals" (Character Education Partnership 2008) Moral character: "those qualities needed to be ethical—to develop just and caring relationships, contribute to community, and assume the responsibilities of democratic citizenship" (Character Education Partnership 2008)
Personality qualities	Openness, conscientiousness, extraversion, agreeableness, and neuroticism or emotional stability
21st century skills	Measures of (a) learning and innovation skills, including creativity and innovation, critical thinking and problem solving, and communication and collaboration; (b) information, media, and technology skills including the ability to access, evaluate, use, and manage information; analyze media; create media products; and apply technology effectively; (c) life and career skills such as flexibility and adaptability, initiative and self-direction, social and cross-cultural skills, productivity and accountability, and leadership and responsibility
Life skills	Loose groups of three broad categories of skills: (a) cognitive skills for analyzing and using information; (b) personal skills for developing personal agency and managing oneself; and (c) interpersonal skills for communicating and interacting effectively with others (These skills are linked to health, peace education, human rights, citizenship education, and other social issues.)

Note: This table is for illustration purposes only. It is not intended to be comprehensive.

http://dx.doi.org/10.1596/978-1-4648-0872-2

However, this review does not seek to convey supremacy to the term socioemotional skills or claim that it is the ideal terminology to describe the concepts.[9]

Notes

1. Borghans and others (2008) define personality traits as patterns of thought, feelings, and behavior.
2. Accessed April 16, 2015, http://novofoundation.org/advancing-social-and-emotional-learning/what-is-social-and-emotional-learning/.
3. Accessed January 20, 2014, http://www.oxforddictionaries.com/definition/english/soft-skills?q=soft+skills.
4. Duckworth and Yeager (2015) mention that self-control, for example, is affected by the representation of temptations in the mind—a cognitive event.
5. See http://www.apa.org/topics/personality/.
6. The Big Three inventory captures three high-order dimensions: extraversion, neuroticism, and psychoticism. It usually is measured using the Eysenck Personality Questionnaire. The Big Five is a five-factor scheme that measures extraversion, conscientiousness, agreeableness, neuroticism, and openness to experience. The Big Nine measures affiliation, potency, achievement, dependability, agreeableness, adjustment, intellectance, rugged individualism, and locus of control. Finally, the MPQ measures social closeness, social potency, achievement, control, aggression, stress reaction, and absorption (Blum and Noble 1996).
7. The Partnership for 21st Century Learning (P21) was founded in 2002 bringing together the business community, education leaders, and policy makers to analyze the skills required in the 21st century. They created the 21st century skills, which are widely known in the field. See http://www.p21.org/about-us/our-history.
8. Accessed April 16, 2015, http://www.unicef.org/lifeskills/index_7308.html.
9. This is done for consistency with various other materials and programs currently sponsored by the World Bank, such as the STEP (Skills Toward Employment and Productivity) Skills Measurement Program (Pierre and others 2014) and other reviews (Guerra, Modecki, and Cunningham 2014). We acknowledge that the terminology is fluid and subject to change.

References

Almlund, Mathilde, Angela L. Duckworth, James J. Heckman, and Tim D. Kautz. 2011. "Personality Psychology and Economics." NBER Working Paper 16822, National Bureau of Economic Research, Cambridge, MA.

Bancino, Randy, and Claire Zevalkink. 2007. "Soft Skills: The New Curriculum for Hard-Core Technical Professionals." *Techniques: Connecting Education and Careers* 82 (5): 20–22.

Blum, Kenneth, and Ernest P. Noble, eds. 1996. *Handbook of Psychiatric Genetics*.Vol. 236. Boca Raton, FL: CRC Press.

Borghans, Lex, Angela Lee Duckworth, James J. Heckman, and Bas ter Weel. 2008. "The Economics and Psychology of Personality Traits." *Journal of Human Resources* 43 (4): 972–1059.

http://dx.doi.org/10.1596/978-1-4648-0872-2

Character Education Partnership. 2008. "Performance Values: Why They Matter and What Schools Can Do to Foster Their Development." Position paper, Character Education Partnership, Washington, DC.

Colman, Andrew M. 2009. *A Dictionary of Psychology.* 3rd ed. Oxford, U.K.: Oxford University Press.

Duckworth, Angela L., and David Scott Yeager. 2015. "Measurement Matters: Assessing Personal Qualities other than Cognitive Ability for Educational Purposes." *Educational Researcher* 44 (4): 237–51.

Durlak, Joseph A., Roger P. Weissberg, Allen B. Dymnicki, Rebecca D. Taylor, and Kriston B. Schellinger. 2011. "The Impact of Enhancing Students' Social and Emotional Learning: A Meta-Analysis of School-Based Universal Programs." *Child Development* 82 (1): 405–32.

Guerra, Nancy, Kathryn Modecki, and Wendy Cunningham. 2014. "Developing Social-Emotional Skills for the Labor Market: The PRACTICE Model." World Bank Policy Research Working Paper 7123, World Bank, Washington, DC.

Heckman, James J., and Tim D. Kautz. 2012. "Hard Evidence on Soft Skills." *Labour Economics* 19 (4): 451–64.

———. 2013. "Fostering and Measuring Skills: Programs That Improve Character and Cognition." NBER Working Paper 19656, National Bureau of Economic Research, Cambridge, MA.

Heckman, James J., and Yona Rubinstein. 2001. "The Importance of Noncognitive Skills: Lessons from the GED Testing." *American Economic Review Papers and Proceedings* 91 (2): 145–49.

Ibarrarán, Pablo, Laura Ripani, Bibiana Taboada, Joan Miguel Villa, and Brígida García. 2012. "Life Skills, Employability and Training for Disadvantaged Youth: Evidence from a Randomized Evaluation Design." IZA Discussion Paper 6617, Institute for the Study of Labor, Bonn.

Kaplan, Steve, Mark Klebanov, and Morten Sorensen. 2012. "Which CEO Characteristics and Abilities Matter?" *Journal of Finance* 67 (3): 973–1007.

Kaplan, Steve, Morten Sorensen, and Mark Klebanov. 2007. "In Leadership, 'Hard' Skills Trump 'Soft' Skills." *Harvard Business Review HBR.org.* https://hbr.org/2007/12/in-leadership-hard-skills-trum.

Messick, Samuel. 1978. "Potential Uses of Noncognitive Measurement in Education." *ETS Research Bulletin* 1978 (1): i–25.

Payton, John, Roger P. Weissberg, Joseph A. Durlak, Allison B. Dymnicki, Rebecca D. Taylor, Kriston B. Schellinger, and Molly Pachan. 2008. "The Positive Impact of Social and Emotional Learning for Kindergarten to Eighth-Grade Students: Findings from Three Scientific Reviews—Technical Report." Collaborative for Academic, Social, and Emotional Learning, Chicago.

Pierre, Gaëlle, Maria Laura Sánchez Puerta, Alexandria Valerio, and Tania Rajadel. 2014. "STEP Skills Measurement Surveys: Innovative Tools for Assessing Skills." Social Protection and Labor Discussion Paper 1421, World Bank, Washington, DC.

Rothbart, Mary K., Stephan A. Ahadi, and David E. Evans. 2000. "Temperament and Personality: Origins and Outcomes." *Journal of Personality and Social Psychology* 78 (1): 122–35.

Sanson, Ann, Margot Prior, and Michael Kyrios. 1990. "Contamination of Measures in Temperament Research." *Merrill-Palmer Quarterly* 36 (2): 179–92.

Singh, Madhu. 2003. "Understanding Life Skills." Paper commissioned for the *Education for All Global Monitoring Report 2003/04 Gender and Education for All: The Leap to Equality,* United Nations Educational, Scientific, and Cultural Organization Institute for Education, Hamburg, Germany.

WHO (World Health Organization). 1999. "Partners in Life Skills Education: Conclusions from a United Nations Inter-Agency Meeting." WHO, Department of Mental Health, Geneva.

http://dx.doi.org/10.1596/978-1-4648-0872-2

CHAPTER 4

Conceptual Framework

A number of programs foster socioemotional skills to achieve diverse objectives, such as child development or labor market–related outcomes. Such programs offer a range of different services and target diverse population groups. For example, some programs offer monthly home visits to provide early stimulation activities for children who live in marginalized households and communities. Other programs focus on providing classroom instruction to develop specific skills for youths or young adults. Those differences, along with where and how a given program is implemented, must be taken into account when determining the program's overall success. Drawing lessons from diverse program offerings and target groups is complex and calls for a way to organize a program's characteristics, results, and outcomes.

The first and most important task in categorizing programs is to identify whether they occur inside or outside the formal education system. Programs that take place in a school tend to have a different set of characteristics than those that happen outside of school. For example, school-based programs typically target universal populations. Out-of-school programs focus on specific groups, with a vulnerability criterion attached to participation.

Another important distinction is the age of participants. Programs built around the school system usually target students ranging from ages 4 to 18—those in preschool through grade 12. Out-of-school programs are more likely to target (a) infants and younger children for early childhood development programs or (b) adolescents and young adults ages 11 to 25.

The programs included in this review are organized into three categories, according to when they are implemented in the life cycle: (a) before school (infants and young children), (b) school based (preschool to secondary education), and (c) out of school (usually targeted, vulnerable populations).

As a general rule, programs for infants and young children tend to have longer follow-ups on participants that generate more and richer information on outcomes and effects. School-based programs target enrolled students with a separate curriculum that focuses solely on socioemotional skills. Programs outside the school usually focus on objectives (including labor market–related outcomes) that are above and beyond the development of socioemotional skills.

Figure 4.1 presents the conceptual framework that will be used throughout this book. This stylized image organizes the programs in this review according to age of beneficiaries and relationship with the formal education system.

To launch the review of programs, we identified what matters most in program features and participant characteristics for achieving program objectives and outcomes (figure 4.2). Every program is immersed in an environment that inevitably mediates its outcomes. An analysis of the broad social, cultural, economic, and political context in which each program takes place is beyond the scope of this review.

Program Characteristics

The review analyzes evidence from programs with randomized or quasi-randomized evaluations that included the information needed to calculate the statistical significance of the effect sizes.

We will carefully assess the main features of each program, including (a) objectives, (b) components and complementary elements, (c) program setting, and (d) program quality levels. Although all programs selected for this review aim to foster socioemotional skills, they have a wide range of objectives, including (a) promoting young children's learning potential, (b) improving school readiness, (c) reducing children's developmental risks associated with poverty, (d) reducing high school dropout rates, and (e) improving the economic prospects (labor participation, earnings, socioeconomic status) of jobless youths. This wide range of objectives translates into different program designs and, ultimately, outcomes and effects. Few of the programs reviewed focus exclusively on the development of

Figure 4.1 Conceptual Framework

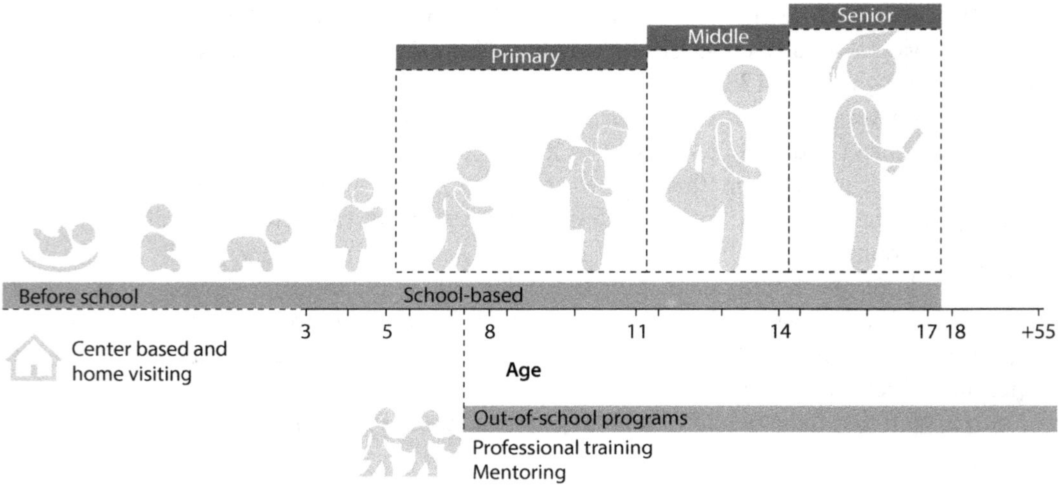

http://dx.doi.org/10.1596/978-1-4648-0872-2

Figure 4.2 Basic Elements Analyzed in Each Program

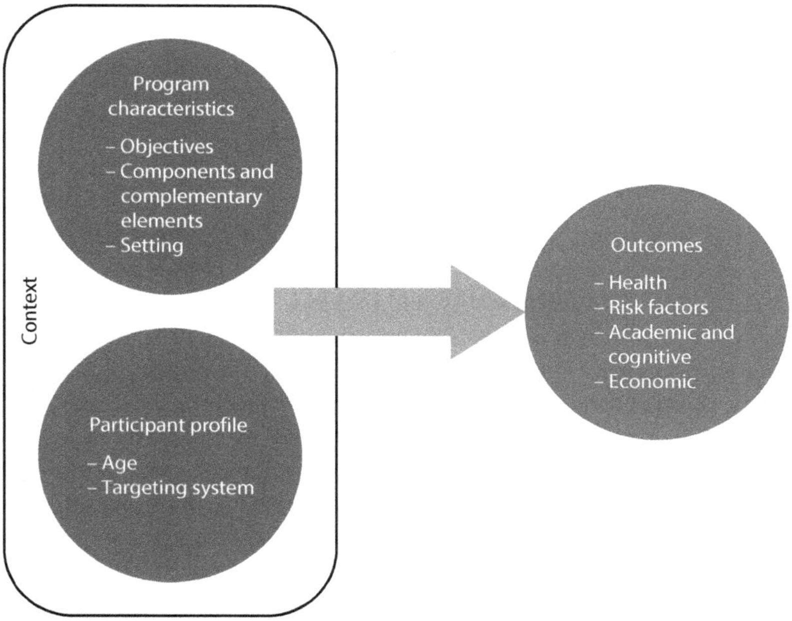

socioemotional skills. However, all programs included in this review have socioemotional skills as one of their explicit objectives, and all have a clear component or activity to develop such skills.

The second factor that we will analyze is the program components and complementary elements. Although programs have a commonly shared goal (fostering socioemotional skills), no two programs are alike. Some programs are narrowly constructed with only one component, whereas other programs are broad based and include multiple components. In some cases, components of the broad-based programs have elements that are intertwined. Examples of component activities include family or community training, classroom instruction, and experiential learning. Complementary elements can include, for example, health access stemming from participating in early childhood services to mentoring and networking opportunities for eligible beneficiaries of training.

We also study the setting in which program services are provided. The setting is important given that socioemotional skills are usually moderated by diverse environmental characteristics. Bearing this fact in mind, we analyze the different effects of programs that occur in diverse environments. For example, programs that are implemented in institutions (nurseries, schools, or the workplace) occur in controlled, structured, and organized environments compared with programs implemented at home or in multipurpose community or training centers.

Another important feature that we analyze relates to the quality of programs. The analysis will show that (a) program content (for example, curricula),

http://dx.doi.org/10.1596/978-1-4648-0872-2

(b) delivery method (for example, pedagogy, duration, intensity, and class or group size), and (c) characteristics of individuals delivering the program (for example, their qualifications, professional training, and experience) are all critical elements of any program and determine the achievement of desired outcomes.

Participants' Characteristics

An essential distinction among programs is related to the characteristics of eligible participants (for example, age, socioeconomic background, educational attainment, vulnerability, personality, and previous work experience). Our analysis will focus on two main aspects: age group and targeting mechanisms.

As stated previously, most of the available research on the process of skills formation is structured around specific ages. The consensus is that the skills-formation process is dynamic, and compelling evidence indicates that the life cycle contains critical or sensitive periods for optimal learning (Cunha and Heckman 2007). This evidence lends support to using age group as an area of interest, since it has important effects on the dynamics of a program and the program's objectives. Both the literature and our review of programs indicate that program participation early in life usually involves small groups or even one-on-one interactions with parents or caregivers and their children. Such programs tend to have a strong health component and aim to foster both cognitive and socioemotional development in ways that differ greatly from school-based programs that focus on children between the ages of 4 and 18. Similarly, our review of programs shows that those aimed at adults most often seek to foster socioemotional skills as a way to shape participants' immediate labor market outcomes.

Our analysis finds that even though programs target specific age groups, most programs use intense screening processes to select their beneficiaries, targeting those with low socioeconomic status, high risk, vulnerability, or unemployment. A program's targeting mechanism is important insofar as it moderates outcomes and objectives. For example, early childhood programs targeting infants with few environmental resources attempt to diminish inequity in cognitive and socioemotional development; programs that target the unemployed usually develop traits that ease labor market–related outcomes.[1]

Outcomes

Although programs (or their components) share the common goal of fostering socioeconomic skills, each is unique in the outcome indicators that are selected to determine success. Also, the monitoring and evaluation strategies attached to each program and the data collection mechanisms vary considerably. For example, some programs rely on self-reported beneficiary data, others use information collected by blind observers or specialists, and many use administrative data.

http://dx.doi.org/10.1596/978-1-4648-0872-2

To facilitate the review, reported outcomes are classified into the following four broad categories:

- *Health related:* Targeted outcomes include substance use (tobacco, alcohol, and drugs), fertility decisions and HIV (human immunodeficiency virus) risk behaviors, mental and physical health, and mortality.
- *Risk factor related:* Targeted outcomes include number of crimes committed, number of arrests, recidivism, running away, internalizing behavior problems (depression, stress, and so forth), externalizing behavior problems (aggression, cooperation), social competencies, attention, domestic violence, hyperactivity disorders, self-control, bullying, parental practices, marital status, and workplace satisfaction.
- *Academic/cognitive related:* Targeted outcomes include academic performance (grades), IQ (intelligence quotient), language and literacy skills, standardized test results, visual-spatial memory, reading ability, vocabulary development, school enrollment, school attendance, high school completion, postsecondary enrollment, use of school remedial services, dropout rates, grade retentions, progress on training programs, and classroom climate and support.
- *Economic related:* Targeted outcomes include migration, employment, earnings, salary, employment status, high-skilled job, reemployment, marital status, cost–benefit analysis and rates, workplace satisfaction, voucher earnings, and progress in training programs.

Note

1. Being born into a disadvantaged environment leads to skill gaps between children even before school age (Paxson and Schady 2007; Rubio-Codina and others 2014).

References

Cunha, Flavio, and James J. Heckman. 2007. "The Technology of Skill Formation." *American Economic Review* 97 (2): 31–47.

Paxson, Christina, and Norbert Schady. 2007. "Cognitive Development among Young Children in Ecuador: The Roles of Wealth, Health, and Parenting." *Journal of Human Resources* 42 (1): 49–84.

Rubio-Codina, Marta, Orazio Attanasio, Costas Meghir, Natalia Varela, and Sally Grantham-McGregor. 2014. "The Socio-Economic Gradient of Child Development: Cross-Sectional Evidence from Children 6–42 Months in Bogota." *Journal of Human Resources* 50 (2): 464–83.

http://dx.doi.org/10.1596/978-1-4648-0872-2

CHAPTER 5

Search Methodology

In this chapter, we describe the search strategy applied to identify relevant literature and programs seeking to foster socioemotional skills. Given our program classification, a methodologically comprehensive review had to be conducted in three stages according to life cycle. In the first stage, we identified literature and program evaluations of early childhood development programs, that is, those undertaken with children before they enter the formal and compulsory education system. In the second stage, we focused on school-based programs (from preschool to secondary education). And in the third stage, we reviewed literature on programs that take place outside the formal and compulsory school environment. Segmenting our search strategy was deemed necessary as key definitions, relevant programs, and associated literature vary according to the age of the population and program settings.

Within each stage, the search contained three phases:

- *Identification:* During this phase, we identified potential studies by examining specialized and multidisciplinary databases, analyzing the references section of pertinent papers, searching the websites of universities and international development institutions, and consulting with experts, among others. Papers and programs selected in this phase aimed to affect socioemotional skills.
- *Screening:* The papers selected in the first phase were further analyzed to determine if the complete program file and component details were readily accessible, if they were written in English after the year 2000, if they kept a strict methodological approach (randomized or quasi-randomized control trials), if they had sufficient sample sizes, and if they reported information on standard errors.
- *Inclusion:* The screening phase usually resulted in the identification of more than one paper evaluating the effects of a particular program. When that was the case, we kept the relevant follow-ups and papers that had a wider variety of outcomes analyzed with a rigorous approach.

http://dx.doi.org/10.1596/978-1-4648-0872-2

Search Phase 1: Programs before Formal Education

For this segment of the literature, we reviewed four different sources: (a) papers identified using the search engine of the American Economic Association under the sole keyword *early childhood*, (b) papers and policy documents referenced by international development agencies, (c) programs identified by University of Chicago professor James Heckman,[1] and (d) papers referenced in revised meta-analyses or in other documents analyzed. During each of these phases, special effort was made to include credible research that took place in developing countries.

That effort resulted in the identification of 118 potential studies that aimed to affect socioemotional skills. Of those studies, 111 were accessible, written in English, and methodically strict. After eliminating multiple follow-ups for the same program, 82 studies were included in the early childhood stage.

Search Phase 2: School-Based Programs

For the school-based portion of the literature, a set of relevant keywords and search terms were used to scan a short list of online newspapers and websites to identify relevant programs, researchers, and institutions working on socioemotional skills at a school level.[2] Three sources were useful (Gelles 2015; Kahn 2013; Kimball and Smith 2013). All were written for a general audience, referenced academic institutions, and cited researchers working on the topic. From those articles, we identified nine relevant institutions, six researchers who were repeatedly mentioned, and four programs directly related to our topic of interest.

Using this information, we searched for relevant academic literature in peer-reviewed journals and electronic databases. In particular, we extended our initial list of keywords with the names of the programs previously identified and conducted systematic searches on electronic databases and policy discussion websites. The following electronic databases and institutions were reviewed:

- *Databases:* ERIC, EBSCOhost, EconPapers, JSTOR, Web of Science, Web of Knowledge, ProQuest, and Google Scholar.
- *Institutions:* American Psychological Association; Collaborative for Academic Social, and Emotional Learning; Office of Juvenile Justice and Delinquency Prevention of the U.S. Department of Justice; and the Inter-American Development Bank.

We analyzed 247 reports and found 98 academic articles evaluating the effects of different programs aimed at fostering socioemotional skills. We kept only those that were written after the year 2000 and targeted universal population groups.

http://dx.doi.org/10.1596/978-1-4648-0872-2

Excluded from our search strategy were programs that targeted specific conditions or groups of individuals. We acknowledge the limitation of excluding programs that target specific conditions or groups of individuals, but the available alternatives were not time efficient and cost-effective. However, we decided to include some insights from targeted programs that were mentioned in other compilations or meta-analyses.

In cases where more than one paper was written about a specific program, we decided to keep only those that were relevant follow-ups and those that used a wider variety of outcomes.

We ended up managing a sample of 48 different studies and 45 different programs. Most of those 45 programs were conducted in a school environment and targeted populations between the ages of 3 and 18.

Search Phase 3: Out-of-School Programs

Our search strategy for out-of-school programs was broader than in the first two phases. The reason was that no unified pattern existed to organize the literature by a small set of words, concepts, or ideas,[3] and therefore there was no unique place to compile all programs.

Our approach was as follows:

- We identified papers and policy documents that most international development agencies highlighted in their reports on youth employability. We were particularly careful to include evidence regarding developing countries.
- We reviewed the programs examined by Heckman and Kautz (2013).
- We created a database of effective out-of-school violence-prevention programs as suggested by the Office of Juvenile Justice and Delinquency Prevention[4] and the National Registry of Evidence-Based Programs and Practices of the U.S. Substance Abuse and Mental Health Services Administration.[5]

Of the 130 documents initially identified, 42 records were screened. All others were neither up-to-date nor high-quality research (randomized control trial or quasi-experiment) written in English. Once we eliminated the multiple evaluations of the same program, the resulting list of out-of-school, labor market–related programs included 20 different programs and eight compilations.

Figure 5.1 illustrates the flow of the literature review process that we conducted to identify studies and literature of socioemotional skills. As a result, the analysis includes more programs than previous systematic reviews. Further, it includes as much evidence from developing countries as possible. Finally, it does not concentrate on one particular socioemotional skill or one particular life stage.

http://dx.doi.org/10.1596/978-1-4648-0872-2

Figure 5.1 Literature Review Process to Identify Socioemotional Programs

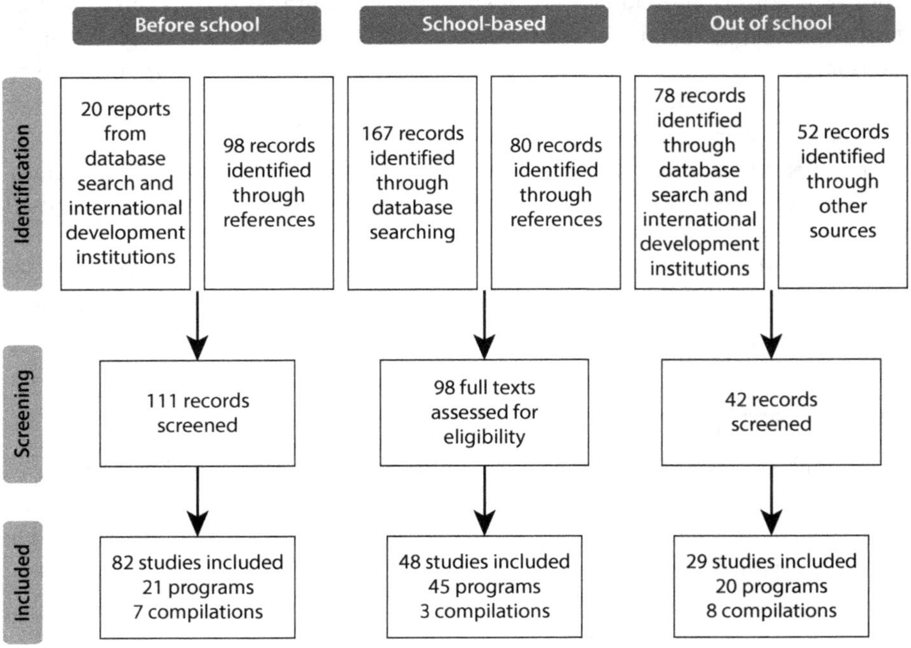

Notes

1. See http://heckman.uchicago.edu/page/early-childhood-interventions-0.
2. The following set of keywords were searched: *noncognitive* (with and without a hyphen), *socioemotional, social-emotional learning, self-restraint, persistence, self-awareness, perseverance, self-esteem, locus of control, internalities, Big Five personality traits, youth behavior problems, moral capital, consistency, dependability, persistence, emotional intelligence, emotional skills,* and *socioemotional learning.* The online papers and websites that were used are the *New York Times, Washington Post, Boston Globe, Huffington Post, Financial Times,* and *Quartz.*
3. To our knowledge, Heckman and Kautz (2013) provide the only unified framework in the literature.
4. National Institute of Justice, Crime Solutions web page, http://www.crimesolutions .gov.
5. Substance Abuse and Mental Health Services Administration website, http://nrepp .samhsa.gov.

References

Gelles, David. 2015. *Mindful Work: How Meditation Is Changing Business from the Inside Out.* Boston: Eamon Dolan/Houghton Mifflin Harcourt.

Heckman, James J., and Tim Kautz. 2013. "Fostering and Measuring Skills: Programs That Improve Character and Cognition." NBER Working Paper 19656, National Bureau of Economic Research, Cambridge, MA.

http://dx.doi.org/10.1596/978-1-4648-0872-2

Kahn, Jennifer. 2013. "Can Emotional Intelligence Be Taught?" *New York Times*, September 11. http://www.nytimes.com/2013/09/15/magazine/can-emotional-intelligence-be-taught.html?pagewanted=all&_r=0.

Kimball, Miles, and Noah Smith. 2013. "There's One Key Difference between Kids Who Excel at Math and Those Who Don't." *Quartz*, October 27. http://Qz.Com/139453/Theres-One-Key-Difference-Between-Kids-Who-Excel-At-Math-And-Those-Who-Dont/.

http://dx.doi.org/10.1596/978-1-4648-0872-2

CHAPTER 6

Program Analysis throughout the Life Cycle

Before-School Programs

The early stages of life are critical for an individual's healthy development. However, the unequal opportunities faced by the most vulnerable at-risk infants lead to an achievement gap that emerges even before preschool (Melmed 2008; Rubio-Codina and others 2014; Shady and Paxson 2007). Early childhood programs that improve nutrition, cognitive skills, and socioemotional skills have gained the attention of scholars and policy makers, as these programs have the potential to prevent this achievement gap from forming early in children's lives and, therefore, to promote equality. Additionally, such programs have a high rate of return and yield greater results for vulnerable children than do equal investments made during a later stage in life (Heckman 2008; Heckman, Stixrud, and Urzua 2006; Heckman and others 2009; Rolnick and Grunewald 2007). Because initial levels of skills affect skill acquisition (a phenomenon described as "skills beget skills"), investments early in life provide the foundation to increase the efficiency of further investments (Cunha and others 2005).

Seeking to capture the existing evidence regarding the effectiveness of early childhood programs on socioemotional skills, we analyze the effects of 21 before-school programs, 10 of which take place outside the United States.[1] All of the programs that were included were rigorously evaluated through randomized control trials or quasi-experimental techniques, with follow-up periods that range from two months to 37 years. Almost half of the analyzed programs measure results more than five years after program implementation.

Programs that begin before the formal schooling begins typically target children younger than 5 years old, and some begin even before birth (see tables 6.1, 6.2, and 6.3). These programs focus not only on young children or newborns but also on their families. Outside the United States, all these programs target at-risk families (in the United States, seven programs have universal coverage).

http://dx.doi.org/10.1596/978-1-4648-0872-2

Table 6.1 Distribution of Programs by Age Covered

			Months												Years				
Program name	*Country*	*Pregnancy*	*1*	*2*	*3*	*4*	*5*	*6*	*7*	*8*	*9*	*10*	*11*	*12*	*2*	*3*	*4*	*5*	*6*
Home visiting programs																			
Nurse-Family Partnership	United States																		
Healthy Families	United States																		
Parenting Practices	Canada																		
Parents as Teachers (PAT)	United States																		
Attachment and Biobehavioral Catch-Up Intervention (ABC)	United States																		
Comprehensive Child Development Program	United States																		
Durham Connects	United States																		
Early Childhood Parenting Programme	Bangladesh																		
Positive Action	United States																		
Play and Learning Strategies	United States																		
Jamaican Study	Jamaica																		
Integrated Early Childhood Development Intervention	Colombia																		
Parent-Child Home Program	United States																		
Child-Parent Psychotherapy	United States																		
HIPPY	United States																		
Center-based programs																			
Early Childhood Education and Development program	Indonesia																		
Early Childhood Development Program	Philippines																		

table continues next page

http://dx.doi.org/10.1596/978-1-4648-0872-2

Table 6.1 Distribution of Programs by Age Covered *(continued)*

			Months												*Years*				
Program name	*Country*	*Pregnancy*	*1*	*2*	*3*	*4*	*5*	*6*	*7*	*8*	*9*	*10*	*11*	*12*	*2*	*3*	*4*	*5*	*6*
Abecedarian	United States																		
PIDI	Bolivia																		
ECD intervention	Mozambique																		
Early Enrichment Project	Turkey																		
Total		7	8	7	7	7	7	10	9	9	10	10	10	11	11	10	9	6	3

Note: Shading indicates that the program includes that particular age group. ECD = early childhood development; HIPPY = Home Instruction Program for Preschool Youngsters; PIDI = Proyecto Integral de Desarrollo Infantil.

Table 6.2 Salient Characteristics of Home Visiting Programs before Formal Education

Program characteristics	*Participant profile*	*Outcomes*
Objectives Teach parents responsive parenting skills to support their child's socioemotional and cognitive development; provide early childhood care ***Components and complementary elements*** Parental training Health assistance ***Setting*** Home visiting program ***Quality*** **Personnel:** Coaches, nurses, community health workers, paraprofessional trainers, trained parent educators, college graduates **Intensity:** 1.5 hours per week for 3 months; 1 hour per week for 2 years; 46 twice-weekly visits **Cost:** US$500–US$13,600 per child	***Age*** 0 to 5 years old ***Targeting mechanisms*** Socioeconomic status, marital status (single mothers), young age (teenagers), educational attainment of parents, nutritional status (stunted), unemployment status	**Health:** Substance abuse by both mothers and children; risky sexual behavior; childhood mortality; children's injuries; mothers' subsequent live births **Risk factors:** Parent–child cooperation; emotional support from parents; quality of language inputs; social engagement; arrest and conviction; aggression; emotional and behavioral problems; child abuse and neglect; risky behavior **Academics:** Verbal communication; mathematical grade point average; achievement tests; enrollment in school care; graduation rates; expulsion from school; classroom adaptation **Economic-related factors:** Use of welfare; employment; earnings

Source: Based on 21 rigorously evaluated programs described in detail in appendix A.

Table 6.3 Salient Characteristics of Center-Based Programs before Formal Education

Program characteristics	*Participant profile*	*Outcomes*
Objectives Guarantee school readiness; foster a child's inclination to learn; support cognitive, social, physical, and emotional development; improve health and well-being; improve parent–child relationship ***Components and complementary elements*** Classroom curriculum Health assistance Parental training ***Setting*** Center-based program ***Quality*** **Personnel:** Teachers, trained women from the community, pediatric nurses with master's degrees **Intensity:** 2.5-hour preschool program plus weekly home visits; 3 to 10 hours/day of day care; 90-minute weekly education sessions for parents; four to seven sessions for families **Cost:** US$516–US$67,000	***Age*** 0 to 5 years old ***Targeting mechanisms*** Socioeconomic status, marital status (single mothers), young age (teenagers), educational attainment of parents, nutritional status (stunted), IQ levels	**Health:** Mortality; emergency care episodes; maternal anxiety disorder; overnight hospital stay; substance abuse; teenage parenting; child insurance coverage; health status; weight and height changes; anemia; hemoglobin; wasted condition **Risk factors:** Arrests; externalizing behavior; risky behavior; relationships between children and parents; hyperactivity; social skills at age three; problem solving through fairness; positive peer play; positive parenting behaviors; self-help; self-development; self-concept; aggression **Academics:** IQ; grade point average; vocabulary; oral comprehension; reading and math achievement; grade repetition; assignment to special education; school enrollment; high school graduation; college attendance; educational attainment; school dropout rate; school adjustment **Economic-related factors:** Maternal and child earnings; homeownership; high-skilled job; asset ownership; age at first employment; parental labor engagement

Source: Based on 21 rigorously evaluated programs described in detail in appendix A.
Note: IQ = intelligence quotient.

Overall, before-school programs can be categorized into two broad groups: (a) home visiting programs and (b) center-based programs.

Home Visiting Programs

Home visiting programs occur in the home, where children's most relevant interactions take place. Most of these programs aim to foster child development by improving parenting practices, increasing sensitive responses, and raising the level of stimulation (language and cognitive opportunities) at home. Basic health services and the provision of micronutrients complement some programs.

Program services are delivered by a wide variety of individuals, ranging from nurses to trained parent educators. They also vary in their intensity, with some

http://dx.doi.org/10.1596/978-1-4648-0872-2

lasting three months and others up to two years. The associated cost also varies considerably: some programs cost US$500 per child per year, whereas others cost US$13,600 per participant over a three-year period.

Home visiting programs have the advantage of allowing for ample participation, since providers can reach difficult-to-access locations and can adapt the services to families' schedules. In addition, when entering a home the provider gains a comprehensive view of the child and his or her family, which facilitates tailoring the service to meet the child's specific needs. (For examples of home visiting programs, see boxes 6.1 and 6.2.)

Center-Based Programs

Center-based programs typically provide a combination of education and stimulation services with nutrition at a child care center. As these programs take place before formal schooling, they can be strongly oriented toward promoting school readiness or more heavily oriented toward providing care and guaranteeing child well-being, depending on the curriculum. They sometimes include health checkups and a parental education component. Although they promote early childhood care and stimulation, these programs also facilitate the ability of the child's main caregiver to get a job. (For examples of home visiting programs, see boxes 6.3 and 6.4.)

Box 6.1 Home Visiting Program: The Jamaican Study

The Jamaican Study was a home visiting program that targeted growth-stunted children ages nine months to 24 months living in poor neighborhoods in Jamaica. Participants were randomly assigned into one of four groups: (a) psychosocial stimulation, consisting of two years of weekly home visits with trained community health aides (paraprofessionals) with a curriculum that promoted language development (for example, mother–child conversations, labeling things and actions), parenting skills, educational games, the use of praise, and improvement in the self-esteem of both the child and the mother; (b) nutritional supplementation, consisting of one kilogram of milk formula provided weekly for two years; (c) both psychosocial stimulation and nutritional supplementation; and (d) a control group.

Short-term outcomes suggested that all three groups improved early cognitive development, but in general, psychosocial stimulation outperformed nutritional supplementation. In the long term, only the psychosocial stimulation group improved cognitive and character skills, increasing the average earnings of participants at age 22 by 42 percent relative to the control group. Findings suggest psychosocial stimulation can have substantial effects on labor market outcomes and might reduce inequality in later life.

Source: Gertler and others 2013.

http://dx.doi.org/10.1596/978-1-4648-0872-2

Box 6.2 Home Visiting Program: Nurse-Family Partnership, United States

The Nurse-Family Partnership is a home visiting program that targets first-time, unmarried, low-income mothers (usually adolescents) with the objective of improving prenatal conditions and early parenting. Trained nurses do the following: (a) encourage mothers to improve their health-related behaviors, (b) improve children's health and development by helping parents provide more competent care, and (c) improve families' economic self-sufficiency by helping parents make appropriate choices regarding family planning, finishing their education, and finding work.

The program has been replicated in several locations and is one of the few programs with long-term follow-ups. Treated families receive between 0 and 16 home visits during pregnancy and between 0 and 59 home visits from birth through the child's second birthday.[a] During the first month, prenatal visits are weekly, after which they taper off to biweekly visits until the child is born. After birth, weekly visits resume for the first six weeks, and then biweekly visits continue until the child is approximately 20 months old. The final four visits, leading up to the child's second birthday, occur monthly.

Treated children improved their vocabulary skills, their grade point averages, and their results in achievement tests relative to the control group. Furthermore, they had a lower rate of behavioral problems in the borderline or clinical range 9 years later, and they had a lower probability of arrest and conviction 15 years later. Girls in the program had fewer children and used less Medicaid than the comparison group. Effects were stronger for girls.

Sources: Eckenrode and others 2010; Kitzman and others 2010; Olds 2006; Olds, Henderson, Cole, and others 1998; Olds, Henderson, and Kitzman 1994; Olds, Henderson, Tatelbaum, and others 1986; Olds and others 1986; Olds and others 1997; Olds and others 2007; Olds and others 2010; Olds and others 2014; Zielinski, Eckenrode, and Olds 2009; Nurse-Family Partnership website, http://www.nursefamilypartnership.org.

a. The evaluations of the program measure intention to treat. Therefore, if families who were assigned to the treatment group were not visited, their outcomes are still captured in the treatment group.

The characteristics of center-based programs vary immensely. For example, the service providers of Proyecto Integrado de Desarrollo Infantil in Bolivia are mothers in the community, whereas the service providers of the Parenting Practices program in Canada are pediatric nurses with master's degrees. Additionally, some of the programs involve four to seven counseling sessions for parents, whereas others involve 10 hours of daily care. These differences are reflected in the costs, which range from US$500 for 18 months (Integrated Early Childhood Development Intervention in Colombia) to US$67,000 for five years of the program (Abecedarian).

Outcomes in the literature usually include child abuse and neglect, child health and safety, home environment, parental responsibility and sensitivity, parental harshness, depression, parental stress, child cognition, and child internalizing and externalizing behavior problems. Programs usually exhibit short-term positive results, and outcomes vary from modest to multiple, positive, and persistent among treated children (see boxes 6.3 and 6.4).

Box 6.3 Center-Based Program: Save the Children's Early Childhood Development Programme, Mozambique

Save the Children's Early Childhood Development Programme, carried out in rural areas of Gaza Province in Mozambique, seeks to improve children's cognitive, social, emotional, and physical development. It has two main components: (a) high-quality early stimulation, psychosocial support, and literacy and numeracy instruction in community-based preschool centers that take care of children for 3 hours and 15 minutes every day; and (b) monthly parenting meetings oriented toward strengthening positive parenting practices.

Communities are ultimately responsible for managing and sustaining the centers, which are staffed with volunteer teachers who are mentored, trained, and supervised. The program costs about US$2.50 per month per child.

Among other effects, an evaluation of the program found significant increases in primary school enrollment, improvements in cognitive and problem-solving abilities, and progress in motor skills and socioemotional and behavioral outcomes. However, language, stunting, and wasting did not show significant improvements.

Source: Martinez, Nadeau, and Pereira 2012.

Box 6.4 Center-Based Program: HighScope Perry Preschool Program, United States

The HighScope Perry Preschool Program had two components: a 2.5-hour preschool curriculum on weekdays during the school year and weekly home visits by teachers. The latter component was designed to involve parents with the classroom curriculum and to improve the household environment. The program targeted low-income African American children who were at high risk of school failure, and it is well-known for the outcomes it was found to have during long-term follow-up (participants were followed until they were age 40).

Impact evaluations found that participants faced less grade repetition than nonparticipants; scored better on intellectual and language tests from ages 3 to 7; scored better on school achievement tests at ages 9, 10, and 14; and scored better on literacy tests at ages 19 and 27. Furthermore, they achieved higher levels of schooling and greater high school graduation rates. At ages 15 and 19, participants had significantly better attitudes toward school than did nonparticipants.

With regard to economic performance, at age 40 participants had higher employment rates and greater median annual earnings. They were also significantly more likely to own a house or a car and reported having more in savings accounts than did nonparticipants.

Importantly, participants had significantly fewer lifetime arrests and arrests for violent crimes than did nonparticipants, as well as fewer arrests for property and drug crimes and fewer subsequent prison or jail sentences.

Sources: Heckman and others 2010; "HighScope Perry Preschool Study" web page, http://www.highscope.org/content.asp?contentid=219.

Outcomes of Before-School Programs

The discussion that follows presents the main findings of programs that occur before formal schooling and that have among their components improvement in participants' socioemotional skills. The task is particularly challenging because, as Heckman and Kautz (2013) suggest, there are more differences among evaluations than there are evaluations, making it difficult to understand exactly why some programs are more successful than others.

In particular, (a) programs target different populations; (b) specific program components are not usually tested or evaluated; (c) even within a particular population, samples are heterogeneous in many aspects; (d) identification problems might be present in some evaluations; (e) small samples decrease the statistical power and make it hard to detect significant impacts even when they exist; (f) not all programs measure the same outcomes; and (g) most programs have only short-term follow-ups. In other words, because of external validity considerations, caution was necessary when giving general conclusions.

We will face this challenge using two basic inputs: our own compilation of program characteristics, outcomes, and results (see appendixes); and (b) a group of selected reports and compilations available in the literature. Findings and conclusions will be presented using the same framework that we used in the previous section, that is, organizing programs according to their relation with the formal education system and the ages of the participants involved.

This section starts by presenting the primary outcomes documented in the programs analyzed and the available meta-analysis. It will then provide an overview of the program characteristics that mediate the achievement of those particular results, and, finally, it will describe consistent findings regarding the effect of the participant's profile over the results of the programs.

To get an approximate idea of the kinds of results that were captured by program evaluations at each stage of the life cycle, we first grouped the statistically significant and unique outcomes of each program by whether they relate to health, risk factors, academics, or economic aspects. For example, for Proyecto Integral de Desarrollo Infantil in Bolivia, we counted one result for health (increments in weight and height for children), two results related to academics (motor skills and language skills), one result for risk factors (statistically significant effect in psychosocial skills), and another result related to economics (future earnings). Then, we added the number of outcomes in each category across programs. Finally, we calculated the percentages by dividing the outcomes measured in each category by the total number of results (measured in the sum of all of the categories).[2]

Most of the outcomes documented by our sample of studies of before-school programs are related to academics or risk factors. As mentioned before, programs that target individuals before formal schooling tend to have longer follow-up periods than do other types of programs. In particular, (a) 38 percent of the effects were related to academic activities, such as schooling, literacy, math skills, intelligence quotient (IQ), school performance, and graduation rates; (b) 31 percent of

http://dx.doi.org/10.1596/978-1-4648-0872-2

the effects were related to risk factors, such as criminal activity, arrests, and externalizing and internalizing behavior; (c) 18 percent were related to health variables, such as drug use, fertility, and physical health; and (d) 13 percent were related to economic variables, such as welfare use, employment status, earnings, and marital status (see figure 6.1).

In the short term, before-school programs foster cognitive skills. In the long term, they improve behaviors and reduce welfare use, which indicates that they affect socioemotional skills. A careful analysis of the studies shows that child care and preschool education programs implemented in different contexts and with different methodologies appear to have consistent short-term effects on cognitive and academic performance. Long-term studies find that the cognitive gains diminish over time, but the programs yield increased rates of high school graduation and lower rates of teen pregnancy, arrests, and substance use and abuse. As suggested by Heckman and Kautz (2013), these findings are indicative of the benefits that early prevention can bring by promoting socioemotional skills during early childhood.[3]

For example, for the Project Student/Teacher Achievement Ratio (STAR) program in the United States, the effects of class quality on test scores fade by eighth grade, but gains in noncognitive measures persist. A relationship exists between cognitive and noncognitive skills, and, for example, being more persistent leads to individuals' studying for longer periods, which in turn yields higher test scores. Both the HighScope Perry Preschool Program and the Abecedarian program (also in the United States) find lasting effects on adult outcomes as well, including criminal activity and graduation, despite the fact that effects on test scores fade.

Figure 6.1 Outcomes of Before-School Programs

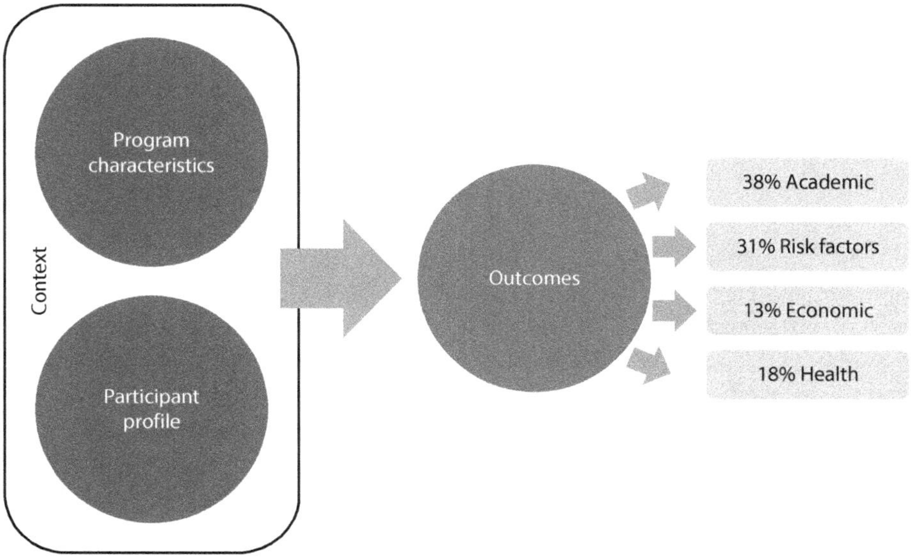

http://dx.doi.org/10.1596/978-1-4648-0872-2

Finally, combined data from Abecedarian and Project CARE (character actualization requires education) in the United States show that the effect of early childhood programs on the IQs of eight-year-old children is mediated by improvements in infants' responsiveness to people and objects in their surroundings.

Reported rates of return for early childhood programs are extremely high. For example, Heckman and others (2010) and Heckman and Kautz (2013) estimate that the rate of return of the HighScope Perry Preschool Program is about 7 percent to 10 percent a year. Behrman, Cheng, and Todd (2004) estimate that Proyecto Integrado de Desarrollo Infantil in Bolivia has a ratio of earning benefits to cost of 1.7 to 3.7. Additionally, the Abecedarian program was found to have benefits of US$2.50 for every US$1.00 invested. Finally, evaluations of the Nurse-Family Partnership find that the cost of the program was recovered from low-socioeconomic families before the children reached age four (Eckenrode and others 2010; Olds, Henderson, Cole, and others 1998; Olds, Henderson, and Kitzman 1994; Olds, Henderson, Tatelbaum, and others 1986; Olds and others 1986; Olds and others 1997; Zielinski, Eckenrode, and Olds 2009.

However, some early childhood programs do not work as envisioned and even have negative results. For example, Loeb and others (2007) find that although exposure to a center-based program before kindergarten had positive results in prereading and math skills for children, it had similar-sized but negative effects on a teacher-reported behavioral measure that captured self-control and a variety of interpersonal skills. Similarly, Magnuson, Ruhm, and Waldfogel (2007) find that prekindergarten intervention increases reading and mathematics skills at school entry but also increases behavioral problems and reduces self-control. Finally, Bouguen and others (2014) find that a preschool program in Cambodia had negative or insignificant effects on some indicators of child development.

The extensive differences in results might derive from the heterogeneity of the program characteristics (the dissimilar design elements and implementation realities behind each intervention). As illustrated in figure 6.2, six elements that the literature finds alter the effects of before-school programs include (a) a program's components, (b) its curriculum, (c) its intensity, (d) the qualifications of its personnel, (e) its teacher-to-child ratio, and (f) the fidelity of its implementation (including context-specific responses to the intervention). The effects of each of these six elements are reviewed next.

First, programs with multiple components that target health, cognitive development, and emotional development tend to produce greater and longer-lasting effects. These conclusions may suffer from confounding factors, since multiple-component programs tend to be more intense. Additionally, the Jamaican Study and the Integrated Early Childhood Development Intervention show that nutritional programs tend to be less effective than stimulation programs.

Furthermore, as mentioned by Kautz and others (2014), programs that involve parents are usually more effective. That finding can be explained by the fact that if the parent changes his or her practices, the home environment is transformed. After the program ends, the child still benefits from a more

http://dx.doi.org/10.1596/978-1-4648-0872-2

Figure 6.2 Selected Program Characteristics That Affect the Outcomes of Before-School Programs

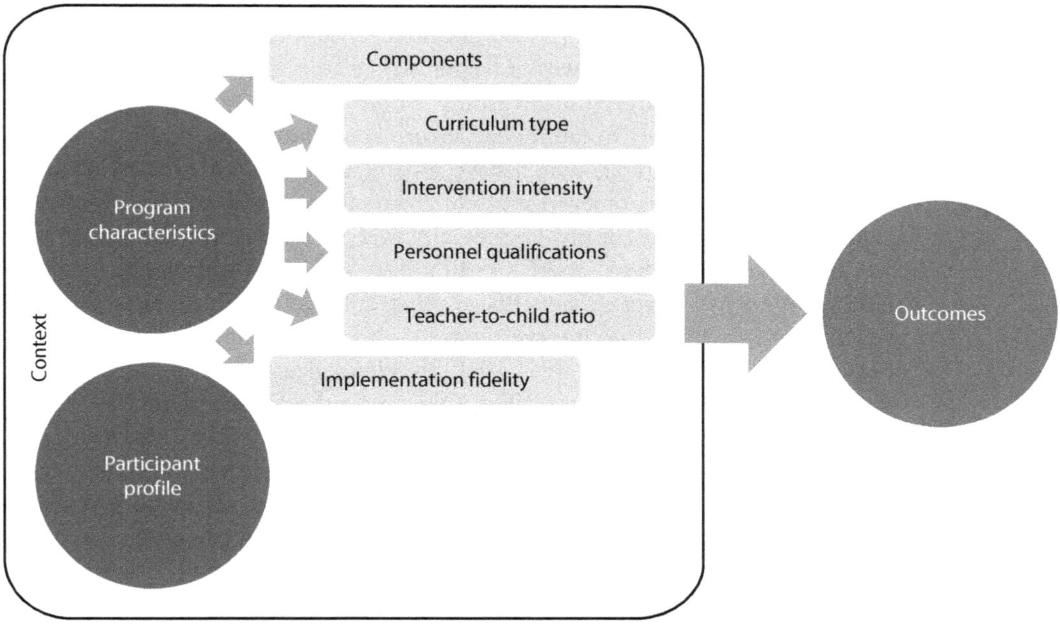

supportive or stimulating environment, thereby increasing the effect and the persistence of the programs.

Second, as expected, the type of curriculum a program follows affects the program's effectiveness. The HighScope Preschool Curriculum Comparison Study (Schweinhart and Weikart 1997) in the United States measured the effect of implementing three different curricula: (a) the HighScope model, where children planned, carried out, and reviewed their own activities while engaging in active learning; (b) a traditional nursery school model in which teachers responded to children's self-initiated play in a loosely structured, socially supportive setting; and (c) a direct instruction model that involved teachers following a script to directly teach children academic skills. This study found that people born in poverty experienced fewer emotional problems and felony arrests if they attended a preschool program that used either the HighScope model or a traditional nursery school model than if they attended a preschool with the direct instruction model. No significant differences were found between the effects of the HighScope and the nursery school models when participants were 23 years old. When compared with the direct instruction model, beneficiaries of the HighScope and the nursery school models required less treatment for emotional impairment or disturbance, had engaged in fewer acts of misconduct, had experienced fewer arrests for felonies, had committed fewer property crimes, were more tolerant, were more involved in volunteer work, and were more likely to plan to

http://dx.doi.org/10.1596/978-1-4648-0872-2

graduate from college. The three models had similar effects on IQ, school achievement, and high school graduation rates.

Howard and Brooks-Gunn (2009) find that for home visiting programs, using a clearly defined curriculum with a formal structure is key to inducing and promoting optimal program results. Programs where the content of the visits varied dramatically from family to family had inconsistent outcomes.

Third, intense programs, which have greater coverage with regard to hours per day, days per week, or even years of coverage, result in greater effects. For example, in the Nurse-Family Partnership trial in New York, the group that received home visits from public health nurses during both pregnancy and infancy experienced greater benefits in most child-related outcomes than the groups that received the intervention in either pregnancy or infancy but not both (Eckenrode and others 2010; Olds, Henderson, Cole, and others 1998; Olds, Henderson, and Kitzman 1994; Olds and others 1986; Olds and others 1997; Zielinski, Eckenrode, and Olds 2009.

Fourth, programs with more qualified personnel tend to be more effective. In the Nurse-Family Partnership in the United States, having a paraprofessional in charge of the visits instead of a nurse led to the program losing its effect for the general population (effects were found only for high-risk children) (Kitzman and others 2010; Olds and others 2007; Olds and others 2010). In the STAR program in the United States, students with more experienced teachers in kindergarten had higher earnings (Chetty and others 2010). Howard and Brooks-Gunn (2009) state that home visitors' credentials matter, but their importance depends on the objectives or goals. In general, professional home visitors such as nurses are preferred, but for those programs that seek primarily to improve mother–infant attachments (as opposed to promoting healthy behaviors), social workers or trained paraprofessionals can also be beneficial.

Fifth, programs with greater teacher-to-child ratios are more effective. In the STAR program in the United States, students in small classes (13 to 17 students) performed better on standardized tests, such as the SAT, and were more likely to attend college than were those in larger classes (22 to 25 students) (Chetty and others 2010; Krueger and Whitmore 2001). These results were stronger when the small class size occurred during the child's earliest school years and diminished when small class size occurred after first grade. Being in a small class did not affect student self-concept and motivation (Word and others 1990). According to Epstein (1993), the HighScope Perry Preschool Program in the United States showed this positive effect of small class size with up to two adults teaching in a class of up to 20 students.

Sixth, critically, having a well-designed program is insufficient: interventions that do not follow the designed standards and practices have fewer or even negative effects. The fidelity of implementation (understood as faithfulness to a program's standards and practices) can be low because of administrative or operational limitations. Countries should ensure that they have the capacity to implement the programs that they design successfully. In Cambodia, Bouguen and others (2014) attribute the negative effects of the program they evaluated to implementation constraints, low take-up rates, and context-specific behavioral responses to the intervention.[4]

In many early childhood programs, implementation fidelity is low. Araujo, López-Bóo, and Puyana (2013) find that the quality standards stipulated by early childhood programs in Latin America do not translate into the daily practices of the operators of these services. In particular, they identify that (a) center-based programs usually involve more children and fewer adults than those reported by program directors, forcing a child-to-caregiver ratio that might hinder beneficial outcomes; (b) although programs are de jure completely funded by local authorities, parents are usually "encouraged" to pay a fee for the services they receive from the centers; and (c) great heterogeneity exists in the daily schedule of activities. Further, they suggest that ensuring positive effects requires ensuring fidelity or compliance with implementation standards.

Another important finding is that the effects of before-school programs tend to yield superior benefits among the most vulnerable populations (see figure 6.3). This finding strongly supports the use of early childhood programs as mechanisms to decrease countries' inequality levels.

Even when effects are widespread, they tend to be greater for children born in high-risk environments (with younger, single, or uneducated parents; in families with few socioeconomic resources; or with low birth weight). For

Figure 6.3 Participant Characteristics That Affect the Outcomes of Before-School Programs

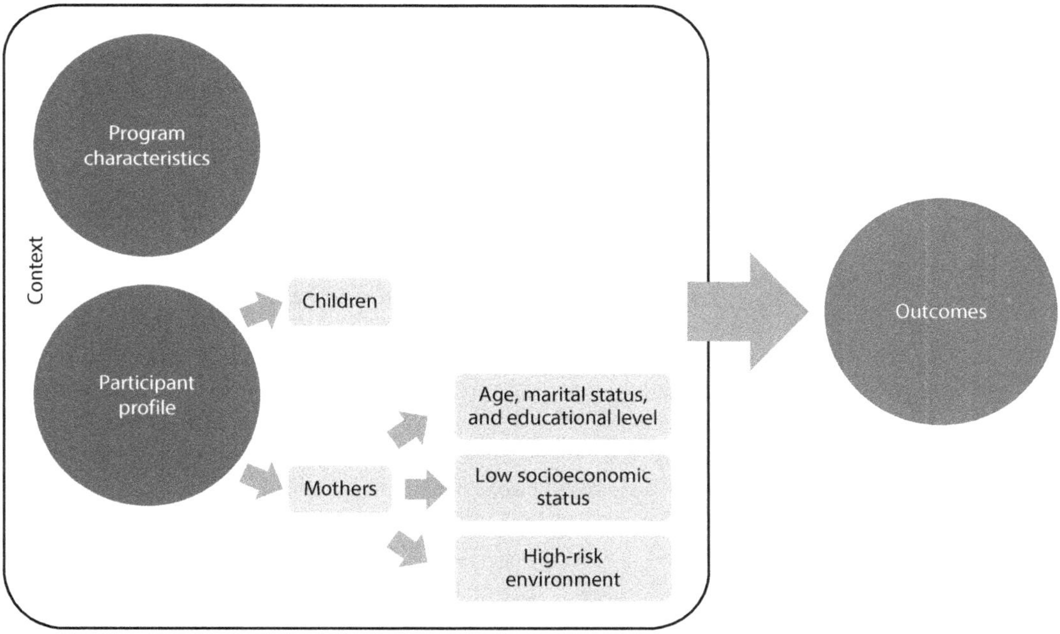

http://dx.doi.org/10.1596/978-1-4648-0872-2

example, for the Nurse-Family Partnership in Tennessee (United States), significant effects were found for children at risk in the areas of grade point average at age 12, achievement tests, arithmetic achievement, and aggression, among others (Kitzman and others 2010; Olds and others 2007; Olds and others 2010). The Parents as Teachers (PAT) program in the United States also achieved greater benefits for very low-income parents and their children, as well as for Latino groups who were less educated (Wagner and Clayton 1999; Wagner, Spiker, and Linn 2002). For the Parent-Child Home Program (United States), infants that started with the lowest IQs also obtained the most benefits (Levenstein and others 1998).

Further, effects tend to be greater for low-income, first-time adolescent mothers and for those who are psychologically vulnerable. Howard and Brooks-Gunn (2009) find that programs targeting adolescent mothers tended to differ in effectiveness from programs that enrolled mothers with other backgrounds. The greatest effects were usually found among low-income, first-time adolescent mothers. Another important group that benefited most from this type of intervention was psychologically vulnerable mothers (that is, mothers who were rated high in depressive symptoms and low in self-mastery).

The greater effect of programs on vulnerable beneficiaries could be attributable to early childhood programs leveling the playing field. That is, it could be that these programs level out the preexisting differences in stimulation and even in nutrition among children and parents of varying socioeconomic strata. Before-school programs offer a stimulating environment for infants and toddlers of all backgrounds. In their absence, children from low-resource households would face a harsher environment, so the programs provide a setting that is more productive than their homes. In contrast, infants with plentiful resources would have been highly stimulated at home even if the programs did not exist, so they benefit less from them.

School-Based Programs

Programs that foster socioemotional skills during the school year are both abundant and strategic. On the one hand, Heckman and others (2010) and Heckman and Kautz (2012) have found that important periods of brain malleability occur during the school years. Additionally, since vital personality traits—such as conscientiousness[5]—increase monotonically from childhood into late adulthood, school environments allow for continuous skills development (Borghans and others 2008). For instance, school-based programs analyzed in this book, such as Montessori and Family Check-Up, target a broad range of school grades (kindergarten through 12) as potential beneficiaries with classroom curricula that follow a yearly sequence, have grade-specific content, and adjust program length and intensity to children's school progression. Finally, these programs multiply the impacts of investments made in disadvantaged children during early childhood.[6]

http://dx.doi.org/10.1596/978-1-4648-0872-2

Operational or practical advantages result from working with groups of beneficiaries who are already present in an organized school atmosphere. According to Rutter (1987), the structured and supportive environment developed in classroom settings eases the implementation of socioemotional programs. Furthermore, since elementary school participation is widespread in most countries, school-based socioemotional programs have higher enrollment and retention rates. Besides, since schools are already established and working, programs that are built on top of school curricula can be implemented and scaled up more quickly. Finally, as Lösel and Beelmann (2003) state, school-based programs may have relatively low costs as they can involve group training delivered by regular teachers.

Even though myriad programs aim to develop socioemotional skills in schools, in this book we analyze 45 programs that are widely mentioned in the literature and that have been rigorously evaluated with follow-up periods that range from nine weeks to 23 years.[7] Ten of these programs are located outside the United States.

Unlike most early childhood development programs, school-based programs tend to be universal at a school or classroom level, benefiting all children and adolescents attending the institution. When targeting exists, it occurs mostly at a geographical level. For example, the Linking the Interests of Families and Teachers program covers all first- and fifth-grade elementary school children and their families living in neighborhoods characterized by high rates of juvenile delinquency.

These programs use different nomenclatures to refer to their objective population: some define specific age groups, others particular school grades or taxonomies, and others explicit life periods. To facilitate the analysis, we refer mostly to the grade taxonomy (from prekindergarten to 12th grade, for children ages 3 to 18). When analyzing the school grades covered by the programs, two basic conclusions emerge. First, curricula for the entire system from prekindergarten to 12th grade are scant. Second, the availability of socioemotional curricula is greater for early childhood and childhood age cohorts. In our sample of 45 programs, only 2 covered the whole schooling range. Additionally, whereas 7 programs exclusively target prekindergarten and kindergarten students, only 2 programs focus explicitly on adolescents.[8]

This outcome can be easily observed in table 6.4, which illustrates the distribution of the programs according to the school grades offered. It is organized so that programs that include higher grades are located at the top of the list. Horizontally, it shows the grade range covered by each program in our sample. Vertically, it shows the supply of curricula by grade.

Table 6.5 presents the school grades that were included in the impact evaluations. The pattern is similar to that shown in table 6.4 in the sense that most of the empirical evidence is available for early childhood and childhood ages, precisely where the supply of programs is greater. Information is limited regarding the impact on adolescent populations.

http://dx.doi.org/10.1596/978-1-4648-0872-2

Table 6.4 Distribution of Programs by School Grade–Range Covered

		Grade													
Program	*Country*	*Pre-K*	*K*	*1*	*2*	*3*	*4*	*5*	*6*	*7*	*8*	*9*	*10*	*11*	*12*
Montessori	United States														
Family Check-Up	United States														
Positive Action	United States														
SEAL	United Kingdom														
Raising Healthy Children	United States														
Michigan Model for Health	United States														
KIPP	United States														
Mato-Oput5	Uganda														
Learn and Serve America	United States														
Teen Outreach	United States														
Becoming a Man	United States														
Second Step	United States														
Open Circle	United States														
RULER program	United States														
Social and Emotional Training	Sweden														
Bal Sabha	India														
Aerobic Running	United States														
ISFP and PDFY	United States														
MindUp	Canada														
Fast Track PATHS	United States														
Responsive Classroom	United States														
Project CARE Child Development Project	United States														
Resolving Conflict Creatively	United States														
Steps to Respect	United States														

table continues next page

http://dx.doi.org/10.1596/978-1-4648-0872-2

Table 6.4 Distribution of Programs by School Grade–Range Covered *(continued)*

		Grade													
Program	*Country*	*Pre-K*	*K*	*1*	*2*	*3*	*4*	*5*	*6*	*7*	*8*	*9*	*10*	*11*	*12*
Chicago Child-Parent Center	United States														
I Can Problem Solve	United States														
Incredible Years	United States														
LEAD	United States														
4Rs Program	United States														
Unique Minds	United States														
Project SAFE	United States														
Intervention on Grit	Istanbul														
Drama in Finland	Finland														
LIFT	United States														
MAPs	United States														
Attention Academy Program	United States														
STAR	United States														
Al's Pals	United States														
School-based programs	Colombia														
HighScope Perry Preschool Program	United States														
Head Start	United States														
Tools of the Mind	United States														
Child Health Project	Mauritius														
Preschool program	Cambodia														
Peace Works	United States														
Total		15	27	28	28	27	26	27	23	16	15	12	11	10	10

Note: Darker areas represent higher school grades. 4Rs = reading, writing, respect, and resolution; CARE = character actualization requires education; ISFP = Iowa Strengthening Families Program; KIPP = Knowledge Is Power Program; LEAD = Leadership Education Through Athletic Development; LIFT = Linking the Interests of Families and Teachers; MAPs = Mindful Awareness Practices; PATHS = Promoting Alternative Thinking Strategies; PDFY = Preparing for the Drug Free Years; RULER = recognizing, understanding, labeling, expressing, and regulating emotions; SAFE = Strategies Aimed at Family Empowerment; SEAL = Social and Emotional Aspects of Learning; STAR = Student/Teacher Achievement Ratio.

http://dx.doi.org/10.1596/978-1-4648-0872-2

Table 6.5 Distribution of Programs by School Grade Tested

		Grade													
Program	*Country*	*Pre-K*	*K*	*1*	*2*	*3*	*4*	*5*	*6*	*7*	*8*	*9*	*10*	*11*	*12*
Learn and Serve America	United States								■	■	■	■	■	■	■
Teen Outreach	United States												■	■	■
Becoming a Man	United States												■		
Bal Sabha	India								■	■	■				
Aerobic Running	United States								■	■	■				
Positive Action	United States					■									
MindUp	Canada						■	■	■	■					
Intervention on Grit	Istanbul						■								
KIPP	United States							■	■						
SEAL	United Kingdom									■					
Social and Emotional Training	Sweden			■	■	■	■	■	■						
Resolving Conflict Creatively	United States			■	■	■	■	■	■						
RULER program	United States							■	■						
Second Step	United States								■						
Family Check-Up	United States								■						
Montessori	United States								■						
ISFP and PDFY	United States								■						
LEAD	United States		■	■	■	■	■	■							
Project CARE Child Development Project	United States					■	■	■							
Responsive Classroom	United States					■	■	■							
Steps to Respect	United States					■	■	■							
Michigan Model for Health	United States						■	■							
Drama in Finland	Finland						■	■							
LIFT	United States			■				■							
Mato-Oput5	Uganda							■							
Open Circle	United States						■								
Unique Minds	United States						■								
STAR	United States		■	■	■	■									
Fast Track PATHS	United States	■		■	■	■									
Attention Academy Program	United States			■	■	■									
MAPs	United States				■	■									
4Rs Program	United States					■									

table continues next page

http://dx.doi.org/10.1596/978-1-4648-0872-2

Table 6.5 Distribution of Programs by School Grade Tested *(continued)*

		Grade													
Program	*Country*	*Pre-K*	*K*	*1*	*2*	*3*	*4*	*5*	*6*	*7*	*8*	*9*	*10*	*11*	*12*
Raising Healthy Children	United States														
School-based programs	Colombia														
Al's Pals	United States														
Project SAFE	United States														
I Can Problem Solve	United States														
Incredible Years	United States														
HighScope Perry Preschool Program	United States														
Chicago Child-Parent Center	United States														
Head Start	United States														
Tools of the Mind	United States														
Preschool program	Cambodia														
Peace Works	United States														
Child Health Project	Mauritius														
Total		10	10	12	9	12	12	13	12	6	4	2	3	2	2

Note: Darker areas represent higher school grades. 4Rs = reading, writing, respect, and resolution; CARE = character actualization requires education; ISFP = Iowa Strengthening Families Program; KIPP = Knowledge Is Power Program; LEAD = Leadership Education Through Athletic Development; LIFT = Linking the Interests of Families and Teachers; MAPs = Mindful Awareness Practices; PATHS = Promoting Alternative Thinking Strategies; PDFY = Preparing for the Drug Free Years; RULER = recognizing, understanding, labeling, expressing, and regulating emotions; SAFE = Strategies Aimed at Family Empowerment; SEAL = Social and Emotional Aspects of Learning; STAR = Student/Teacher Achievement Ratio.

Analysis of the impact evaluations shows that knowledge of these programs is limited by the fact that the majority of the evaluations focus on a subgroup of the academic grades covered by each intervention (see boxes 6.5 and 6.6). Since the evaluations cover a smaller grade range than the programs themselves, they leave important gaps in the *longitudinal* understanding of these types of programs. That is, questions remain unanswered regarding cumulative impacts, variations of intensity along different years, and the effects of a particular sequence of curriculum content over the process of skills development, among other matters.

The short follow-up periods in the evaluations do little to increase the understanding of the real impact of these programs. Among the 45 programs that were studied, only 8 analyzed the situation of the beneficiaries five or more years later, and only 2 of those (Family Check-Up and Positive Action) targeted children older than age five. Furthermore, close to half of them followed participants for a year or less after the beginning of implementation.[9] Consequently, questions remain regarding whether or how the results will persist over time.

http://dx.doi.org/10.1596/978-1-4648-0872-2

Box 6.5 School-Based Program: Al's Pals

Lynch, Geller, and Schmidt (2004) evaluated the effectiveness of the Al's Pals early childhood program's outcomes associated with socioemotional learning. The program combines a two-day teacher training component, in-class curriculum, and parent awareness. Thirty-three classrooms were preselected (unclear criteria), 17 were randomly assigned to receive the Al's Pals curriculum (218 children), and 16 remained as control groups (181 children).

Classrooms that received the Al's Pals intervention showed significant positive changes in socioemotional competence and prosocial skills as measured by the Preschool and Kindergarten Behavior Scales and Child Behavior Rating Scale–30. They also showed improvement in positive measures of coping. Control classrooms showed no significant changes in any of these measures.

Sources: Lynch 1998; Lynch, Geller, and Hunt 1998; Lynch, Geller, and Schmidt 2004.

Box 6.6 School-Based Program: I Can Problem Solve, United States

Boyle and Hassett-Walker (2008) present the results of a two-year evaluation of the I Can Problem Solve (ICPS) program. The goal of ICPS is to teach children to think about solutions, anticipate consequences, and solve problems. It comprises a specific curriculum of activities, a two-day teacher training component, and instructional sheets for parents. The intervention was implemented in kindergarten and first-grade classrooms in a racially and ethnically diverse urban school district (city and state not disclosed).

The district's schools were matched according to (a) the number of students and kindergarten classrooms, (b) racial and ethnic student body composition, (c) socioeconomic status, and (d) language proficiency of students. Treatment was randomly assigned at the school level (226 students) to one of three groups: a two-year ICPS group ($n = 96$), a one-year ICPS group ($n = 106$), and a control group ($n = 24$). (None of the control group participants were African American.)

Teachers were required to assess baseline and postevaluation student behaviors using two different behavior rating scales. The findings suggest that the results were positive and monotonically increasing with years of implementation. That is, the authors claimed the effectiveness of ICPS in increasing prosocial behaviors and in reducing aggressive behaviors. (Those outcomes are not directly related to the program's objective.)

Sources: Boyle and Hassett-Walker 2008; Kumpfer and others 2002.

The objective of most programs that tackle socioemotional skills in a school environment is to enhance prosocial characteristics in participants, such as the ability to solve conflicts and be assertive.[10] Some also have the intention of decreasing risk factors related to early aggressive, violent, or antisocial behaviors or related to substance abuse. Others seek to improve the classroom climate and conduct as well. The importance of improving the classroom climate is explained

http://dx.doi.org/10.1596/978-1-4648-0872-2

by Brown and others (2010), who suggest that a positive classroom climate has been associated with greater self-esteem, perceived cognitive competence, internal locus of control, mastery motivation, school satisfaction, academic performance, and less acting-out behavior. Moreover, positive teacher–child relationships have also been associated with classroom quality and the process of learning (NICHHD 2003).

To teach all students in a classroom or school to identify and effectively handle emotions or social situations that could generate problems or conflicts in the absence of proper training or awareness, the programs that were studied have three main components. First and foremost, they are often based on a socioemotional syllabus that is integrated into the educational curriculum. Second, since teachers usually deliver the curriculum, the programs usually include teacher training on implementing the socioemotional component (incorporating specific dynamics or exercises into their existing school classes), as well as on class and group management. Third, the programs usually have a set of household activities that reinforce concepts learned at the school and that involve parents in their children's education.

For example, the 4Rs (reading, writing, respect, and resolution) Program is a literacy-based curriculum in conflict resolution and socioemotional learning, composed of 21 to 35 grade-specific lessons. To teach this curriculum and achieve positive rules and norms and safe and secure classroom environments, teachers receive 25 hours of training and ongoing coaching. Finally, a component called 4Rs Family Connections consists of activities for children and parents at home (see box 6.7).

Box 6.7 School-Based Program: 4Rs Program, New York City

Brown and others (2010) used a novel measurement tool and a clustered, randomized control trial evaluation strategy to assess the short-term effectiveness of the 4Rs (reading, writing, respect, and resolution) Program on classroom quality. The 4Rs Program includes a comprehensive class curriculum, teacher training, and take-home activities to develop social and emotional skills. Participants were 82 third-grade teachers in 18 urban public elementary schools in the New York City area.

Classroom quality was measured using the CLASS assessment tool, which combines three different dimensions of the class environment: (a) classroom organization, (b) classroom emotional support, and (c) classroom instructional support. Results showed positive improvements on their measure of *classroom quality*, and effects were robust to differences in teacher's socioemotional factors. Among the study's limitations pointed out by the authors were (a) the small sample, which limited the ability to control observable factors in the estimation; and (b) the nature of the intervention and the design of the evaluation, which made it impossible to map specific components of the intervention to classroom quality.

Sources: Brown and others 2010; Jones and others 2010; Jones, Brown, and Aber 2011.

http://dx.doi.org/10.1596/978-1-4648-0872-2

By implementing each of these components, programs alter various environments where people learn and interact. Curricular modifications and teacher trainings alter classroom norms or school-wide practices (or both) to induce specific behaviors indirectly. Household activities alter parenting practices and modify the family environment. Other programs, not included in this review, encourage extracurricular activities (usually sports or music) as a way to create an environment that requires sharing responsibilities with others and to boost the learning of socioemotional skills (see box 6.8).[11] Most programs foster skills directly, through a school curriculum, and indirectly, through parenting and the household environment.

An analysis of the frequency of each of these components shows that class curriculum and teacher training are the most recurrent features of socioemotional programs in school environments. Figure 6.4 illustrates how many programs in our sample include each of these four components. Since programs usually target one or more components, the number of programs for some components is more than 30.

Box 6.8 After-School Program: Big Brothers Big Sisters of America, United States

Some programs, like Big Brothers Big Sisters of America, are extracurricular and might involve only a portion of all students. In this intervention, children attending school who were referred by school staff were matched to a trained volunteer mentor, who spent 45–60 minutes with the child about once a week.

Matches often chose how they spent their time together, although all of the programs had some degree of structure (that is, the activities from which matches could choose are at least partly outlined by the program). In a few cases, the activities in which matches engaged were predetermined. More often, programs offered suggestions for the meetings. Most of the contents did not focus on academics but instead emphasized creative activities (such as drawing and arts and crafts), playing games, and talking about various topics (such as friends, family, academic issues, and the importance of staying in school).

A randomized control trial involving 1,139 youths in grades four through nine in 71 schools nationwide found positive and significant effects of the program on (a) academic performance (overall, in science and in written and oral language), (b) the quality of classwork and the number of assignments turned in by students, (c) scholastic efficacy (feeling more competent academically), (d) students' college expectations, (e) the level of serious school misconduct, (f) the number of absences without an excuse, and (g) children's willingness to start skipping school. The program found no benefits in the out-of-school areas that were examined, including substance use, misconduct outside of school, relationships with parents and peers, social acceptance, self-esteem, and assertiveness. The program cost is an estimated US$1,000 per student per year.

Source: Herrera and others 2008.

http://dx.doi.org/10.1596/978-1-4648-0872-2

Figure 6.4 Program Components in the Sample of Programs

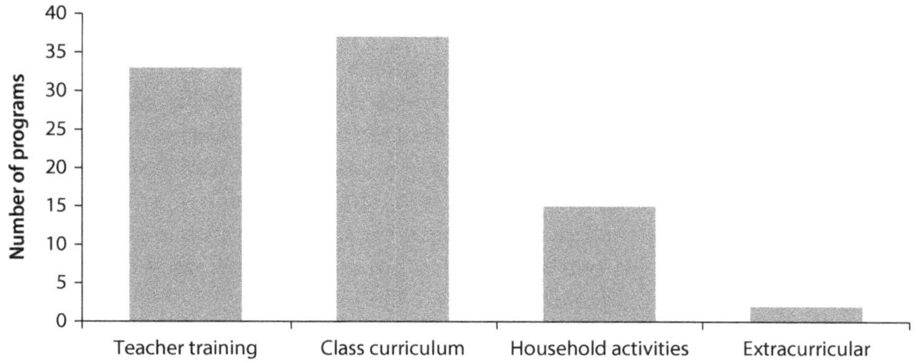

Table 6.6 Salient Characteristics of School-Based Programs

Program characteristics	*Participant profile*	*Outcomes*
Objectives Develop socioemotional skills; improve classroom climate; increase protective factors; and decrease risk factors related to aggressive, violent, or antisocial behaviors and substance abuse ***Components and complementary elements*** Classroom curriculum Teacher training Household activities ***Setting*** School ***Quality*** **Personnel:** Primarily schoolteachers; some programs also use volunteers with some level of education **Intensity:** From 20-minute lessons delivered three to five times a week to four to nine classroom sessions **Cost:** Almost never reported	***Age*** 5 to 18 years old ***Targeting mechanisms*** Primarily universal programs at a school level. Geographic targeting may occur for select schools in riskier or poorer areas.	**Health:** Risk of initiating substance use; substance abuse; sexual behavior; depression; anxiety **Risk factors:** Hostile attribution bias; attention/hyperactivity symptoms; problem or antisocial behavior; disruptive behaviors; conduct problems; oppositional behavior; bullying behaviors; aggressive fantasies; physical aggression; verbal abuse; arrests; delinquent behavior; victimization; executive control; attention seeking; autonomy; interpersonal negotiation and coping strategies; social withdrawal; prosocial behavior; social and interpersonal skills; social cooperation; social independence; self-management skills; behavioral and emotional self-regulation; self-esteem; optimism; positive affect; authority acceptance; parenting skills; emotional support **Academics:** Teacher–student relations; classroom quality; classroom management; school bonding; educational aspirations and expectations; grade point average; achievement test scores; reading; math; writing; metacognition; academic engagement; effort and discipline in class; expected graduation rates; school absences; suspensions; disciplinary referrals

Source: Based on 45 rigorously evaluated programs described in detail in appendix B.

Unfortunately, little evidence illustrates the relative effectiveness of each of these components. The reason for the lack of evidence is that school-based programs that seek to promote socioemotional skills do not normally test the effectiveness or intensity of their specific components. Out of the 45 programs included in the analysis, only the evaluations of Project SAFE, school-based programs in Colombia, and Becoming a Man evaluate the relative effect of the different components. Furthermore, only the evaluation of I Can Problem Solve incorporates the level of exposure in the evaluation design, allowing for an analysis of the persistence of the results (in particular, one can compare a group that has been in a program for two years with a group that was treated only during the first year, along with a control group for the two years).

The remaining programs capture the effect of exposure time by analyzing the impacts of the program after the first year and comparing them with the impacts in the second year. However, this method does not allow one to see how long the effects persist once the program is no longer delivered.

Outcomes of School-Based Programs

This section focuses on the main findings from evaluations of school-based programs that foster socioemotional skills. The primary outcomes of these types of programs will be discussed, followed by important program and participant characteristics.

Most of the impacts of school-based programs are related to risk factors (figure 6.5). In fact, our list of statistically significant outcomes for school-based

Figure 6.5 Outcomes of School-Based Programs

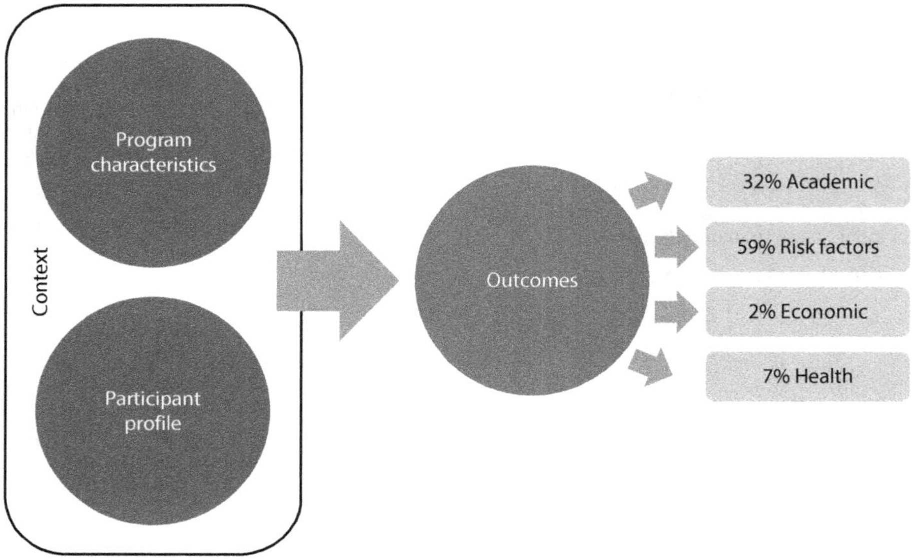

http://dx.doi.org/10.1596/978-1-4648-0872-2

programs was distributed as follows: 59 percent related to behavioral variables, such as internalizing and externalizing behavior, aggression to peers, and cooperation; 32 percent were academic-related outcomes, such as grades, standardized test results, and classroom climate; and 7 percent related to health variables, such as drug use and high-risk sexual behavior. The minimal evidence related to important economic variables indicates the lack of longer follow-up periods in the evaluations of this part of the literature.

Durlak and others (2011) conducted a meta-analysis with 213 studies and conclude that those programs significantly improved students' socioemotional skills and attitudes toward self, school, and others. Both internalizing behaviors (such as self-esteem, depression, and emotional distress) and externalizing behavior problems (such as aggression toward others and conduct problems) were also effectively addressed with these types of programs. In a systematic review of 87 rigorous research reports, Lösel and Beelmann (2003) find that a large number of programs revealed positive and statistically significant outcomes with regard to antisocial behavior, social skills, and social-cognitive skills. In a meta-analysis of only programs that sought to reduce aggressive and disruptive behavior, Wilson and Lipsey (2007) find that all outcomes were positive and statistically significant.[12] The impact of these programs on academic performance (standardized test scores and grades) is also significant, and as documented by Payton and others (2008, 6), there is "an average gain on achievement test scores of 11 to 17 percentile points."[13] Finally, the programs have effects on the health of participants.

The positive effects of these programs are generalizable for both in-school and after-school settings and in diverse geographical contexts (urban, suburban, and rural areas). However, after-school programs tend to have smaller outcomes than school-based programs (Durlak and others 2011; Payton and others 2008).

When measured, these programs also seem to have positive rates of return. Belfield and others (2015) conducted a benefit–cost analysis of six prominent socioemotional learning programs: (a) 4Rs, (b) Positive Action, (c) Life Skills Training, (d) Student Success through Prevention (Second Step), (e) Responsive Classroom, and (f) Social and Emotional Training (the first five programs are in the United States; the last one was implemented in Sweden). They find that all of the programs have a positive return, as their benefits exceed their costs. In particular, the average benefit–cost ratio is almost 11 to 1, which means that for every dollar invested in the programs, there is a return of US$11.

However, even though school-based programs appear to have positive impacts on risk factors, they have certain limitations on their effectiveness. For example,

- *Programs might be effective in inducing changes only in evident and not complex risk factors*. The evaluation of Second Step (United States) shows that programs might be more effective at reducing evident forms of disruptive and aggressive behaviors, such as physical aggression, rather than more complex forms of aggression, such as homophobic teasing and sexual violence (Espelage and others 2013).

- *The effectiveness of some programs might depend on the incorporation of school-wide or community-wide components*. After analyzing programs aimed at fighting bullying in school, Vreeman and Carroll (2007) find that programs that aim to change behavior based strictly on social cognitive principles are not effective. They suggest that effective programs need to address systemic issues and social environments. Thus, effective programs tend to incorporate a whole-school approach that involves the entire school community.

- *The Cambridge-Somerville Program (United States) had negative effects on its participants.* This program provided medical assistance, tutoring, summer camps, and parent–teacher meetings for 13-year-old children who had behavioral problems (Kautz and others 2014). A randomized control trial that measured the impact of the program found increases in the drinking habits, serious mental diseases, heart problems, blood pressure, crime rates, and mortality rates of its participants. According to McCord (1978), the program did not create a sense of autonomy among participants. Once removed, it led to the original unfavorable behaviors while generating rejection and resentment for the lack of support.

Further research is needed to evaluate whether the documented effects are permanent or transitory. Many studies have not included postprogram follow-up assessments, and existing evidence related to the subject is mixed. Using 24 studies with a median follow-up period of 52 weeks, Payton and others (2008) find that the effects of the programs on socioemotional skills, positive attitudes and social behaviors, conduct problems, and academic performance persist over time. However, they also find that those long-term effects are less strong than the effects immediately after the intervention. By contrast, upon evaluating Across Ages, Aseltine, Dupre, and Lamlein (2000) find that the impacts of the program (designed to reduce substance use in high-risk youth) disappeared in a six-month follow-up.

Additionally, the question of *what works better* and *under which circumstances* has not been properly answered in the literature. As mentioned before, evaluations vary profoundly, which increases the difficulty of pinpointing the characteristics that drive program success (figure 6.6). Hahn and others (2007) argue that although some school programs are likely to have greater impacts than others, the characteristics (or the setting) that make programs more effective are not clearly understood. Jones and Bouffard (2012) note that research linking specific program components to outcomes is rarely found in the literature.

Wilson and Lipsey (2007) find that multicomponent programs do not have a greater impact on the reduction of problematic behaviors than single-component school-based programs. Payton and others (2008) and Durlak and others (2011) find that this observation can derive from the challenges associated with the implementation of multicomponent programs.

Furthermore, the programs in our sample that analyze the effect of complementing the school-based component with a parental-home component have mixed results. As box 6.9 describes, the Project SAFE program found greater results when targeting both the school and the home environments. However, the

Figure 6.6 Selected Program Characteristics That Affect the Outcomes of School-Based Programs

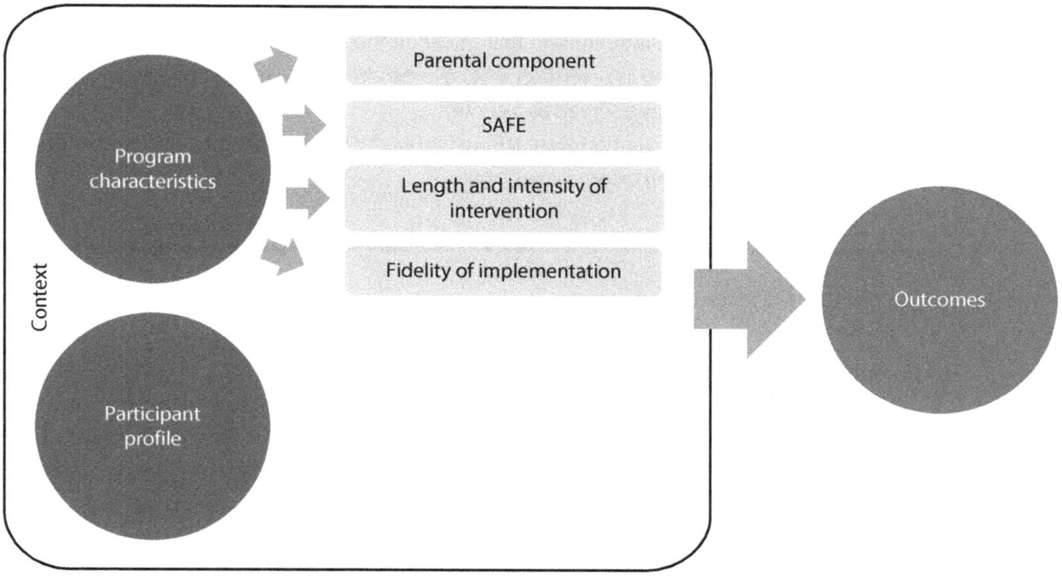

Note: SAFE = sequenced, active, focused, and explicit.

Box 6.9 Impact Evaluations That Include an Analysis of an Intervention's Components: Project SAFE and a School-Based Intervention in Colombia

To evaluate the impact of Project SAFE (Strategies Aimed at Family Empowerment), Kumpfer and others (2002) compare four groups of students: (a) children receiving the I Can Problem Solve (ICPS) intervention, a school-based universal primary prevention curriculum delivered by trained teachers in classes three to five times a week in 20-minute lessons; (b) students receiving the ICPS intervention combined with the Strengthening Families (SF) Program (a 14-session family skills training program that consists of skills training for the parents, skills training for their children, and skills training for the family); (c) students receiving the ICPS intervention and only the parenting component of the SF Program; and (d) control students not participating in any of the programs.

The authors find that the most effective program delivery was the simultaneous administration of ICPS and SF. The ICPS intervention alone affected school bonding and self-regulation. The ICPS with the parenting component of the SF had significant effects on social competence and self-regulation. Finally, the implementation of ICPS and the full SF Program affected school bonding, parenting skills, family relationships, social competency, and behavioral self-regulation, all of which are associated with the risk of substance abuse.

For the impact evaluation of a school-based intervention in Colombia (Klevens and others 2009), students were divided into three groups: (a) some received the teacher-only intervention, where teachers received 10 four-hour weekly workshops on standard classroom management techniques and strategies for shaping children's behaviors; (b) some received a

box continues next page

http://dx.doi.org/10.1596/978-1-4648-0872-2

Box 6.9 Impact Evaluations That Include an Analysis of an Intervention's Components: Project SAFE and a School-Based Intervention in Colombia *(continued)*

teacher/parent combined intervention that included the same teacher's training as well as a one-hour weekly parenting intervention that covered almost the same topics as the teacher's training; and (c) a third group served as a control.

The results of the intervention were surprising, as the teacher/parent combined intervention had a smaller effect on prosocial behavior.

Sources: Klevens and others 2009; Kumpfer and others 2002.

results of the school-based programs in Colombia found that involving schools alone had greater effects than combining parent and teacher intervention.

Several authors (Durlak and others 2011; Payton and others 2008) agree that the most successful socioemotional programs in school settings are *sequenced, active, focused,* and *explicit* (grouped together under the acronym SAFE). Sequenced programs have a planned set of activities that develop skills in a step-by-step approach. Active programs use active forms of learning like role playing, which provide the opportunity to use the recently acquired skills. Focused programs devote a sufficient amount of time and attention to socioemotional skills training. Finally, explicit programs clearly identify and specify the socioemotional skills that they aim to develop as a result of the intervention (Arthur and others 1998; Bond and Hauf 2004; Durlak 1997; Durlak, Weissberg, and Pachan 2010; Dusenbury and Falco 1995; Gresham 1995). These authors find that those four characteristics reinforce one another; an intervention that is focused but not sequenced or active will not be as effective as one that is sequenced, active, focused, and explicit. Durlak, Weissberg, and Pachan (2010) explain that the presence or absence of those characteristics in different programs moderates the programs' effects.

Complementing the finding regarding SAFE programs, Weissberg and Greenberg (1998) report that programs will most likely promote and sustain socioemotional skills formation when they are relevant to the challenges faced by children; when they have longer implementation periods (teaching skills over several years); and when they accompany socioemotional skills training with the opportunity to use the skills learned, a characteristic captured under the SAFE approach as "active."

The length and intensity of the programs also appear to have important effects. For example, the evaluation of the STEPS to Respect program finds that children who are part of the program for two years experience greater improvements in problem behavior on the playground than children who participate for only one year (Frey and others 2009). Something similar is found with the Unique Minds program, where the level of program exposure directly influenced the results for cognitive, social, and emotional skills and grade gains; self-efficacy; and problem solving. Finally, Boyle and Hassett-Walker (2008) find that students who participated in the I Can Problem Solve program for two years showed less

http://dx.doi.org/10.1596/978-1-4648-0872-2

relational aggression than both students who had only one year of the program and students in the control group.

As with programs focused on early childhood development, implementation fidelity appears to affect a program's outcomes. Humphrey, Lendrum, and Wigelsworth (2010) argue that the lack of significant effects of the Social and Emotional Aspects of Learning program results from implementation problems. Chang and Muñoz (2006) find that varying degrees of implementation fidelity of the Child Development Project implemented by Project CARE led to different results: when including all schools, there were no differences between all treated schools and controls. However, when comparing high-quality treatment and control schools, statistically significant effects were found in variables that included reading and number of student referrals. Finally, Payton and others (2008) and Durlak and others (2011) find that the absence of a careful record of implementation problems might hinder the promotion of better results in school-based programs. Further, they state that programs with reported implementation problems yielded fewer positive outcomes than those with no reported problems.

Multiple evaluations find that school-based programs that target socioemotional skills development are effective both for the general population and for particular ethnic groups. For example, the evaluation of Fast Track PATHS (Promoting Alternative Thinking Strategies) documents effects both for students of multiple ethnicities in elementary schools located in neighborhoods where delinquency and juvenile arrests are high and for students in more typical American public schools (CPPRG 2010; Domitrovich, Cortes, and Greenberg 2007). Similarly, significant outcomes are achieved by Family Check-Up, a program implemented both among children in urban schools and among ethnic-minority adolescents (Connell and Dishion 2008; Connell, Klostermann, and Dishion 2012; Fosco and others 2013; Stormshak, Connell, and Dishion 2009; Stormshak and others 2011; Van Ryzin, Stormshak, and Dishion 2012; Fosco and Dishion 2012). Further, the evaluation of Positive Action also documents impacts for racially diverse students in both Hawaii and Chicago (Lewis and others 2013; Snyder and others 2013).

However, the effect of school-based programs on socioemotional skills is greater for students who exhibit higher initial levels of problem behavior or more risk factors (see figure 6.7). Some programs—such as 4Rs, Linking the Interests of Families and Teachers, and Mindful Awareness Practices—find effects on the entire population but report effects of greater magnitude on highly vulnerable students (those with the greatest levels of initial aggression or with the lowest level of executive functions). The greater effects of these programs on groups with multiple risk factors are also documented by Lösel and Beelmann (2003). They explain that universal programs have lesser impacts on behavior because they affect the learning process of children who would not develop serious behavioral problems even in the absence of the program. Thus, in the long run, this group exhibits no major differences in behavior from those exhibited by a control group.

http://dx.doi.org/10.1596/978-1-4648-0872-2

Lösel (2001) warns against generalizing this finding to extremely high-risk youngsters, stating that an inverted U-shaped relationship between risk level and program effect appears to be most plausible. Following this theory, the most effective school-based programs would target those youngsters who are at risk, but not at extreme risk (see figure 6.8).

For their part, Hahn and others (2007) suggest that program effectiveness might decrease with the age of participants. Payton and others (2008) and Durlak and others (2011) also report that a student's mean age is usually significantly and negatively related to skill outcomes. However, they do not provide tentative channels or explanations for this result.

Figure 6.7 Selected Participant Characteristics That Affect the Outcomes of School-Based Programs

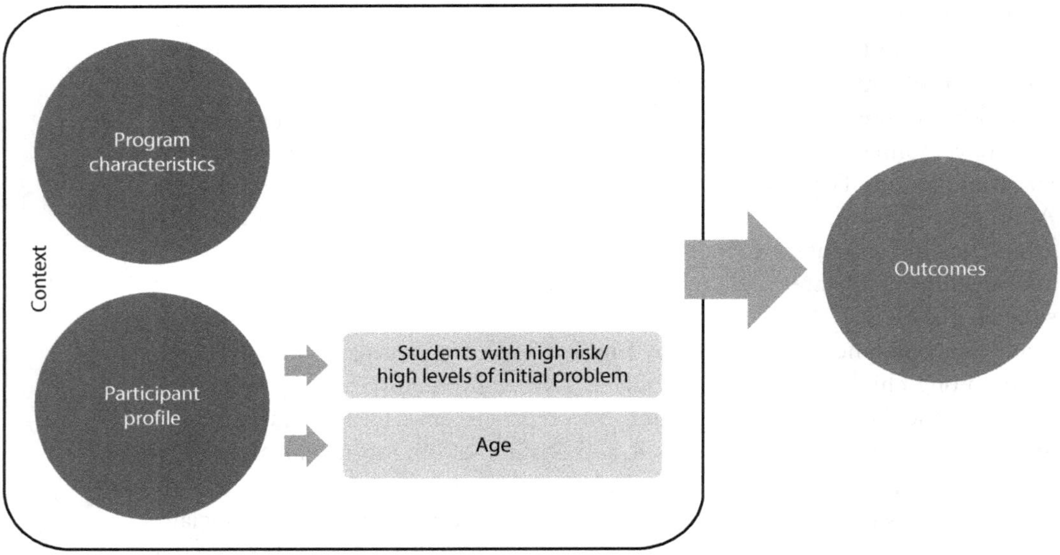

Figure 6.8 Plausible Relationship between Risk Level and Program Effects

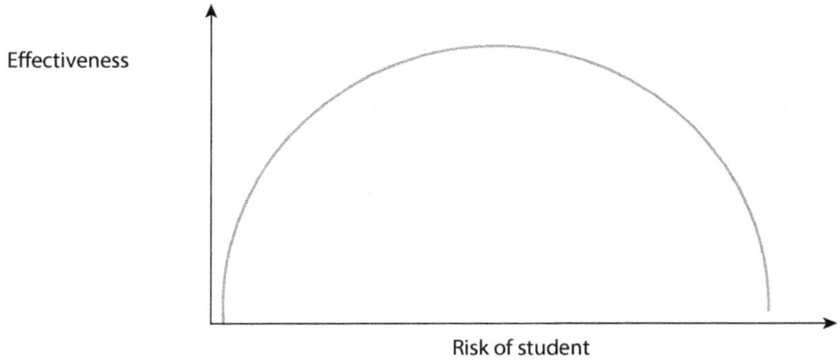

http://dx.doi.org/10.1596/978-1-4648-0872-2

Out-of-School Programs

This section characterizes a set of programs that aim to promote socioemotional skills outside the school environment. As Kuckulenz (2007, 1) states, "Post-school learning is an important source of skill formation that accounts for as much as one-third to one-half of all skill formation in a modern economy." That conclusion is driven not only by the fact that most of the world's population is out of school,[14] but also by the documented productivity of skill investment in teenage and adult populations (Kautz and others 2014). Socioemotional skills are particularly relevant in this life cycle, since as Kautz and others (2014, 78) mention, "If the early years have been compromised, it is more effective in the adolescent years to focus on developing non-cognitive skills rather than cognitive skills."

Having said this, out-of-school programs with socioemotional skill components have an ample range of objectives. For example, some seek to promote job placement for the unemployed, others intend to reduce gender violence or to improve stress-related coping strategies, whereas still others aim to decrease recidivism among individuals with substance dependence or conduct disorders. Although all of these programs play important roles in social protection systems around the world, this book will not cover programs specifically designed for people who have expressed addictions or conduct disorders. Additionally, of the out-of-school programs analyzed in this section, 75 percent are in countries other than the United States.

Most (75 percent) of the programs analyzed in this section seek to improve labor market outcomes. These programs usually include the promotion of socioemotional skills as part of a larger set of components, such as work-related skills training, mentoring, and on-the-job training. Of the programs studied, 10 percent aim to prevent gender-based violence by fostering socioemotional skills and providing educational activities and communication campaigns. Another 5 percent are oriented toward the reduction of risky sexual behaviors among Latino immigrants in the United States, and, finally, 5 percent provide intensive remedial education, social skills training, and personal development.

The group of individuals targeted by out-of-school programs range from age 10 to over age 55. However, since most of the programs included in the sample have job placement as an objective, they focus on potentially economically active populations (adolescents and young adults). Furthermore, as can be seen in table 6.7, which illustrates the distribution of programs in our database organized by targeted age, most programs focus on younger cohorts. Although all of the programs in our sample include youths ages 16 to 30 as part of their target audiences, only 30 percent include individuals over age 30.

A careful analysis of the participant profiles of these programs shows that most focus on unemployed or underemployed youths with a low socioeconomic background. Some programs, such as National Guard Youth ChalleNGe (United States), Apprenticeship Training for Vulnerable Youth (Malawi), Juventud y Empleo (Dominican Republic), and Kingston Young Men's Christian Association (YMCA) Youth Development Programme (Jamaica), explicitly benefit

http://dx.doi.org/10.1596/978-1-4648-0872-2

Table 6.7 Distribution of Out-of-School Programs by Age

		Targeted age				
Program	*Country*	*≤ 15*	*≤ 20*	*≤ 25*	*≤ 30*	*≥ 31*
Team Awareness	United States		■	■	■	■
JOBS program	United States		■	■	■	■
Jordan NOW	Jordan		■	■	■	■
Ninaweza	Kenya		■	■	■	■
Apprenticeship Training for Vulnerable Youth	Malawi			■	■	■
Galpão Aplauso	Brazil				■	■
Procajoven	Panama		■	■	■	
Juventud y Empleo	Dominican Republic			■	■	
entra21	Argentina			■	■	
EPAG program	Liberia			■	■	
Questscope Non-Formal Education	Jordan	■	■	■	■	
Program H	Brazil		■	■		
Jóvenes en Acción	Colombia		■	■		
Year Up	United States		■	■		
Job Corps	United States		■	■		
ELA program	Uganda	■	■			
Involucrando Hombres Jóvenes en el Fin de la Violencia de Género	Chile	■	■			
Kingston YMCA Youth Development Programme	Jamaica	■	■			
Joven Noble	United States	■	■			
National Guard Youth ChalleNGe Program	United States		■			
Total		6	18	14	11	6

Note: Darker areas represent older age groups. ELA = Empowerment and Livelihood for Adolescents; EPAG = Economic Empowerment of Adolescent Girls and Young Women; NOW = New Opportunities for Women; YMCA = Young Men's Christian Association.

adolescents who have dropped out of school. These programs have the intention of reintegrating youths into the education system or equipping them with the necessary skills to enter the labor market. A wide variety of programs benefit women; 20 percent of them were exclusively aimed at women, contributing to the amelioration of gender inequality in the labor market.[15]

The following components are included in most programs that seek to improve labor market outcomes for vulnerable groups:

- *Classroom instruction:* Instruction normally includes technical and theoretical training in a particular field, as well as academic education in math, language, and writing. Professional training services are usually provided only for low-skill occupations like bakery work, bartending, hair styling, tailoring, and carpentry.

- *Counseling or mentoring:* Programs often provide their beneficiaries with the opportunity to contact a professional, role model, or more experienced individual to advise them on how to interview, where to seek jobs, and how to pursue additional training.
- *Internships or other workplace-based training activities:* Many programs offer hands-on training opportunities in the workplace, including internships or apprenticeships. Internship programs are more common in developing countries and consist of less-intensive interactions that usually last from three to six months and that do not involve classroom training. Apprenticeship programs, which are very common in Europe, last for three to four years and involve highly structured training that combines in-class knowledge (that relates to the particular occupation) with workplace practice (Kautz and others 2014).
- *Socioemotional training:* Among others, this component fosters self-esteem, work habits, social harmony, team-building and teamwork skills, negotiation and conflict resolution, time management and punctuality, dress and body language, positive thinking, sense of control, and stress management (see table 6.8). Occasionally, socioemotional training is delivered through an

Table 6.8 Main Characteristics of Socioemotional Skills Components in Out-of-School Programs

Program name	*Country*	*Duration (hours)*	*Contents*
Ninaweza	Kenya	40	Emotional intelligence, self-care, decision making, motivation, communication (listening, body language), cooperation and competition, teamwork, personal planning and goal setting, work ethics and perspectives, job searching
Juventud y Empleo	Dominican Republic	75	Values, self-esteem, group integration, conflict resolution, social risk management, communication, work planning and organization, life project development and a plan for job acquisition, job-search orientation
Galpão Aplauso	Brazil	120	Basic principles of "social harmony," which emphasize civics and certain shared values along with socioemotional development, for example, concepts, principles, and values such as ethics; civic responsibility; respect; environmental education; solidarity; health; and honesty
Jordan NOW	Jordan	45	Effective communication and business writing skills (for example, making presentations, writing business reports and different types of correspondence), team-building and team work skills (for example, characteristics of a successful team, how to work in different roles within a team), time management, positive thinking and how to use it in business situations, excellence in providing customer service, and résumé writing and interviewing skills
entra21	Argentina	64	Life skills

http://dx.doi.org/10.1596/978-1-4648-0872-2

explicit classroom curriculum. Other times, it is incorporated in the classroom dynamic and taught simultaneously with the particular field or the academic subject. Some programs also transmit socioemotional skills during the apprenticeship, internship, or job-training periods.

Seeking to offset some of the opportunity costs associated with leaving the labor force while training, programs like Jóvenes en Acción in Colombia and Juventud y Empleo in the Dominican Republic also provide stipends to their participants. Additionally, programs like Jordan New Opportunities for Women (NOW) provide subsidies to employers that hire the programs' graduates. Previous evaluations of such wage subsidies have found limited results, which are normally attributed to low usage rates of subsidies and to possible stigma effects (Groh and others 2012).

Figure 6.9 illustrates the components found in the set of programs gathered in our literature review and their frequency. Classroom training is by far the most commonly recurring feature of the programs analyzed. It is followed by counseling and mentoring, and by workplace-based job training. Few programs include a subsidy component.

The average length of the programs in our database is 10 months (median of 6 months). However, programs vary substantially: whereas Team Awareness lasts only five hours, the Kingston YMCA Youth Development Programme can take up to four years to complete. Sixty percent of the programs are full time and last more than a week. When present, the on-the-job training component lasts from one to six months. Only two programs (Job Corps and the National Guard Youth ChalleNGe Program) involve high-intensity arrangements where beneficiaries live on the program's premises. As Honorati and McArdle (2013) document, life skills training can last 45 hours (as in Jordan NOW), 75 to 80 hours (as in Juventud y Empleo in the Dominican Republic and the Youth Empowerment Program in Kenya), or even 200 to 400 hours, combining life skills and technical training (as in the Jóvenes programs for youth training in Latin America).

Figure 6.9 Program Components in Sample of Out-of-School Programs

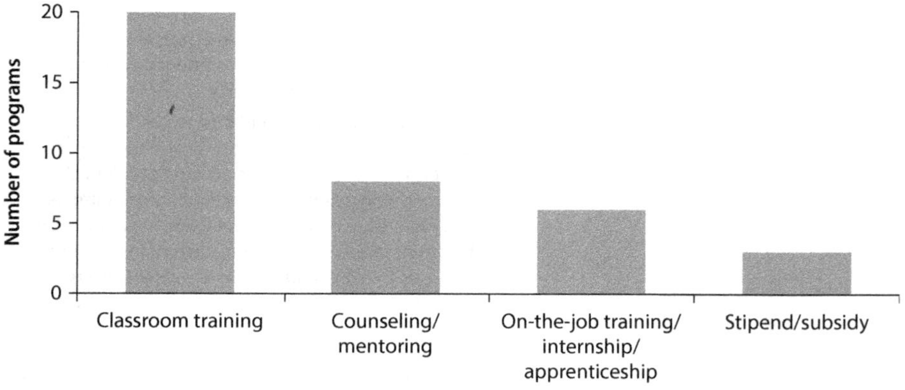

http://dx.doi.org/10.1596/978-1-4648-0872-2

Information on costs was available for 45 percent of the programs. Cost information normally includes the entire program, not just the socioemotional skills formation module or component. For these programs, investments ranged from US$85 to US$16,500 per participant. Taking into account that the higher costs are associated with the two residency-based programs in our sample, the costs of out-of-school programs are low when compared with programs in the other stages of the life cycle. On the basis of an analysis of job-oriented programs in Latin America, González-Velosa, Ripani, and Rosas-Shady (2012) suggest that the small per capita investment should be associated with modest expected results. The programs they analyzed cost between US$330 and US$750.

Outcomes of Out-of-School Programs

This section synthesizes the central findings regarding out-of-school programs with components that strengthen socioemotional skills. Following a description of the main outcomes of these types of programs is a discussion on the aspects of program design and implementation that alter a program's impacts. Finally, the ways that various participant characteristics can hinder or facilitate the attainment of positive results are summarized.

The majority of the out-of-school programs analyzed in this book are oriented toward improving labor market outcomes (see box 6.10 and table 6.9). Consequently, most of the documented program outcomes are related to job status and earnings and to behavior. In fact, 38 percent of the outcomes fall under the economic-related category and a similar percentage of the outcomes (35 percent) are related to behavioral aspects, such as leadership skills, self-esteem, conflict resolution abilities, confidence, and arrests and convictions. Furthermore, 17 percent of the outcomes are related to health (such as obesity, and drug and alcohol consumption), and 10 percent are related to academic aspects (such as enrollment, hours in education, and certification). See figure 6.10.

Box 6.10 Out-of-School Program: Juventud y Empleo, Dominican Republic

Juventud y Empleo is a workplace-based intervention that targets Dominican adolescents between ages 16 and 29 who live in poor neighborhoods; are not attending school; lack a high school diploma; and are unemployed, underemployed, or inactive. The program provides them with 150 hours of vocational training, 75 hours of socioemotional (life skills) training, and a three-month internship to increase the likelihood of their finding a job, to reintegrate them productively into society, and to prevent them from participating in delinquent activities. While participating in the training, participants receive a stipend of close to US$3 per day.

box continues next page

http://dx.doi.org/10.1596/978-1-4648-0872-2

Box 6.10 Out-of-School Program: Juventud y Empleo, Dominican Republic *(continued)*

At 18 to 24 months after the intervention, overall employment showed few effects, but job quality for males was affected significantly (17 percent increase in formal employment, 7 percent increase in monthly earnings for those employed), especially in Santo Domingo. The program also had a positive effect on teenage pregnancy, and in women's expectations and perceptions about the future. With regard to socioemotional skills, the program improved leadership skills, persistency of effort, and conflict resolution.

Six years after the intervention started, employment and earnings continued to show no significant effects. However, formal employment for men had sustained positive effects (25 percent more men in the treatment group have a job with health insurance) and for both genders in Santo Domingo (when comparing the participants and the control group, 30 percent more individuals participating in the intervention have jobs with health insurance). In Santo Domingo, the program also increases earnings by 25 percent for women participants over the control group.

Sources: Fazio 2011; Ibarrarán and others 2012; Ibarrarán and others 2015.

Table 6.9 Salient Characteristics of Out-of-School Programs

Program characteristics	*Participant profile*	*Outcomes*
Objectives Improve the prospects (labor capacity, earning levels, socioeconomic status) of jobless youths and disadvantaged groups by making youths more responsible, employable, and productive Integrate school dropouts into society Empower women along economic and reproductive health dimensions Prevent and reduce the negative effects associated with unemployment and job-seeking stress. Reduce violence against women Prevent risk-related sexual behaviors ***Components and complementary elements*** Counseling Classroom curriculum On-the-job training/ internship, subsidy ***Setting*** Community training centers, firms ***Quality*** Personnel: Trained facilitators Intensity: 5 hours to 4 years Costs: US$85 to US$16,500	***Age*** 10 to over 55 years old ***Targeting mechanisms*** Socioeconomic and employment status, age, educational attainment, geographical location, race, gender	**Health**: Use of tobacco and other drugs; teenage pregnancy; mental health; depressive symptoms; overweight; sexually transmitted diseases; HIV risk knowledge; condom and birth control use; safe sexual activity; delay in marriage and births; health insurance **Risk factors:** Arrests and conviction rates; violent incidents; stalking incidents; aggressive behavior; attitudes about gender roles; expectations and anxiety about the future; leadership skills; self-esteem; confidence and empowerment; prosocial behavior; positive unwinding; conflict resolution; self-organization; persistency and effort; happiness and life satisfaction; stress; social support; collective civic efficacy; cultural esteem **Academics:** Knowledge of ICT and life skills; enrollment; hours in education; degrees, certificates, or diplomas **Economic-related factors**: Employment (formal and informal); hours worked per week; earnings; tenure; savings; perception of entrepreneurship; credit standing; welfare dependency; retirement benefits; spending

Source: Based on 20 rigorously evaluated programs that have socioemotional skills formation as one of their components.
Note: See appendix C for program descriptions. HIV = human immunodeficiency virus; ICT = information and communication technology.

http://dx.doi.org/10.1596/978-1-4648-0872-2

Figure 6.10 Outcomes of Out-of-School Programs

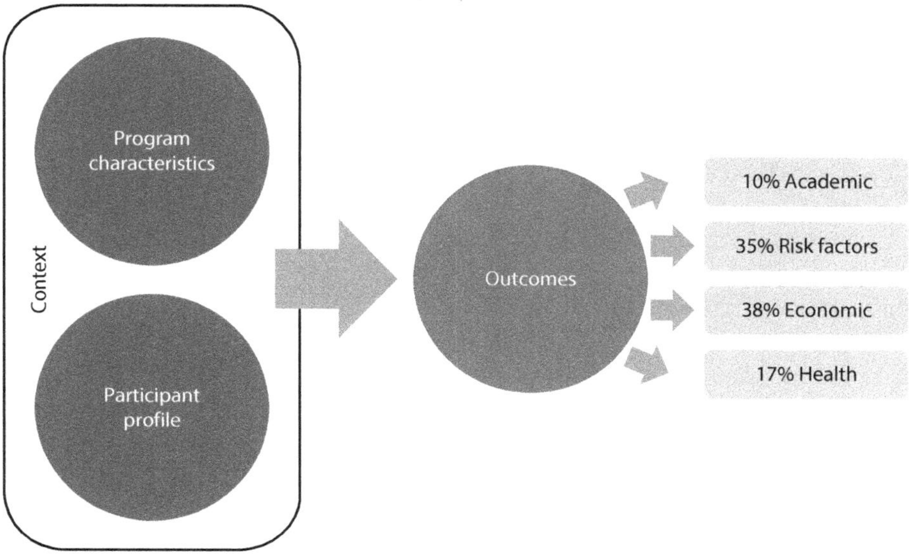

The programs' effects on employment, formality levels, number of hours worked per week, and wages or earnings tend to be small but statistically significant. However, evidence regarding program effects on employment levels and quality of employment is mixed. For example, the impact evaluations of Juventud y Empleo (Dominican Republic), Jóvenes en Acción (Colombia), and entra21 (Argentina) found no significant effects on employment levels, but they found significant improvements in formality (employment with health insurance, a written contract, formal wages) and earnings for those employed. Similarly, the Year Up program (United States) significantly increased the annual earnings of beneficiaries, primarily through higher hourly wages and better job placements, but with no significant changes in employment rates. In contrast, programs like Job Corps (United States) and Galpão Aplauso (Brazil) increased employment rates but had no effect on the quality of the jobs offered to participants.[16]

When measured, job-oriented programs had mixed effects on risk factors. For example, after 75 hours of basic or life skills training that aimed to strengthen trainees' self-esteem and work habits, Juventud y Empleo had an effect on participants' aspirations, conflict resolution skills, leadership, self-esteem, and order and self-organization.[17] It also affected persistence of effort among women and leadership skills among men. In Jordan, Questscope Non-Formal Education was found to have had significant effects on conduct problems (as measured by the Strengths and Difficulties Questionnaire, which screens for behavioral issues in five domains of psychological attributes),[18] men's prosocial behaviors, connectedness, and hyperactivity, although the effects on self-efficacy and social skills

http://dx.doi.org/10.1596/978-1-4648-0872-2

were not statistically significant. Further, programs targeting women, such as Ninaweza in Kenya, EPAG (Economic Empowerment of Adolescent Girls and Young Women) in Liberia, and ELA (Empowerment and Livelihood for Adolescents) in Uganda significantly bolstered the confidence levels and empowerment of teenage girls.[19] By contrast, Galpão Aplauso in Brazil found no significant effects on grit, on participants' score on the competencies covered by the Social and Personal Competencies Scale, on their social activities, or on risky behavior.[20]

Interestingly, the two programs that offer residential services in our sample (Job Corps and National Youth Guard ChalleNGe) have short-term effects on arrests and conviction rates. However, the effects of both programs on criminal behavior fade over time. Kautz and others (2014) attribute this phenomenon to the fact that since youths are housed in the program, they are "incapacitated" from committing any crime in the short term. Once they return to their original environment, they revert to their usual behaviors and criminality. That, however, does not mean that modifying aggression should not be considered a viable program outcome for programs that target extremely disadvantaged youth: the Kingston YMCA Youth Development Programme in Jamaica finds statistically significant effects on the aggressive behavior and aggressive propensity of its participants.

Finally, some of the programs have statistically significant effects on academics-related variables, such as knowledge of information and communication technology; knowledge of life skills; enrollment in educational institutions; number of hours spent on education; and attainment of degrees, certificates, or diplomas. Those effects were expected, as most of the programs have a component that trains participants on particular job-related skills.

Cost–benefit analyses find that out-of-school programs that target labor market outcomes and are not residential appear to be cost-effective (see figure 6.11). As Card, Kluve, and Weber (2010) mention, few studies include the information required to conduct a cost–benefit analysis. However, the impact evaluations that do capture cost-effectiveness have found positive results. For example, the evaluation of Procajoven (Panama) found that the overall costs of the program were recovered in 12.6 months. Additionally, Attanasio, Kugler, and Meghir (2011) estimate that Jóvenes en Acción (Colombia) yielded internal rates of return of 35 percent overall and 21.6 percent for women. Further, Alzúa, Cruces, and Lopez Erazo (2013) calculate that entra21 (Argentina) had an internal rate of return of 19 percent, which, although positive, was lower than the rate found for similar programs in the region. Finally, several studies of apprenticeship training in European countries find high rates of return for participants, in the range of 9 percent to 15 percent (Adda and others 2013; Bougheas and Georgellis 2004; Clark and Fahr 2002; Winkelmann 1996). Consistent with those findings, Hollenbeck (2008) estimates that in the state of Washington (United States), social and governmental returns (for example, taxes received on earnings and reductions in spending on unemployment insurance, Temporary Assistance for Needy Families, food stamps, and Medicaid benefits) to apprenticeship programs administered by the

Figure 6.11 Selected Program Characteristics That Affect the Outcomes of Out-of-School Programs

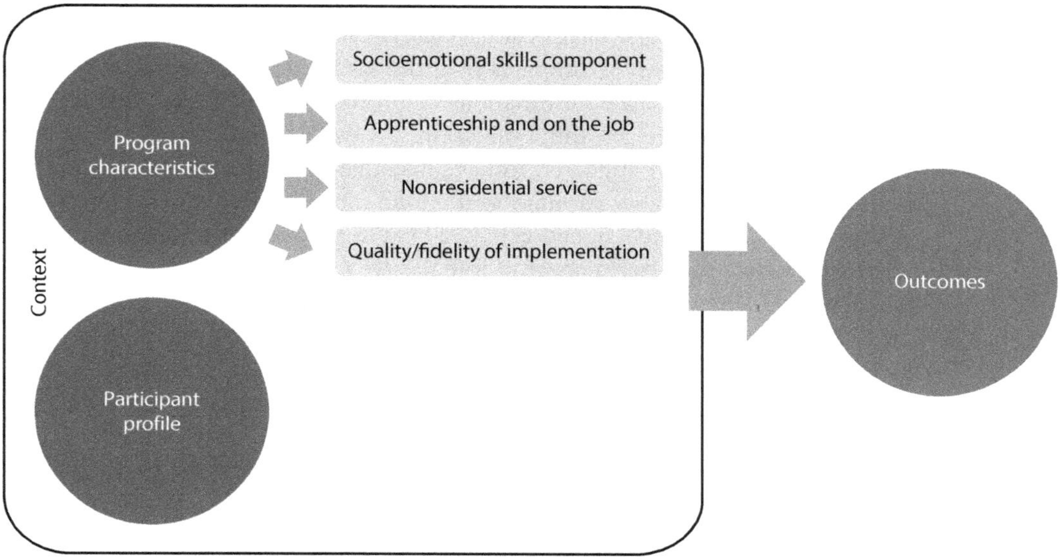

state's Department of Labor and Industries are greater than 20 percent within the first 2.5 years after apprentices leave the program.

By contrast, residential programs that foster job placement do not appear to be cost-effective. Programs such as Job Corps and National Guard Youth ChalleNGe have very high costs for trainee housing and meals and for teaching costs. Even with important benefits, those costs lead to net earnings effects of close to zero (Bloom, Gardenhire-Crooks, and Mandsager 2009; Millenky, Bloom, and Dillon 2010; Millenky and others 2011; Perez-Arce and others 2012; Schochet, Burghardt, and McConnell 2008).

These results are limited by the fact that out-of-school programs have short follow-up periods. In fact, only 25 percent of the programs analyzed in this book have a follow-up period that exceeds two years. Shorter follow-up periods may lead to an underestimation of the effects of active labor market programs[21] and may limit the number of outcomes that can be measured. For example, evaluations that cover only two months after an intervention cannot reasonably expect to find effects on fertility outcomes. This limitation restricts the accuracy of the rates of return calculated for these programs. In addition, it also increases the difficulty of making claims regarding the longevity of the results. For example, the evaluation of Jordan NOW found extremely large immediate effects from providing a subsidy to employers as an incentive to hire graduates of the program. Nevertheless, the effects disappeared 14 months after the start of the intervention. This finding is consistent with reports from Calero and others (2014), who report that the impact of wage subsidies peaks at 12 months and then fades.

http://dx.doi.org/10.1596/978-1-4648-0872-2

Kautz and others (2014) argue that this lack of long-term evaluation might be incorrectly fueling the perception that programs targeting adolescents are not as effective as programs that target earlier life cycles. For instance, if labor market–oriented programs have low impacts over the short run but significant impacts over the long run, calculated estimations might underestimate their effects. This problem is observable in the evaluation of the United States' Workforce Investment Act, which appeared to have negative impacts in the short run but actually resulted in higher earnings in the long run (Heinrich and others 2013). Caliendo, Schmidl, and Uhlendorff (2011) observe a similar phenomenon in Germany, where short-term negative impacts are followed by positive significant impacts after 10 months. Card, Kluve, and Weber (2015) analyze 200 econometric evaluations of active labor market programs and find that long-term evaluations seem more favorable: even though average impacts are close to zero in the short-term, impacts become positive and significant two or three years after the intervention.

Because of the diversity of out-of-school programs, identifying their effective elements is difficult. However, evidence suggests that program components matter, and that "workplace-based programs that teach non-cognitive skills appear to be the most effective remediation programs for adolescents" (Kautz and others 2014, 82). In particular,

- There appears to be a greater benefit from including socioemotional skills compared with having mainly cognition and academic learning (Kautz and others 2014). In the evaluation of Jordan NOW, Groh and others (2012) find that although life skills training had only slight effects on employment (no effects in the short term and a slight effect one year after program completion but only for those outside of Amman), it improved life outlook and reduced depression. Additionally, in the evaluation of the Ninaweza program (Kenya), Alvarez de Azevedo, Davis, and Charles (2013) find that the inclusion of a socioemotional skills component had a significant effect on knowledge acquisition, life skills, and the probability of obtaining a job. Oddly, the group in this program that went without life skills training experienced greater increases in their weekly income.
- Furthermore, on-the-job training appears to be a constant component of effective out-of-school programs (Calero and others 2014; Urzua and Puentes 2010). One reason could be that this type of program involves the transmission of field-specific job-related skills, as well as noncognitive skills, such as punctuality, personal presentation, and teamwork. Furthermore, workplace-oriented training eases matching of workers and firms. The prospect of future employment may also serve as an important incentive for participating youth, increasing their effort to meet the requirements of the particular profession. However, because these programs integrate cognitive and socioemotional education with particular incentives for satisfactory performance, they do not allow one to discern the relative effectiveness of each of these elements.

http://dx.doi.org/10.1596/978-1-4648-0872-2

Our limited evidence on the use of residential services to boost labor market outcomes is not promising. Only two programs in our sample of preventive programs offer residential services: Job Corps and National Guard Youth ChalleNGe. These programs take place in the United States, target at-risk youth and high-school dropouts, usually take more than a year to complete, and include training and remedial education as well as mentoring. Over the short term, they have substantial impacts on employment, educational attainment, and crime. However, the effects of Job Corps on earnings and the effects of National Guard Youth ChalleNGe on high school graduation and criminality fade over time.

Further analysis of the programs included in this book shows that, as expected, the quality of the programs mediates the magnitude of their effects. For example, the impact evaluation of Questscope Non-Formal Education (Jordan) found both significant negative effects in low-quality centers and important positive effects in high-quality centers. Also, the low-intensity socioemotional intervention called Jordan NOW was found to have a limited effect on women's graduation from public community colleges.[22]

Most programs appear to work better for younger individuals and females, and when implemented in cities (see figure 6.12). The impact of both Procajoven (Panama) and Jóvenes en Acción (Colombia) on the probability of employment, number of hours worked weekly, and labor earnings is limited to women. Procajoven also has greater effects in Panama City. Ibarrarán and others (2012) also find that Juventud y Empleo (Dominican Republic) has greater benefits for younger individuals and for those living in Santo Domingo, but more in men's formal employment. entra21 (Argentina), Questscope Non-Formal Education

Figure 6.12 Selected Participant Characteristics That Affect the Outcomes of Out-of-School Programs

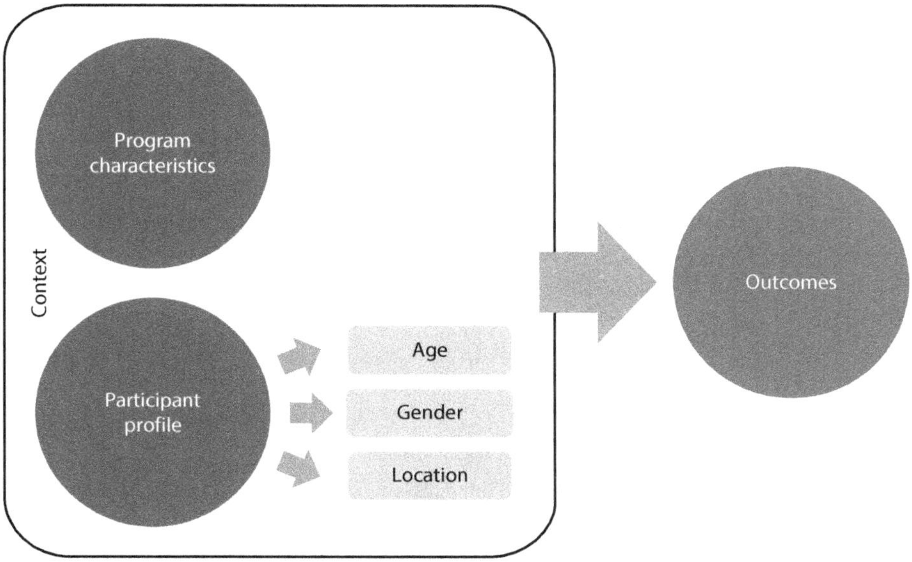

http://dx.doi.org/10.1596/978-1-4648-0872-2

(Jordan), and Job Corps (United States) also have greater impacts on younger cohorts. In contrast, the effects of entra21 and Team Awareness (United States) are greater for men. Additionally, Card, Kluve, and Weber (2010) report that youth programs lead to fewer and less positive results in labor outcomes. In an analysis of more than 200 econometric evaluations, Card, Kluve, and Weber (2015) find larger gains for females and participants that enter the program after long-term unemployment.

With regard to location, multiple authors argue that programs aimed at improving labor market outcomes appear to have greater effects in developing countries. For example, Urzua and Puentes (2010) and Ñopo and Saavedra (2003) find more positive evidence in Latin America and the Caribbean than in more industrialized countries. Betcherman, Olivas, and Dar (2004) document similar results after reviewing 69 impact evaluations of unemployed and youth training; the impacts they found in the 19 programs implemented in developing countries were greater than those found in the United States and Europe.

Notes

1. Appendix A describes the before-school programs that were analyzed.
2. The calculation focused on statistically significant outcomes only. Including both significant and nonsignificant outcomes would have been ideal, as that would have provided information on the objectives of the programs and their effectiveness. However, most evaluations do not report nonsignificant outcomes, resulting in no knowledge regarding further program objectives.
3. Only the Nurse-Family Partnership and the Jamaican Study find effects on cognitive abilities that persist over time.
4. Wealthier children who first attended primary school switched to preschool, but children from poorer families who were attending primary school left the formal education system when the official age of primary school was enforced.
5. Conscientiousness is defined as the degree to which a person is willing to comply with conventional rules, norms, and standards.
6. Currie and Thomas (1995) document that Head Start's impact on vulnerable minorities decreases significantly when these children stop attending the program and return to their initial environment.
7. Appendix B describes the school-based programs that were analyzed.
8. To avoid redundancy, prekindergarten and kindergarten programs were included in the preceding section concerning early childhood programs in an institutional setting.
9. See appendix B for further details.
10. According to Eisenberg and Mussen (1989, 3), prosocial behavior refers to "voluntary actions that are intended to help or benefit another individual or group of individuals."
11. Because of space and time limitations, this book does not analyze programs that take place during after-school hours or in the summer.
12. Standardized mean difference is defined as the difference between the treatment and control group means on an outcome variable divided by their pooled standard deviation.

http://dx.doi.org/10.1596/978-1-4648-0872-2

13. See, for example, Battistich, Schaps, and Wilson (2004) and Brock and others (2008).
14. According to the *World Development Indicators*, 73.6 percent of the world's population was over age 15 in 2013.
15. These programs are Ninaweza, Jordan NOW (New Opportunities for Women), EPAG (Economic Empowerment of Adolescent Girls and Young Women), and ELA (Empowerment and Livelihood for Adolescents).
16. In the case of Galpão Aplauso, Brazil faced high levels of formality (*com carteira assinada*), and the program did not rely on subsidized internships with a formal job (Calero and others 2014).
17. The impact evaluation of Juventud y Empleo captured socioemotional skills in two ways. First, it developed the Social and Personal Competencies Scale to capture leadership, behavior in conflict situations, self-esteem, abilities to relate to others, order, empathy, and communication skills. Second, it used Rosenberg's self-esteem scale and Duckworth's Grit scale.
18. For more information, see Goodman, Meltzer, and Bailey (1998).
19. Ninaweza provides 40 hours of life skills training, including attention to emotional intelligence, self-care, decision making, motivation, communication, cooperation and competition, goal setting, and teamwork. ELA provided life skills training that included materials on sexual and reproductive health, menstruation and menstrual disorders, pregnancy, sexually transmitted diseases, HIV/AIDS (human immunodeficiency virus/acquired immune deficiency syndrome) awareness, family planning, rape, management skills, negotiation and conflict resolution, leadership among adolescents, bride price, child marriage, and violence against women.
20. The impact evaluation of Galpão Aplauso uses the Social and Personal Competencies Scale developed for the evaluation of Juventud y Empleo in the Dominican Republic.
21. When analyzing more than 200 studies of active labor market programs, Card, Kluve, and Weber (2015) find that average impacts may be close to zero in the short run, but become more positive two to three years after program completion.
22. Jordan NOW provides 45 hours of socioemotional training over a nine-day period, with a maximum of 30 participants in each training group. The course covers effective communication and business writing skills (for example, making presentations and writing business reports and different types of correspondence), team building and teamwork skills (for example, characteristics of a successful team, how to work in different roles within a team), time management, positive thinking and how to use it in business situations, excellence in providing customer service, and résumé and interviewing skills.

References

Adda, Jerome, Christian Dustmann, Costas Meghir, and Jean-Marc Robin. 2013. "Career Progression, Economic Downturns, and Skills." NBER Working Paper 18832, National Bureau of Economic Research Cambridge, MA.

Alvarez de Azevedo, Thomaz, Jeff Davis, and Munene Charles. 2013. "Testing What Works in Youth Employment: Evaluating Kenya's Ninaweza Program." Global Partnership for Youth Employment, Washington, DC.

Alzúa, María Laura, Guillermo Cruces, and Carolina Lopez Erazo. 2013. "Youth Training Programs beyond Employment: Evidence from a Randomized Controlled Trial." https://www2.unine.ch/files/content/sites/irene/files/shared/documents/seminaires/Alzua.pdf.

http://dx.doi.org/10.1596/978-1-4648-0872-2

Araujo, María Caridad, Florencia López-Bóo, Juan Manuel Puyana. 2013. *Overview of Early Childhood Development Services in Latin America and the Caribbean*. Washington, DC: Inter-American Development Bank, Social Protection and Health Division.

Arthur, Winfred Jr., Winston Bennett Jr., Pamela L. Stanush, and Theresa L. McNelly. 1998. "Factors That Influence Skill Decay and Retention: A Quantitative Review and Analysis." *Human Performance* 11 (1): 57–101.

Aseltine, Robert H. Jr., Matthew Dupre, and Pamela Lamlein. 2000. "Mentoring as a Drug Prevention Strategy: An Evaluation of 'Across Ages.'" *Adolescent and Family Health* 1 (1): 11–20.

Attanasio, Orazio, Adriana Kugler, and Costas Meghir. 2011. "Subsidizing Vocational Training for Disadvantaged Youth in Colombia: Evidence from a Randomized Trial." *American Economic Journal: Applied Economics* 3 (3): 188–220.

Battistich, Victor, Eric Schaps, and Nance Wilson. 2004. "Effects of an Elementary School Intervention on Students' 'Connectedness' to School and Social Adjustment during Middle School." *Journal of Primary Prevention* 24 (3): 243–62.

Behrman, Jere R., Yingmei Cheng, and Petra E. Todd. 2004. "Evaluating Preschool Programs When Length of Exposure to the Program Varies: A Nonparametric Approach." *Review of Economics and Statistics* 86 (1): 108–32.

Belfield, Clive, Brooks Bowden, Alli Klapp, Henry Levin, Robert Shand, and Sabine Zander. 2015. "The Economic Value of Social and Emotional Learning." Center for Benefit-Cost Studies in Education, Teachers College, Columbia University, New York.

Betcherman, Gordon, Karina Olivas, and Amit Dar. 2004. "Impacts of Active Labor Market Programs: New Evidence from Evaluations with Particular Attention to Developing and Transition Countries." Social Protection Discussion Paper 0402, World Bank, Washington, DC.

Bloom, Dan, Alissa Gardenhire-Crooks, and Conrad Mandsager. 2009. "Reengaging High School Dropouts: Early Results of the National Guard Youth Challenge Program Evaluation." Report, MDRC, New York.

Bond, Lynne A., and Amy M. Carmola Hauf. 2004. "Taking Stock and Putting Stock in Primary Prevention: Characteristics of Effective Programs." *Journal of Primary Prevention* 24 (3): 199–221.

Borghans, Lex, Angela Lee Duckworth, James J. Heckman, and Bas ter Weel. 2008. "The Economics and Psychology of Personality Traits." *Journal of Human Resources* 43 (4): 972–1059.

Bougheas, Spiros, and Yannis Georgellis. 2004. "Early Career Mobility and Earnings Profiles of German Apprentices: Theory and Empirical Evidence." *Labour* 18 (2): 233–63.

Bouguen, Adrien, Deon Filmer, Karen Macours, and Sophie Naudeau. 2014. "Preschools and Early Childhood Development in a Second Best World: Evidence from a Scaled-Up Experiment in Cambodia." CEPR Discussion Paper 10170, Center for Economic Policy Research, Washington, DC.

Boyle, Douglas, and Connie Hassett-Walker. 2008. "Reducing Overt and Relational Aggression among Young Children: The Results from a Two-Year Outcome Study." *Journal of School Violence* 7 (1): 27–42.

Brock, Laura L., Tracy K. Nishida, Cynthia Chiong, Kevin J. Grimm, and Sara E. Rimm-Kaurman. 2008. "Children's Perceptions of the Classroom Environment and Social and Academic Performance: A Longitudinal Analysis of the Contribution of the Responsive Classroom Approach." *Journal of School Psychology* 46 (2): 129–49.

Brown, Joshua L., Stephanie M. Jones, Maria D. LaRusso, and J. Lawrence Aber. 2010. "Improving Classroom Quality: Teacher Influences and Experimental Impacts of the 4Rs Program." *Journal of Educational Psychology* 102 (1): 153–67.

Calero, Carla, Carlos Henrique Corseuil, Veronica Gonzales, Jochen Kluve, and Yuri Soares. 2014. "Can Arts-Based Interventions Enhance Labor Market Outcomes among Youth? Evidence from a Randomized Trial in Rio de Janeiro." IZA Discussion Paper 8210, Institute for the Study of Labor, Bonn.

Caliendo, Marco, Ricarda Schmidl, and Arne Uhlendorff. 2011. "Social Networks, Job Search Methods and Reservation Wages: Evidence for Germany." *International Journal of Manpower* 32 (7): 796–824.

Card, David, Jochen Kluve, and Andrea Weber. 2010. "Active Labour Market Policy Evaluations: A Meta-Analysis." *Economic Journal* 120 (548): F452–F477.

———. 2015. "What Works? A Meta-Analysis of Recent Active Labor Market Program Evaluations." NBER Working Paper 21431, National Bureau of Economic Research, Cambridge, MA.

Chang, Florence, and Marco A. Muñoz. 2006. "School Personnel Educating the Whole Child: Impact of Character Education on Teachers' Self-Assessment and Student Development." *Journal of Personality Evaluation in Education* 19: 35–49.

Chetty, Raj, John N. Friedman, Nathaniel Hilger, Emmanuel Saez, Diane W. Schanzenbach, and Danny Yagan. 2010. "How Does Your Kindergarten Classroom Affect Your Earnings? Evidence from Project STAR." NBER Working Paper 16381, National Bureau of Economic Research, Cambridge, MA.

Clark, Damon, and René Fahr. 2002. "The Promise of Workplace Training for Non-College-Bound Youth: Theory and Evidence from German Apprenticeship." Discussion Paper 518, Centre for Economic Performance, London School of Economics.

Connell, Arin M., and Thomas J. Dishion. 2008. "Reducing Depression among At-Risk Early Adolescents: Three-Year Effects of a Family-Centered Intervention Embedded within Schools." *Journal of Family Psychology* 22 (4): 574–85.

Connell, Arin M., Susan Klostermann, and Thomas J. Dishion. 2012. "Family Checkup Effects on Adolescent Arrest Trajectories: Variation by Developmental Subtype." *Journal of Research on Adolescence* 22 (2): 367–80.

CPPRG (Conduct Problems Prevention Research Group). 2010. "The Effects of a Multiyear Universal Socio-Emotional Learning Program: The Role of Student and School Characteristics." *Journal of Consulting and Clinical Psychology* 78 (2): 156–68.

Cunha, Flavio, James J. Heckman, Lance Lochner, and Dimitriy V. Masterov. 2005. "Interpreting the Evidence on Life Cycle Skill Formation." In *Handbook of the Economics of Education*, vol. 1, edited by Eric A. Hanushek and Finis Welch, 697–812. Amsterdam and New York: North-Holland.

Currie, Janet, and Duncan Thomas. 1995. "Does Head Start Make a Difference?" *American Economic Review* 85 (3): 341–64.

Domitrovich, Celene E., Rebecca C. Cortes, and Mark T. Greenberg. 2007. "Improving Young Children's Social and Emotional Competence: A Randomized Trial of the Preschool PATHS Curriculum." *Journal of Primary Prevention* 28 (2): 67–91.

Durlak, Joseph A. 1997. *Successful Prevention Programs for Children and Adolescents.* New York: Plenum Press.

http://dx.doi.org/10.1596/978-1-4648-0872-2

Durlak, Joseph A., Roger Weissberg, Allison Dymnicki, Rebecca Taylor, and Kriston Schellinger. 2011. "The Impact of Enhancing Students' Social and Emotional Learning: A Meta-Analysis of School-Based Universal Programs." *Child Development* 82 (1): 405–32.

Durlak, Joseph A., Roger Weissberg, and Molly Pachan. 2010. "A Meta-Analysis of After-School Programs That Seek to Promote Personal and Social Skills in Children and Adolescents." *American Journal of Community Psychology* 45 (3–4): 294–309.

Dusenbury, Linda, and Mathea Falco. 1995. "Eleven Components of Effective Drug Abuse Prevention Curricula." *Journal of School Health* 65 (10): 420–25.

Eckenrode, John, Mary Campa, Dennis W. Luckey, Charles R. Henderson, Robert Cole, Harriet J. Kitzman, Elizabeth Anson, Kimberly Sidora-Arcoleo, and David L. Olds. 2010. "Long-Term Effects of Prenatal and Infancy Nurse Home Visitation on the Life Course of Youths: 19-Year Follow-Up of a Randomized Trial." *Journal of the American Medical Association* 164 (1): 9–15.

Eisenberg, Nancy, and Paul Henry Mussen, eds. 1989. *The Roots of Prosocial Behavior in Children*. Cambridge: Cambridge University Press.

Epstein, Ann S. 1993. *Training for Quality: Improving Early Childhood Programs through Systematic In-Service Training*. Ypsilanti, MI: HighScope Press.

Espelage, Dorothy L., Sabina Low, Joshua R. Polanin, and Eric C. Brown. 2013. "The Impact of a Middle School Program to Reduce Aggression, Victimization, and Sexual Violence." *Journal of Adolescent Health* 53 (2): 180–86.

Fazio, Maria Victoria. 2011. "Programa Juventud y Empleo en República Dominicana: Análisis de la percepción de los empleadores acerca ee las pasantías y ee las perspectivas ee inserción laboral de los jóvenes." Técnical Note IDB-TN-240, Inter-American Development Bank, Washington, DC.

Fosco, Gregory M., Jennifer L. Frank, Elizabeth A. Stormshak, and Thomas J. Dishion. 2013. "Opening the 'Black Box': Family Check-Up Intervention Effects on Self-Regulation That Prevents Growth in Problem Behavior and Substance Use." *Journal of School Psychology* 51 (4): 455–68.

Frey, Karin S., Miriam K. Hirschstein, Leihua Van Schoiack Edstrom, and Jennie L Snell. 2009. "Observed Reductions in School Bullying, Non-Bullying Aggression, and Destructive Bystander Behavior: A Longitudinal Evaluation." *Journal of Educational Psychology* 101: 466–81.

Gertler, Paul, James Heckman, Rodrigo Pinto, Arianna Zanolini, Christel Vermeerch, Susan Walker, Susan Chang-Lopez, and Sally Grantham-McGregor. 2013. "Labor Market Returns to Early Childhood Stimulation: A 20-Year Follow Up to an Experimental Intervention in Jamaica." Policy Research Working Paper 6529, World Bank, Washington, DC.

González-Velosa, Carolina, Laura Ripani, and David Rosas-Shady. 2012. "How Can Job Opportunities for Young People in Latin America Be Improved?" Technical Note IDB-TN-345, Inter-American Development Bank, Washington, DC.

Goodman, Robert, Howard Meltzer, and V. Bailey. 1998. "The Strengths and Difficulties Questionnaire: A Pilot Study on the Validity of the Self-Report Version." *European Child and Adolescent Psychiatry* 7 (3): 125–30.

Gresham, Frank M. 1995. "Best Practices in Social Skills Training." In *Best Practices in School Psychology III*, edited by Alex Thomas and Jeff Grimes, 1021–30. Washington, DC: National Association of School Psychologists.

http://dx.doi.org/10.1596/978-1-4648-0872-2

Groh, Matthew, Nandini Krishnan, David McKenzie, and Tara Vishwanath. 2012. "Soft Skills or Hard Cash? The Impact of Training and Wage Subsidy Programs on Female Youth Employment in Jordan." Policy Research Working Paper 6141, World Bank, Washington, DC.

Hahn, Robert, Dawna Fuqua-Whitley, Holly Wethington, Jessica Lowy, Alex Crosby, Mindi Fullilove, Robert Johnson, Akiva Liberman, Eve Moscicki, LeShawndra Price, Susan R. Snyder, Farris Tuma, Stella Cory, Glenda Stone, Kaushik Mukhopadhaya, Sajal Chattopadhyay, and Linda Dahlberg. 2007. "Effectiveness of Universal School-Based Programs to Prevent Violent and Aggressive Behavior: A Systematic Review." *American Journal of Preventive Medicine* 33 (2 Suppl.): S114–S129.

Heckman, James J. 2008. "Schools, Skills and Synapses." *Economic Inquiry* 46 (3): 289–324.

Heckman, James J., Lena Malofeeva, Rodrigo Pinto, and Peter A. Savelyev. 2009. "The Powerful Role of Noncognitive Capabilities in Explaining the Effects of the Perry Preschool Program." Unpublished manuscript, University of Chicago, Department of Economics.

Heckman, James J., and Tim Kautz. 2012. "Hard Evidence on Soft Skills." *Labour Economics* 19 (4): 451–64.

———. 2013. "Fostering and Measuring Skills: Programs That Improve Character and Cognition." NBER Working Paper 19656, National Bureau of Economic Research, Cambridge, MA.

Heckman, James J., Jora Stixrud, and Sergio Urzua. 2006. "The Effects of Cognitive and Noncognitive Abilities on Labor Market Outcomes and Social Behavior." *Journal of Labor Economics* 24 (3): 411–48.

Heinrich, Carolyn J., Peter R. Mueser, Kenneth R. Troske, Kyung-Seong Jeon, and Daver C. Kahvecioglu. 2013. "Do Public Employment and Training Programs Work?" *IZA Journal of Labor Economics* 2 (1): 1–23.

Herrera, Carla, Tina J. Kauh, Siobhan M. Cooney, Jean Baldwin Grossman, and Jennifer McMaken. 2008. "High School Students as Mentors: Findings from the Big Brothers Big Sisters School-Based Mentoring Impact Study." Public/Private Ventures, Philadelphia. http://www.childtrends.org/?programs=big-brothersbig-sisters-school-based-mentoring#sthash.NrUcSLm1.dpuf.

Hollenbeck, Kevin. 2008. "Is There a Role for Public Support of Incumbent Worker On-the-Job Training?" Working Paper 08–138, W. E. Upjohn Institute for Employment Research, Kalamazoo, MI.

Honorati, Maddalina, and Thomas P. McArdle. 2013. "The Nuts and Bolts of Designing and Implementing Training Programs in Developing Countries." Working Paper 78980, World Bank, Washington, DC.

Howard, Kimberly S., and Jeanne Brooks-Gunn. 2009. "The Role of Home-Visiting Programs in Preventing Child Abuse and Neglect." *Future of Children* 19 (2): 119–46.

Humphrey, Neal, Ann Lendrum, and Michael Wigelsworth. 2010. "Social and Emotional Aspects of Learning (SEAL) Programme in Secondary Schools: National Evaluation." Research Report DFE-RR049, Department for Education, London.

Ibarrarán, Pablo, Jochen Kluve, Laura Ripani, and David Rosas-Shady. 2015. "Experimental Evidence on the Long-Term Impacts of a Youth Training Program." IZA Discussion Paper 9136, Institute for the Study of Labor, Bonn.

Ibarrarán, Pablo, Laura Ripani, Bibiana Taboada, Juan Miguel Villa, and Brigida Garcia. 2012. "Life Skills, Employability and Training for Disadvantaged Youth: Evidence from a Randomized Evaluation Design." IZA Discussion Paper 6617, Institute for the Study of Labor, Bonn.

Jones, Stephanie M., and Suzanne M. Bouffard. 2012. "Social and Emotional Learning in Schools: From Programs to Strategies." *Social Policy Report* 26 (4): 1–22.

Jones, Stephanie M., Joshua L. Brown, and J. Lawrence Aber. 2011. "Two-Year Impacts of a Universal School-Based Social-Emotional and Literacy Intervention: An Experiment in Translational Developmental Research." *Child Development* 82: 533–54.

Jones, Stephanie M., Joshua L. Brown, Wendy Hoglund, and J. Lawrence Aber. 2010. "A School-Randomized Clinical Trial of an Integrated Social-Emotional Learning and Literacy Intervention: Impacts after One School Year." *Journal of Consulting and Clinical Psychology* 78 (6): 829–42.

Kautz, Tim, James J. Heckman, Ron Diris, Bas ter Weel, and Lex Borghans. 2014. "Fostering and Measuring Skills: Improving Cognitive and Non-Cognitive Skills to Promote Lifetime Success." NBER Working Paper 20749, National Bureau of Economic Research, Cambridge, MA.

Kitzman, Harriet J., David L. Olds, Robert E. Cole, Carole A. Hanks, Elizabeth A. Anson, Kimberly J. Arcoleo, Dennis W. Luckey, Michael D. Knudtson, Charles R. Henderson Jr., and John R. Holmberg. 2010. "Enduring Effects of Prenatal and Infancy Home Visiting by Nurses on Children: Follow-Up of a Randomized Trial among Children at Age 12 Years." *Archives of Pediatrics and Adolescent Medicine* 164 (5): 412–18.

Klevens, Joanne, José William Martínez, Brenda Le, Carlos Rojas, Adriana Duque, and Rafael Tovar. 2009. "Evaluation of Two Interventions to Reduce Aggressive and Antisocial Behavior in First and Second Graders in a Resource-Poor Setting." *International Journal of Educational Research* 48 (5): 307–19.

Krueger, Alan B., and Diane M. Whitmore. 2001. "The Effect of Attending a Small Class in the Early Grades on College Test Taking and Middle School Test Results: Evidence from Project STAR." *Economic Journal* 111 (468): 1–28.

Kuckulenz, Anja. 2007. *Studies on Continuing Vocational Training in Germany: An Empirical Assessment. Vol. 37, ZEW Economic Studies Series*. Heidelberg, Germany: Physica-Verlag.

Kumpfer, Karol L., Rose Alvarado, Connie Tait, and Charles Turner. 2002. "Effectiveness of School-Based Family and Children's Skills Training for Substance Abuse Prevention among 6–8-Year-Old Rural Children." *Psychology of Addictive Behaviors* 16 (45): S65–S71.

Levenstein, Phyllis, Susan Levenstein, James A. Shiminski, and Judith E. Stolzberg. 1998. "Long-Term Impact of a Verbal Interaction Program for At-Risk Toddlers: An Exploratory Study of High School Outcomes in a Replication of the Mother–Child Home Program." *Journal of Applied Developmental Psychology* 19 (2): 267–85.

Lewis, Kendra M., Marc B. Schure, Niloofar Bavarian, David L. Dubois, Joseph Day, Peter Ji, Naida Silverthorn, Alan Acock, Samuel Vuchinich, and Brian R. Flay. 2013. "Problem Behavior and Urban, Low-Income Youth: A Randomized Controlled Trial of Positive Action in Chicago." *American Journal of Preventive Medicine* 4 (6): 622–30.

http://dx.doi.org/10.1596/978-1-4648-0872-2

Loeb, Susanna, Margaret Bridges, Daphna Bassok, Bruce Fuller, and Russell W. Rumberger. 2007. "How Much Is Too Much? The Influence of Preschool Centers on Children's Social and Cognitive Development." *Economics of Education Review* 26 (1): 52–66.

Lösel, Friedrich. 2001. "Evaluating the Effectiveness of Correctional Programs: Bridging the Gap between Research and Practice." In *Offender Rehabilitation in Practice: Implementing and Evaluating Effective Programs*, edited by Gary A. Bernfeld, David P. Farrington, and Alan W. Leschied, 67–92. Chichester, U.K.: Wiley.

Lösel, Friedrich, and Andreas Beelmann. 2003. "Effects of Child Skills Training in Preventing Antisocial Behavior: A Systematic Review of Randomized Evaluations." *Annals of the American Academy of Political and Social Science* 587 (1): 84–109.

Lynch, Kathleen Bodisch. 1998. "Results of Michigan Replication Study 1996–97: Child Outcomes—Al's Pals: Kids Making Healthy Choices." Institute for Development Disabilities, Virginia Commonwealth University, Richmond.

Lynch, Kathleen Bodisch, Susan R. Geller, and Denise R. Hunt. 1998."Successful Program Development Using Implementation Evaluation." *Journal of Prevention and Intervention in the Community* 17 (2): 51–64.

Lynch, Kathleen Bodisch, Susan R. Geller, and Melinda G. Schmidt. 2004. "Multi-Year Evaluation of the Effectiveness of a Resilience-Based Prevention Program for Young Children." *Journal of Primary Prevention* 24 (3): 335–53.

Magnuson, Katherine A., Christopher Ruhm, and Jane Waldfogel. 2007. "Does Prekindergarten Improve School Preparation and Performance?" *Economics of Education Review* 26 (1): 33–51.

Martinez, Sebastian, Sophie Nadeau, and Vitor Pereira. 2012. "The Promise of Preschool in Africa: A Randomized Impact Evaluation of Early Childhood Development in Rural Mozambique." enGender Impact: The World Bank's Gender Impact Evaluation Database, World Bank, Washington, DC.

McCord, Joan. 1978. "A Thirty-Year Follow-Up of Treatment Effects." *American Psychologist* 33 (3): 284–89.

Melmed, Matthew. 2008. Testimony on "Investing in Early Education: Paths to Improving Children's Success" before the House Committee on Education and Labor, 110th Cong., 2nd sess., January 23.

Millenky, Megan, Dan Bloom, and Colleen Dillon. 2010. "Making the Transition: Interim Results of the National Guard Youth Challenge Evaluation." MDRC, New York.

Millenky, Megan, Dan Bloom, Sara Muller-Ravett, and Joseph Broadus. 2011. "Staying on Course: Three-Year Results of the National Guard Youth Challenge Evaluation." MDRC, New York.

NICHHD (National Institute of Child Health and Human Development Early Child Care Research Network). 2003. "Social Functioning in First Grade: Associations with Earlier Home and Child Care Predictors and with Current Classroom Experiences." *Child Development* 74 (6): 1639–62.

Ñopo, Hugo, and Jaime Saavedra. 2003. "Recomendaciones para la mejora del levantamiento de la linea de base de projoven y sugerencias para la construcción de una linea de base aleatorizada como parte de un disen o experimental" (Recommendations to Improve Baseline Data Collection for Projoven and to Construct a Baseline Using Random Assignment as Part of an Experimental Design). Grupo de Análisis para el Desarrollo, Lima.

http://dx.doi.org/10.1596/978-1-4648-0872-2

Olds, David L. 2006. "The Nurse-Family Partnership: An Evidence-Based Preventive Intervention." *Infant Mental Health Journal* 27 (1): 5–25.

Olds, David L., John Eckenrode, Charles R. Henderson Jr., Harriet J. Kitzman, Jane Powers, Robert Cole, Kimberly Sidora, Pamela Morris, Lisa M. Pettitt, and Dennis W. Luckey. 1997. "Long-Term Effects of Home Visitation on Maternal Life Course and Child Abuse and Neglect: Fifteen-Year Follow-Up of a Randomized Trial." *Journal of the American Medical Association* 278 (8): 637–43.

Olds, David L., Charles R. Henderson Jr., Robert Chamberlin, and Robert Tatelbaum. 1986. "Preventing Child Abuse and Neglect: A Randomized Trial of Nurse Home Visitation." *Pediatrics* 78 (1): 65–78.

Olds, David L., Charles R. Henderson Jr., Robert Cole, John Eckenrode, Harriet J. Kitzman, Dennis W. Luckey, and Jane Powers. 1986. "Long-Term Effects of Nurse Home Visitation on Children's Criminal and Antisocial Behavior: 15-Year Follow-Up of a Randomized Controlled Trial." *Journal of the American Medical Association* 280 (14): 1238–44.

Olds, David L., Charles R. Henderson Jr., and Harriet J. Kitzman. 1994. "Does Prenatal and Infancy Nurse Home Visitation Have Enduring Effects on Qualities of Parental Caregiving and Child Health at 25 to 50 Months of Life?" *Pediatrics* 93 (1): 89–98.

Olds, David L., John R. Holmberg, Nancy Donelan-McCall, Dennis W. Luckey, Michael D. Knudtson, and JoAnn Robinson. 2014. "Effects of Home Visits by Paraprofessionals and by Nurses on Children: Follow-Up of a Randomized Trial at Ages 6 and 9 Years." *JAMA Pediatrics* 168 (2): 114–21.

Olds, David L., Harriet J. Kitzman, Robert Cole, Carole Hanks, Kimberly Arcoleo, Elizabeth Anson, Dennis W. Luckey, Michael D. Knudtson, Charles R. Henderson Jr., Jessica Bondy, and Amanda J. Stevenson. 2010. "Enduring Effects of Prenatal and Infancy Home Visiting by Nurses on Maternal Life Course and Government Spending: Follow-Up of a Randomized Trial among Children at Age 12 Years." *Journal of the American Medical Association* 164 (5): 419–24.

Olds, David L., Harriet J. Kitzman, Carole Hanks, Robert Cole, Elizabeth Anson, Kimberly Sidora-Arcoleo, and Jessica Bondy. 2007. "Effects of Nurse Home Visiting on Maternal and Child Functioning: Age-9 Follow-Up of a Randomized Trial." *Pediatrics* 120 (4): e832–e845.

Payton, John, Roger P. Weissberg, Joseph A. Durlak, Allison B. Dymnicki, Rebecca D. Taylor, Kriston B. Schellinger, and Molly Pachan. 2008. "The Positive Impact of Social and Emotional Learning for Kindergarten to Eighth-Grade Students: Findings from Three Scientific Reviews—Technical Report." Collaborative for Academic, Social, and Emotional Learning, Chicago.

Perez-Arce, Francisco, Louay Constant, David S. Loughran, and Lynn A. Karoly. 2012. "A Cost–Benefit Analysis of the National Guard Youth ChalleNGe Program." RAND Research Monograph TR1193, RAND Corporation, Santa Monica, CA.

Rolnick, Arthur J., and Rob Grunewald. 2007. "The Economics of Early Childhood Development as Seen by Two Fed Economists." *Community Investments* 19 (2): 13–14, 30.

Rubio-Codina, Marta, Orazio Attanasio, Costas Meghir, Natalia Varela, and Sally Grantham-McGregor. 2014. "The Socio-Economic Gradient of Child Development: Cross-Sectional Evidence from Children 6–42 Months in Bogota." *Journal of Human Resources* 50 (2): 464–83.

http://dx.doi.org/10.1596/978-1-4648-0872-2

Rutter, Michael, 1987. "Psychosocial Resilience and Protective Mechanisms." *American Journal of Orthopsychiatry* 57 (3): 316–31.

Schochet, Peter Z., John Burghardt, and Sheena McConnell. 2008. "Does Job Corps Work? Impact Findings from the National Job Corps Study." *American Economic Review* 98 (5): 1864–86.

Schweinhart, Lawrence J., and David P. Weikart. 1997. "The High/Scope Preschool Curriculum Comparison Study through Age 23." *Early Childhood Research Quarterly* 12 (2): 117–43.

Shady, Norbert, and Christina Paxson. 2007. "Does Money Matter? The Effects of Cash Transfers on Child Health and Development in Rural Ecuador." Policy Research Working Paper 4226, World Bank, Washington, DC.

Snyder, Frank J., Alan Acock, Sam Vuchinich, Michael W. Beets, Isaac J. Washburn, and Brian R. Flay. 2013. "Preventing Negative Behaviors among Elementary-School Students through Enhancing Students' Social-Emotional and Character Development." *American Journal of Health Promotion* 28 (1): 50–58.

Stormshak, Elizabeth A., Arin M. Connell, and Thomas J. Dishion. 2009. "An Adaptive Approach to Family-Centered Intervention in Schools: Linking Intervention Engagement to Academic Outcomes in Middle and High School." *Prevention Science* 10 (3): 221–35.

Stormshak, Elizabeth A., Arin M. Connell, Marie Hélène Véronneau, Michael W. Myers, Thomas J. Dishion, Kathryn Kavanagh, and Allison S. Caruthers. 2011. "An Ecological Approach to Promoting Early Adolescent Mental Health and Social Adaptation: Family-Centered Intervention in Public Middle Schools." *Child Development* 82 (1): 209–25.

Urzua, Sergio, and Esteban Puentes. 2010. "La evidencia del impacto de los programas de capacitación en el desempeño en el mercado laboral." Inter-American Development Bank, Washington, DC.

Van Ryzin, Mark. J., Gregory M. Fosco, and Thomas J. Dishion. 2012. "Family and Peer Predictors of Substance Use from Early Adolescence to Early Adulthood: An 11-Year Prospective Analysis." *Addictive Behaviors* 37 (12): 1314–24.

Van Ryzin, Mark. J., Elizabeth A. Stormshak, and Thomas J. Dishion. 2012. "Engaging Parents in the Family Check-Up in Middle School: Longitudinal Effects on Family Conflict and Problem Behavior through the High School Transition." *Journal of Adolescent Health* 50 (6): 627–33.

Vreeman, Rachel C., and Aaron E. Carroll. 2007. "A Systematic Review of School-Based Programs to Prevent Bullying." *Archives of Pediatrics and Adolescent Medicine* 161 (1): 78–88.

Wagner, Mary M., and Serena L. Clayton. 1999. "The Parents as Teachers Program: Results from Two Demonstrations." *Future of Children* 9 (1): 91–115.

Wagner, Mary M., Donna Spiker, and Margaret Inman Linn. 2002. "The Effectiveness of the Parents as Teachers Program with Low-Income Parents and Children." *Topics in Early Childhood Special Education* 22 (2): 67–81.

Weissberg, Roger P., and Mark T. Greenberg. 1998. "School and Community Competence-Enhancement and Prevention Programs." In *Handbook of Child Psychology*, 5th ed., vol. 4, edited by William Damon, Richard M. Lerner, Irving E. Sigel, K. Ann Renninger, 877–954. Hoboken, NJ: Wiley.

http://dx.doi.org/10.1596/978-1-4648-0872-2

Wilson, Sandra Jo, and Mark W. Lipsey. 2007. "School-Based Programs for Aggressive and Disruptive Behavior: Update of a Meta-Analysis." *American Journal of Preventive Medicine* 33 (Suppl. 2): S130–S143.

Winkelmann, Rainer. 1996. "Employment Prospects and Skill Acquisition of Apprenticeship-Trained Workers in Germany." *Industrial and Labor Relations Review* 49 (4): 658–72.

Word, Elizabeth, John Johnson, Helen Pate Bain, B. DeWayne Fulton, Jan Boyd Zaharies, Martha Nannette Lintz, Charles M. Achiles, John Folger, and Carolyn Breda. 1990. "Student/Teacher Achievement Ratio (STAR) Tennessee's K–3 Class Size Study: Final Summary Report, 1985–1990." Tennessee State Department of Education, Nashville.

Zielinski, David S., John Eckenrode, and David L. Olds. 2009. "Nurse Home Visitation and the Prevention of Child Maltreatment: Impact on the Timing of Official Reports." *Development and Psychopathology* 21 (2): 441–53.

CHAPTER 7

Program Findings: What Works (or Doesn't Work) in Fostering Socioemotional Skills?

This chapter presents our best effort to synthesize the most important findings of the extensive literature on the rigorous evaluations of programs that seek to promote socioemotional skills, usually alongside fostering several other skills or behaviors. The findings below summarize results along the following dimensions: targeting, focus, impacts, replicability, and evaluation.

Targeting

Most programs reviewed are oriented toward individuals with high vulnerability. Before-school programs tend to benefit (a) children in low socioeconomic strata or who belong to minority groups or (b) children whose parents are poorly educated, have low occupational status, have low cognitive skills, or are in their teenage years. School-based programs are often carried out in institutions located in high-risk areas, including regions with low income, considerable school absenteeism, high mobility, or elevated crime rates. Finally, out-of-school programs focus primarily on low-income unemployed individuals, those who have dropped out of the education system, or women. With regard to age, gender, and location, programs tend to target all age ranges, are mostly gender neutral (although a few out-of-school programs focus on women), and focus on urban areas.

Because of the differences in the age groups covered, the process for entry into the different programs varies greatly throughout the life cycle: whereas before-school programs require parental consent and interest, school-based programs normally require consent only from school officials, though some programs do seek parental consent. Finally, out-of-school programs are sought out by youths and adults who make their own decisions about whether to join.

http://dx.doi.org/10.1596/978-1-4648-0872-2

Focus

Another important finding is that few programs focus exclusively on the development of socioemotional skills. For example, most before-school programs also seek to provide care or to support cognitive development or school readiness; school-based programs seek to improve classroom climate and to decrease aggressive, violent, or antisocial behaviors and substance abuse; and out-of-school programs tend to have labor market–related components. This finding is expected, because socioemotional skills development is normally part of a broader curriculum.

Impacts

Most of the before-school programs focus on highly vulnerable children and their families. They have important effects on cognitive skills and academic outcomes in the short run, whereas in the long run they improve behavior and risk factors, which indicates that they can modify socioemotional skills. These programs appear to be particularly effective when targeting vulnerable populations, as well as when they have multiple components, involve parents, and are intense with regard to instruction time and the teacher-to-child ratio.

Unlike most early childhood development programs, school-based programs tend to be universal at a school or classroom level, benefiting all children and adolescents in the classroom or attending the institution. The evidence regarding these programs is less widespread, but available results show a particularly strong effect on such risk factors as internalizing and externalizing behavior, aggression toward peers, and cooperation. Long and intense programs tend to be more effective, as do those that target vulnerable or at-risk populations.

Programs for out-of-school children and youths are usually designed to achieve immediate labor market outcomes (for example, job placement, formal employment, and higher wages). Although some of these programs show positive and statistically significant effects on socioemotional skills, the impacts tend to be small. These programs seem to be cost-effective, but long-term evaluation is lacking.

Early childhood programs appear to have a greater impact than those that take place later in life. Kautz and others (2014) state that only very early childhood programs (before age three) improve IQ (intelligence quotient) in a lasting way. Further, they suggest that the most promising adolescent programs integrate aspects of work into traditional education, breaking down the rigid separation between school and employment. Kautz and others (2014) explain that early childhood is a sensitive period for cognitive and noncognitive skills development. Furthermore, through dynamic complementarity, investments in the early years make later investments more productive. They also state that the most successful programs target preschoolers (after age three) and primary school children, improving later-life outcomes by developing socioemotional skills. However, as will be explained

http://dx.doi.org/10.1596/978-1-4648-0872-2

below, these results could partially reflect the fact that early childhood programs have longer follow-up periods.

Throughout the life cycle, socioemotional skills acquisition appears to explain important life outcomes. Several programs throughout the life cycle find long-term effects on earnings despite no indication of cognitive gain. This finding suggests that the long-term effects result from a change in beneficiaries' socioemotional skills. Among these programs are the HighScope Perry Preschool Program, the Abecedarian Program, and the Career Academies Program (before- and during-school programs).

Replicability

Finally, there are questions regarding replicability, as small-scale programs appear to be more effective than massive ones, and external research on scaling-up programs frequently shows that positive effects diminish with dissemination (Durlak and DuPre 2008). Kautz and others (2014) find that the reason behind this outcome in early childhood development programs is that large-scale programs are less intensive and involve parents less frequently. Others argue that this outcome is the result of higher levels of program fidelity in impact evaluations of small-scale programs: normally, the researcher or highly trained university students implement the intervention, whereas the program itself is normally run by individuals with lower education attainment levels, less training, or less commitment to the project.

The diminishing positive effects with dissemination might be explained by, among other causes, the following: the programs are seldom designed for universal coverage; and when they are scaled up, they experience lower participation rates and lower retention, have lower levels of quality and fidelity, and are unable to meet families' needs (Dodge and others 2014; Howard and Brooks-Gunn 2009). Lösel and Beelmann find greater effects in rigorous impact evaluations of school-based programs that have smaller sample sizes and state, "in large studies, difficulties in maintaining program integrity and homogeneity of samples or treatments may reduce design sensitivity" (2003, 99). They also find that when small evaluations are taking place, programs tend to be delivered by the study authors, research staff, or other highly qualified individuals—rather than by more typical staff—leading to greater effects than one finds when programs are implemented widely. Hahn and others (2007) also point to the difficulty of providing accurate conclusions because of reporting implementation problems.

However, evidence also shows that some large-scale, massive programs can be effective. For example, the school-based Chicago Child-Parent Center program in the United States had significant effects on high school completion, years of education, juvenile and violent arrests, school dropout rates, grade retention, and use of special-education services. The replicability of the results relies on maintaining such features as expenditure per child, training for providers, and parent involvement. Furthermore, the external validity of the results can be compromised when

http://dx.doi.org/10.1596/978-1-4648-0872-2

a program is replicated in a different context or country with dissimilar conditions. In some developing countries, for example, where malnutrition levels are higher, programs that effectively foster socioemotional skills in more developed countries or settings cannot be expected to achieve the same results.

Evaluation

Programs that target early stages in life have longer follow-up periods. Participant outcomes were recorded for 10 or more years after the intervention for 36 percent of the before-school programs, 3 percent of the school-based programs, and none of the out-of-school programs. The length of the follow-up directly affects the results captured by each program, for the following reasons.

First, the outcomes that can be measured in programs with short follow-up periods are more constrained. Before-school programs often capture effects that can be observed only with the evolution and growth of participants. For example, they measure behavioral effects with outcomes that evolve over time, from playground practices and school suspension to arrests, substance abuse and use, early sexual activity, and even reproductive and childbearing practices. This measure is profoundly richer than what is measured in out-of-school programs, which focus on immediate job-related outcomes.

Second, the persistence of any intervention's effects can be measured only through observations made over an extended period. All evaluations that are restricted to a few months might leave the reader questioning whether the findings might vanish after a certain time frame. Furthermore, this lack of information could mislead those responsible for policy design and implementation. For example, without the 40-year follow-up applied in the Jamaican Study, policy makers could not have learned that providing stimulation was more effective than providing nutrition with regard to cognitive and character achievements for stunted children living in poor, disadvantaged neighborhoods.

Third, programs with extensive follow-up periods provide rich information that allows researchers to understand the process of skills acquisition behind the observed impacts (Kautz and others 2014). For example, one could hypothesize that the HighScope Perry Preschool Program's long-term positive effects on criminality are the result of socioemotional skills acquisition rather than cognitive gains, because the follow-up 37 years later found that the effects on test scores faded, whereas behavioral results did not.

An additional finding is that although the programs explicitly target socioemotional skills development, few explicitly indicate what socioemotional skills they intend to improve. Further, most impact evaluations do not directly measure the skills that the program intends to alter. As discussed throughout this book, the effects of the different programs are captured in the behavior of the beneficiaries, yet rarely do researchers look to see if an intervention modified personality traits, risk behaviors, or mind-sets. Future research should include skills assessment in order to measure whether or not such changes occur as a result of the intervention. The evaluation of Juventud y Empleo and

http://dx.doi.org/10.1596/978-1-4648-0872-2

Galpão Aplauso are exceptions, because they use Rosenberg's self-esteem scale, Duckworth's Grit scale, and the Social and Personal Competencies Scale. The Juventud y Empleo intervention had a statistically significant effect on socioemotional skills, whereas Galpão Aplauso had no effects on this area.

Furthermore, the literature might contain blind spots on socioemotional skills formation, as the effect of environmental investments to improve socioemotional learning appears underexplored. Only one intervention in our sample (Program H in Brazil) evaluated the impact of a community-wide "lifestyle" social marketing campaign to promote condom use and change gender norms and behavior.

Direction for Future Research

Although evidence regarding socioemotional skills is promising, important questions still remain unanswered. Future studies should define and measure socioemotional skills directly so as to identify the triggers that lead to behavioral alterations. As mentioned before, a key area for future research is related to the identification of longer-term effects, particularly for school-age and out-of-school populations. It would also be important to measure the relative effectiveness of program intensity versus program duration as well as the way in which the overall intervention is structured and delivered.

Further, impact evaluations of multicomponent programs should capture the cost-effectiveness of the different components. An important area of research lies in the identification of the ideal variations within programs that achieve maximum effects within dissimilar target populations. Other areas of future research include the documentation of the externalities of the programs, which could be achieved by assessing the effects of school-wide versus classroom-wide programs. Much could be gained by documenting the costs of the programs, by including longer follow-up periods, and by collecting direct measures of socioemotional skills.

References

Dodge, Kenneth A., W. Benjamin Goodman, Robert A. Murphy, Karen O'Donnell, Jeannine Sato, and Susan Guptill. 2014. "Implementation and Randomized Controlled Trial Evaluation of Universal Postnatal Nurse Home Visiting." *American Journal of Public Health* 104 (S1): S136–S143.

Durlak, Joseph A., and Emily P. DuPre. 2008. "Implementation Matters: A Review of Research on the Influence of Implementation on Program Outcomes and the Factors Affecting Implementation." *American Journal of Community Psychology* 41 (3–4): 327–50.

Hahn, Robert, Dawna Fuqua-Whitley, Holly Wethington, Jessica Lowy, Alex Crosby, Mindi Fullilove, Robert Johnson, Akiva Liberman, Eve Moscicki, LeShawndra Price, Susan R. Snyder, Farris Tuma, Stella Cory, Glenda Stone, Kaushik Mukhopadhaya, Sajal Chattopadhyay, and Linda Dahlberg. 2007. "Effectiveness of Universal School-Based Programs to Prevent Violent and Aggressive Behavior: A Systematic Review." *American Journal of Preventive Medicine* 33 (2 Suppl.): S114–S129.

http://dx.doi.org/10.1596/978-1-4648-0872-2

Howard, Kimberly S., and Jeanne Brooks-Gunn. 2009. "The Role of Home-Visiting Programs in Preventing Child Abuse and Neglect." *Future of Children* 19 (2): 119–46.

Kautz, Tim, James J. Heckman, Ron Diris, Bas ter Weel, and Lex Borghans. 2014. "Fostering and Measuring Skills: Improving Cognitive and Non-Cognitive Skills to Promote Lifetime Success." NBER Working Paper 20749, National Bureau of Economic Research, Cambridge, MA.

Lösel, Friedrich, and Andreas Beelmann. 2003. "Effects of Child Skills Training in Preventing Antisocial Behavior: A Systematic Review of Randomized Evaluations." *Annals of the American Academy of Political and Social Science* 587 (1): 84–109.

http://dx.doi.org/10.1596/978-1-4648-0872-2

APPENDIX A

Before-School Program Descriptions

http://dx.doi.org/10.1596/978-1-4648-0872-2

Table A.1 Before-School Programs—Home Visiting Programs

Program		*Evaluation*	
Name	*Description*	*Author/description*	*Results*
Attachment and Biobehavioral Catch-up Intervention (ABC)	**Beneficiaries:** Children younger than age 2 **Objective:** Develop children's regulatory capabilities. **Description:** The program consists of 10 hour-long weekly sessions, where experienced professional social workers or psychologists teach caregivers how to interpret children's alienating behaviors, how to over-ride the issues that interfere with nurturing care, and how to provide an environment that fosters child development. **Cost:** n/a	**Authors:** Dozier and others (2009); Bick and Dozier (2013) **Type:** RCT **Location:** United States **Follow-up:** 1 month after the intervention **Sample:** Children ages 1 to 22 months, randomly assigned to receive the ABC intervention or the Developmental Education for Families intervention (which has the same intensity, but is designed to enhance cognitive development). Dozier and others (2009) evaluate 46 children and Bick and Dozier (2013) include 96 children. **Term used:** Emotional functioning	**Behavior related:** Avoidance (–)**; Maternal sensitivity (+)*
Comprehensive Child Development Program	**Beneficiaries:** Young children (from pregnancy until the child enters the school system) from poor families who need intensive and comprehensive support services **Objective:** "Enhance the physical, social, emotional, and intellectual development of children in low-income families; provide support to their parents and other family members; and assist families in becoming economically self-sufficient" (Pierre and others 1997, 1). **Description:** The program provides comprehensive services for families. The services targeted at parents include prenatal care; parental education in infant and child development, healthcare, nutrition, and parenting; and referral to education, vocational training, and labor counseling. The services targeted at children include early childhood education, health screening treatment and referral, and nutritional services. **Cost:** The average total cost per year was $14,984 per family.	**Authors:** Pierre and others (1997); Pierre and Layzer (1989) **Type:** RCT **Location:** United States **Follow-up:** 5 years later **Sample:** 4,410 families were randomly assigned to either treatment (2,213 families) or control (2,197 families). **Term used:** Social and emotional development	The program had no significant effects. The variables that were measured were mother's employment status, level of employment (number of hours worked) of parents, income, level of dependence on public assistance, mother's educational status, parental attitudes linked to abusive or neglectful behavior, quality of the home environment, parent-child interaction, and health behaviors of mothers during subsequent pregnancies. **Note:** The program was not implemented according to design. Only 33% of the families were enrolled for five or more years.

table continues next page

Table A.1 Before-School Programs—Home Visiting Programs *(continued)*

Program		*Evaluation*	
Name	*Description*	*Author/description*	*Results*
Child-Parent Psychotherapy	**Beneficiaries:** Children ages 3 to 5 years who witnessed marital violence **Objective:** Alleviate symptoms and restore child's development toward healthy functioning **Description:** Child-parent psychotherapy (CPP) is a relationship-based treatment that integrates modalities from psychodynamic, attachment, trauma, cognitive-behavioral, and social learning theories. The treatment consisted of 55 weekly sessions that lasted approximately 60 minutes each, distributed over a 1-year period. **Cost:** n/a	**Authors:** Lieberman, Ippen, and Van Horn (2006) **Type:** RCT **Location:** United States **Follow-up:** 6 months later **Sample:** 75 preschool-age child-mother dyads were randomly assigned to CPP (42) or case management plus community referral (33). **Term used:** Emotional functioning	**Behavior related:** Total behavior problems (–)***; Mother's general distress (–)***
Play and Learning Strategies (PALS) program	**Beneficiaries:** PALS I—mothers with infants ages 6 to 12 months; PALS II—mothers with toddlers ages 24 to 36 months **Objective:** Teach parents responsive parenting skills to support their child's socioemotional cognitive, and language development. **Description:** Each week for three months, families are visited by coaches who implement 1.5-hour sessions that include the discussion of the mother's practice during the preceding week, a description of the behavior targeted in the visit, an observation and discussion of educational videos demonstrating the skill, videotaping of mothers practicing the skill with their child, reviewing the videotaped practice, and planning ways to integrate responsive behavior during the upcoming week.	**Authors:** Landry, Smith, and Swank (2006) **Type:** RCT **Location:** United States: Houston, Texas, and Galveston, Texas **Follow-up:** 3 months later **Sample:** 264 upper-lower-class and lower-middle-class mothers with children ages 6 to 10 months. Sample was divided into two groups: (a) 133 mothers receiving 10 meetings (in developmental laboratories) with the PALS program content, and (b) 131 mothers receiving 10 meetings (in developmental laboratories) where they discussed new infant skills observed in the previous week, measured the children's development with developmental assessment sessions (DASs), and received feedback. **Term used:** Affective-emotional behavior	**Behavior related:** Cooperation in the child (+)*; mother's contingent responsiveness (+)***; improvements in emotional support from mothers (warm sensitivity (+)***; harshness of voice tone (–)**; physical intrusiveness (–)**; support of infant foci of attention from mothers [maintaining (+)*; redirecting (+)***]; and quality of language input from mothers (verbal scaffolding, labeling objects, labeling actions, verbal encouragement—all (+)*** **Academic/cognitive related:** Early communication (+)***

table continues next page

Table A.1 Before-School Programs—Home Visiting Programs *(continued)*

Program		*Evaluation*	
Name	*Description*	*Author/description*	*Results*
	PALS I (the infant curriculum) consists of 10 sessions and is appropriate for parents of infants from about ages five months to one year. PALS II (the toddler curriculum) consists of 12 sessions and is appropriate for parents of toddlers from about ages 18 months to three years. Both versions of the program emphasize similar skills but at an age-appropriate level. **Cost:** According to the U.S. Department of Health and Human Services, approximately US$2,500 per family (2011 dollars)	**Authors:** Landry and others (2008) **Type:** RCT **Location:** United States: Houston, Texas, and Galveston, Texas **Follow-up:** 3 months later **Sample:** 166 upper-lower-class and lower-middle-class mothers with children ages 6 to 10 months. Sample was divided into four groups: (a) 34 mothers who had received PALS I and were to receive PALS II, (b) 33 mothers who had received PALS I and were to receive DASs, (c) 50 mothers who had received DASs and were to receive PALS II, and (d) 49 mothers who had received DASs and would continue to receive DASs. **Term used:** Affective-emotional behavior	**Infant—behavior related:** Cooperation for children receiving PALS II (+)**; social engagement for children who received PALS II (+)*** **Infant—academic/cognitive related:** Use of words for children with PALS II (+)***; coordinating attention for children who received either PALS I or PALS II (+)**; composite language skills for children who received PALS II (+)** **Mother—behavior related:** Contingent responsiveness in group that received PALS I and PALS II (+)**; positive affect for mothers who received PALS I regardless of the intervention condition during toddler-preschool stage (+)***; improvements in emotional support [warm sensitivity for mothers who received PALS I regardless of the intervention condition during toddler-preschool stage (+)**]; support of infant foci of attention [maintaining for mothers who received PALS I regardless of the intervention condition during toddler-preschool stage (+)**]; redirecting for mothers who received PALS I and PALS II (+)***; significant but smaller effect for mothers who received PALS and DASs in any moment; quality of language input

table continues next page

Table A.1 Before-School Programs—Home Visiting Programs *(continued)*

Program		*Evaluation*	
Name	*Description*	*Author/description*	*Results*
			[maternal use of rich language for children who received PALS I and PALS II (+)**]; verbal encouragement for children who received PALS II (+)**. Smaller effects were found with PALS I, even though they were greater than those found with DASs.
Nurse-Family Partnership	**Beneficiaries:** Nulliparous women who were pregnant less than 29 weeks. Most were (a) low income, (b) unmarried, and (c) teenagers. **Objective:** Provide maternal and early childhood health programs to families most in need. **Description:** Families received sensory and developmental screening, as well as transportation services for prenatal and well-child care. Additionally, families received monthly prenatal and infancy home visits by public health nurses (during pregnancy and the first two years of their children's life). The nurses tried to (a) improve pregnancy outcomes by helping women improve their health-related behaviors, (b) improve children's health and development by helping parents provide more competent care, and (c) improve families' economic self-sufficiency by helping parents make appropriate choices regarding family planning, finishing their education, and finding work, and by linking them to appropriate services.	**Authors:** Eckenrode and others (2010); Luckey and others (2008); Olds, Henderson, and Kitzman (1994); Olds and others 1986; Olds and others 1988; Olds and others 1997; Olds and others 1998; Zielinsky, Eckenrode, and Olds (2009) **Type:** RCT **Location:** United States: Elmira, New York **Follow-up:** 19 years later **Sample:** More than 300 youths from the 400 families enrolled in the Elmira Nurse-Family Partnership program. Approximately 90% of the women were white, 60% were low income, and 60% were unmarried. Their average age was 19. The follow-up 19 years later had 352 youths (164 control, 86 receiving a mean of 9 home visits during pregnancy; 102 receiving a mean of 23 home visits during pregnancy, birth, and through the child's second birthday) and 315 youths for the follow-up 15 years later (144 control, 77 receiving home visits during pregnancy, and 94 receiving home visits during pregnancy and infancy). **Term used:** Socioemotional development	**Health related:** Cigarette consumption 15 years later (–)*; alcohol consumption 15 years later (–)**; lifetime sex partners 15 years later (–)**; number of children for girls born to high-risk mothers 19 years later (–)**; condom use for girls born to high-risk mothers 19 years later (+)**; sexual partners for boys 19 years later (+)** **Behavior related:** Instances of running away for children in high-risk families 15 years later (–)**; probability of arrest (–) [15 years later (–)**; 19 years later, girls only (–)**]; probability of being convicted (–) [15 years later (–)**; 19 years later, girls only (–)**]; number of lifetime arrests for girls 19 years later (–)**; number of lifetime convictions for girls 19 years later (–)** **Economic related:** Use of Medicaid for girls born to high-risk mothers 19 years later (–)**; use of food stamps and receiving Aid to Families with Dependent Children (–)**

table continues next page

Table A.1 Before-School Programs—Home Visiting Programs *(continued)*

Program		*Evaluation*	
Name	*Description*	*Author/description*	*Results*
	Cost: US$13,600 per woman (2014 dollars), to deliver program services (that is, three years of home visits by a trained nurse). This cost was offset in two of the trials by reduced government spending on mothers' use of welfare and other public assistance (for example, US$14,500 in lower spending per woman over 12 years in Memphis, Tennessee). Both the Elmira, New York, and Memphis trials found such lower welfare spending, but the Denver, Colorado, trial did not.		**Other:** Child abuse and neglect: during the program, 2 years after the program ended (–); 15 years later (–)*** *Note:* (a) High-risk group defined as being born to an unmarried, low-income mother; (b) impacts in the 19-years-later evaluation based on the 95% confidence interval reported.
		Authors: Kitzman and others (2010); Olds and others (2007); Olds and others (2010) **Type:** RCT **Location:** United States: Memphis, Tennessee **Follow-up:** 9 years later **Sample:** 743 primarily low–income, African American, high-risk women (approximately 90% of the women were African American, 85% were low income, and almost all were unmarried; their average age was 18), who were randomly assigned to receive (a) 255 free developmental screenings and referrals for their child before age two, (b) 245 screenings offered in treatment 2 plus paraprofessional home visiting during pregnancy and the child's first two years of life, (c) 235 screenings offered in treatment 1 plus nurse home visits during pregnancy and infancy. **Term used:** Socioemotional development	**Health related**: Infant and childhood mortality from preventable causes 6 years later(–)*; children's injuries or ingestions before age 2 (–)**; substance use by mothers—cigarettes, alcohol, and marijuana (–)**; mother's subsequent live births (–)**; mother's subsequent low-birth-weight newborns (–)* **Behavior related:** Behavior problems in the borderline or clinical range (–)**; aggression for high-risk children (–)** **Academic/cognitive related**: GPA for children in risk group at age 12 (+)*; results on achievement tests for children in high-risk group at age 11 (+)**; enrollment in formal out-of-school care by ages 2 to 4.5 (+)**; intellectual functioning and receptive vocabulary scores at age 8 (+)**; for high-risk children, arithmetic achievement (+)**

table continues next page

Table A.1 Before-School Programs—Home Visiting Programs *(continued)*

Program		*Evaluation*	
Name	*Description*	*Author/description*	*Results*
			Economic related: Welfare and food stamps for high-risk mothers (–)** *Note:* High-risk group is defined as children born to women who have two of the following three characteristics: unmarried, fewer than 12 years of education, or unemployed.
		Authors: Olds and others (2014) **Type:** RCT **Location:** United States: Denver, Colorado **Follow-up:** 9 years later **Sample:** 490 women with different backgrounds and low levels of income (almost all low income, 46% were Mexican American, 36% were white, 15% were African American, and 84% were unmarried; average age was 20), who were randomly assigned to receive nurse home visits or developmental screening and referral to treatment for their child **Term used**: Socioemotional development	**Health related:** Subsequent pregnancies for mothers (–)**; interval between first and second birth for mothers (–)**; health care encounters for children's injuries or ingestions at age 2 (–)**; says hospitalized for injuries or ingestions at age 2 (–)** **Behavior related:** Emotional/behavioral problems in children under age 6 for children visited by nurses (–)*; internalizing problems at age 9 for children visited by nurses (–)*; dysfunctional attention at age 9 for children visited by nurses (–)**; for high-risk children visited by paraprofessionals: deregulated aggression (–)**; behavioral regulation (+)** **Academic/cognitive related:** For children in high-risk environment who were visited by nurses: receptive language at ages 2, 4, and 6 (+)**; sustained attention at ages 4, 6, and 9 (+)**. Those receiving visits by paraprofessionals presented differences only in visual attention/task switching at age 9 (+)*. **Economic related:** Months using welfare (–)**

table continues next page

Table A.1 Before-School Programs—Home Visiting Programs *(continued)*

Program		*Evaluation*	
Name	*Description*	*Author/description*	*Results*
			Note: High-risk group is defined as children born to women who have two of the following three characteristics: unmarried, fewer than 12 years of education, or unemployed.
Jamaican Study	**Beneficiaries:** Stunted children ages 9 to 24 months who lived in poor disadvantaged neighborhoods **Objective:** Develop children's cognitive and personality skills. **Description:** The stimulation group received one-hour weekly visits from Jamaican community health workers over two years. Visits taught parenting skills and encouraged mothers to interact and play with their children in ways that would develop their children's cognitive and personality skills. The group that received nutritional intervention received weekly nutritional supplements for two years. **Cost:** n/a	**Authors:** Gertler and others (2013) **Type:** RCT **Location:** Kingston, Jamaica **Follow-up:** 20 years later **Sample:** 129 stunted children ages 9 to 24 months who lived in poor disadvantaged neighborhoods assigned to four groups: (a) 32 received psychosocial stimulation, (b) 32 received nutritional supplementation, (c) 32 received both nutritional supplementation and stimulation, and (d) 33 were controls and received neither **Term used:** Psychosocial development	**Behavior related:** Internalizing behavior factor (+)**; expelled from school (–)**; maternal investment in children (+)*** **Academic/cognitive related:** Cognitive development in the stimulation intervention (+); years completed in school (+)*; any college (+)**; enrollment in school (+)*** **Economic related:** Employment (+)*; earnings (+)***; other: migration
Home Instruction Program for Preschool Youngsters (HIPPY)	**Beneficiaries:** Parents who have doubts about or lack confidence in their ability to instruct their children and prepare them for school. Frequently, these parents did not graduate from high school or had only limited formal education, limited English proficiency, limited financial resources, or other risk factors. **Objective:** Help parents with limited formal education prepare their 4- and 5-year-old children for school. Promote preschoolers'	**Authors:** Baker, Piotrkowski, and Brooks-Gunn 1999 **Type:** RCT in New York and a quasi-experimental study in Arkansas with a nonrandomized comparison group **Location:** United States: New York and Arkansas **Follow-up:** 2 years later **Sample:** In New York, 182 families divided in two cohorts: (a) 69 families were part of cohort I, which started in 1990 (37 received HIPPY and 32 were controls) and (b) 113 families were part of cohort II	**Behavior related:** For cohort I in both sites, classroom adaptation in second grade, (+)** in New York, *** in Arkansas **Academic/cognitive related:** For cohort I in New York, cognitive skills (+)** and standardized reading (+)**; promotion to first grade among cohort I in Arkansas (+); for cohort II in Arkansas, school readiness (+)* and standardized achievement (–)**

table continues next page

Table A.1 Before-School Programs—Home Visiting Programs *(continued)*

Program		Evaluation	
Name	*Description*	*Author/description*	*Results*
	school readiness and support parents as their children's first teacher by providing instruction in the home. Although the curriculum is primarily cognitive based, it also fosters socioemotional and physical development. **Description:** In a two-year home-based early education intervention program, paraprofessional trainers visited families bimonthly for 45–60 minutes, providing teaching materials and parenting advice, and supplemented the visits in alternate weeks by group meetings with parents and paraprofessionals led by professional HIPPY program coordinators. **Cost:** According to U.S. Department of Health and Human Services, the average cost per child per year is US$1,500 to US$2,500 (2011 dollars).	(47 in HIPPY and 66 as control), which received services in 1991. Children were randomly assigned to HIPPY or to high-quality preschool. In Arkansas, children who attended HIPPY were matched over several characteristics with those who did not. **Term used:** Social/emotional development **Authors:** Bradley and Gilkey (2002) **Type:** Quasi-experimental design (within classroom matching of HIPPY children with demographically similar children who did not participate) **Location:** United States: Arkansas **Follow-up:** 4 and 6 years later **Sample:** 516 HIPPY children and 516 matched comparison children **Term used:** Social/emotional development	*Note:* Results were not replicated when compared with nonrandomized children who attended high-quality prekindergarten. **Behavior related:** School suspension (–)*; student's adjustment to classroom (+); enjoyment of books; listening and paying attention; task orientation, self-direction in learning, initiative, and interest in school (+) **Academic/cognitive related:** Test on reading and language arts (+); classroom adaptation (+) *Note:* No *p*-values reported in the paper. However, the aspects mentioned above are reported as statistically significant. The following variables were not statistically different between groups: math scores, school attendance, special education, classroom grades, teacher ratings of classroom behavior, curiosity, and using assistance.
Integrated Early Childhood Development Intervention in Colombia	**Beneficiaries:** Children ages 12 to 24 months located in 96 small municipalities in Colombia **Objective:** Reduce some of the developmental risks associated with poverty. **Description:** During 18 months, female community leaders delivered psychosocial stimulation through weekly home visits with play demonstrations or micronutrient sprinkles that were given daily or both combined. **Cost:** US$500 per year per child	**Authors:** Attanasio and others (2014) **Location:** 96 small municipalities in Colombia **Follow-up:** 18 months **Sample:** 1,440 children ages 12 to 24 months and their primary caregivers. These children were divided into four groups: (a) 360 were assigned to a control group, (b) 360 received stimulation, (c) 360 received micronutrients, and (d) 360 received both nutrition and stimulation. **Term used:** Psychosocial	**Academic/cognitive related:** Cognitive scores for stimulated children (+)****; receptive language for stimulated children (+)** *Note:* None of the programs had effects on expressive language, fine motor skills, hemoglobin levels, height, weight, and gross motor scores. Micronutrient supplementation had no significant effect on any outcome. No interaction took place between the programs.

table continues next page

Table A.1 Before-School Programs—Home Visiting Programs *(continued)*

Program		*Evaluation*	
Name	*Description*	*Author/description*	*Results*
Parents as Teachers (PAT) program	**Beneficiaries:** Low-income women with children no older than 6 months. The program starts in pregnancy or infancy and continues through kindergarten entry. **Objectives**: (a) Increase parental knowledge of early childhood development, (b) improve parenting practices, (c) detect developmental delays and health issues early, (d) prevent child abuse and neglect, and (e) increase children's school readiness and success. In addition to home visits, the program provides health and developmental screenings, group meetings, and referrals to resource networks. **Description:** These monthly (or even more frequently if at-risk family) home visitation services are provided by trained parent educators (with at least some college education) who provide information about children's development, model and involve parents in developmentally appropriate activities, and respond to parents' questions and concerns. Additionally, the program involves parent group meetings to discuss child development and to build informal support networks with other parents, periodic developmental screenings, and referrals to community services as needed.	**Authors:** Wagner and Clayton (1999) **Type:** RCT **Location:** United States: RCT 1, Salinas Valley, California; RCT 2, Los Angeles, San Bernardino, San Diego, and Santa Barbara Counties in California **Follow-up:** When children were 2 years old **Sample:** Two RCTs: RCT 1 was composed of 497 Latino families where parents had limited English proficiency; 298 were assigned to treatment (receiving an average of 20 visits of 28–50 minutes) and 199 to control (which received age-appropriate toys and referrals if their children were found with delays); and RCT 2 was composed of 704 families with teenage parents who received (a) 177 PAT services alone, (b) 174 who received case management, (c) 175 who received PAT and case management, and (d) 178 untreated. **Term used:** Social development	**Health related:** Immunization for children receiving the case management intervention (–)**; child abuse or neglect in Teen PAT, for the group receiving PAT and case management (–)** **Behavior related:** Self-help development for Latino families (+)**; social help for Latino families when using multivariate analysis (+)* **Academic/cognitive related:** Cognitive development in Teen PAT, for the group receiving PAT and case management (+)**; when using multivariate analysis, cognitive development measured by DPII for the Latino PAT, and the groups receiving case management and the combined intervention in Teen PAT (+)** *Note:* No benefit with regard to parenting knowledge or practices.

table continues next page

Table A.1 Before-School Programs—Home Visiting Programs *(continued)*

Program		*Evaluation*	
Name	*Description*	*Author/description*	*Results*
	Cost: The average monthly cost of serving a family was determined to be US$170 (1996 dollars). Given that the average length of participation was 30.1 months, the average cost per family was determined to be US$5,117. Those who persisted in the program through the children's third birthdays averaged 35.4 months of participation, for an average per-family cost of US$6,018. Dropouts from the program averaged 17.8 months of participation, for an average per-family cost of US$3,026.	**Authors:** Wagner, Spiker, and Linn (2002) **Type:** RCT **Location:** United States, multisite trial **Follow-up:** When children were 2 years old **Sample:** 665 families **Term used:** Social development	**Behavior related:** Parent's self-reported happiness when caring for their children (+)*** *Note:* No significant effects found for children's development, or for parents' practices or knowledge.
Parent-Child Home Program	**Beneficiaries:** Low-income families with children ages 2 to 4 **Objective:** Improve parent–child interactions to strengthen children's cognitive development and early literacy **Description:** The program consisted of 46 twice-weekly paraprofessional or volunteer home visitation services spread over seven months in each of two years. In this play-filled and nondidactic home-based intervention, the toy demonstrator models verbal interaction with the child centered on toys and books that are permanently assigned to the family and encourages the mother to assume responsibility for the interaction. The program has a cognitive curriculum, a socioemotional behavior curriculum, and a "parenting" curriculum. **Cost:** US$4,500 per child for two-year program	**Authors:** Levenstein and others (1998) **Type:** RCT **Location:** United States: Pittsfield, Massachusetts **Follow-up:** 16–20 years later **Sample:** 123 students who at age 2 (1976–80) had been recruited for the Parent-Child Home Program. The control group is very small (15). **Term:** Socioemotional behavior	**Academic/cognitive related:** Academic achievement, and reading, language, and math scores at eighth grade (+); school dropout at ages 17–22 (–)**; graduation at ages 17–22 (+)***

table continues next page

Table A.1 Before-School Programs—Home Visiting Programs *(continued)*

Program		*Evaluation*	
Name	*Description*	*Author/description*	*Results*
Healthy Families	**Beneficiaries:** New or expectant parents deemed to be at risk of abusing or neglecting their children **Objectives:** (a) promote positive parenting skills and parent–child interaction; (b) prevent child abuse and neglect; (c) support optimal prenatal care, and child health and development; and (d) improve parents' self-sufficiency **Description:** Paraprofessionals make home visits starting in pregnancy and continuing until the child reaches age 5. **Cost:** n/a	**Authors:** Dumont and others (2006); Dumont and others (2008); Dumont and others (2010) **Type:** RCT **Location:** United States: New York **Follow-up:** 2 years later **Sample:** 1,173 families at risk for child abuse and neglect randomly assigned to Healthy Families New York or to a control group that received information and referrals to other services **Term used:** Psychosocial risks	**Health related:** For the subgroup of mothers enrolled by 30 weeks of gestation, incidence of low-birth-weight newborns (–) **Behavior related:** Child abuse/neglect at the end of year 2 (+)**; minor physical aggression during the past year for mothers who engaged in the program at 30 weeks of pregnancy or earlier (–)**; harsh parenting by mothers who engaged in the program at 30 weeks of pregnancy or earlier (–)**; serious abuse or neglect of children by age 2 by psychologically vulnerable mothers (–)***
		Authors: Caldera and others (2007); Duggan and others (2007) **Type:** RCT **Location:** United States: Alaska **Follow-up:** 2 years after birth **Sample:** 325 families with women **Term used:** Psychosocial risks	**Behavior related:** No overall effect on maltreatment or the use of more severe forms of physical discipline. The program had no effects on parental risk.
Parenting Practices Canada	**Beneficiaries:** Children at risk for mental health problems attributable to poverty and/or their parents' inexperience, lack of educational attainment, and young age **Objectives:** Improve the parent–child relationship and indirectly enhance the resilience capacity among at-risk children. **Description:** Two pilot studies were conducted to compare the effects of the following two types of social support for families on parent–child relationships: (a) support with extensive and intense parent training targeted toward adolescent parents in the newborn period	**Authors:** Letourneau and others (2001) **Type:** RCT **Location:** Canada **Follow-up:** 11–13 weeks later **Sample:** 52 families divided into two groups: (a) 18 families received support with extensive and intense parent training, and (b) 34 families received support without extensive and intense parent training. **Term used**: Social skills	**Behavior related:** Improved psychophysiological arousal and orienting at age 11. This is seen through skin conductance amplitudes (+)***; skin conductance rise times (+)***; skin conductance recovery times (+)**; slow-wave electroencephalogram measure during rest (–)***; electroencephalogram measure during continuous performance task conditions (–)***

table continues next page

Table A.1 Before-School Programs—Home Visiting Programs *(continued)*

Program		Evaluation	
Name	*Description*	*Author/description*	*Results*
	(mothers received six weekly home visits delivered by a master's-prepared pediatric nurse); and (b) support without extensive and intense parent training targeted toward other at-risk parents (for example, low-income, low educational attainment, and single-parent status) of 3- to 4-year-old children identified as having developmental delays. **Cost:** n/a		
Durham Connects	**Beneficiaries:** All resident births in Durham, North Carolina, between July 1, 2009, and December 31, 2010 **Objective:** Improve infant health and well-being. **Description:** A four- to seven-session program assesses family needs (parenting and child care, family violence and safety, parental mental health and well-being, and health care) and connects parents with community resources. **Cost:** US$700 per birth	**Authors:** Dodge and others 2014 **Type:** RCT **Location:** United States: Durham, North Carolina **Follow-up:** 6 months **Sample:** All 4,777 resident births in Durham between July 1, 2009, and December 31, 2010, were randomly assigned to intervention and control. A random representative subset of 549 families received blind interviews for impact evaluation. **Term used:** Mental health and well-being	**Health related:** Emergency care episodes (–)***; overnights in hospital (–)***; mother anxiety disorder (–)** **Behavior related:** Positive parenting behaviors (+)* **Academic/cognitive related:** Quality out-of-home child care (+)*** **Other:** Safety of home environment (+)**; community connections (+)***; mother's knowledge of infant development (+)*

Note: DPII = Developmental Profile II; GPA = grade point average; RCT = randomized control trial; n/a = not available. Significance levels of results, positive (+) or negative (–), are reported at 1 percent (*), 5 percent (**), and 10 percent (***).

Table A.2 Before-School Programs—Child Care Centers

Program		Evaluation	
Name	*Description*	*Author/description*	*Results*
Early Childhood Education and Development program in Indonesia	**Beneficiaries:** Children ages 0–6 living in vulnerable villages in Indonesia **Objective:** Improve poor children's overall development and readiness for further education within a sustainable quality early childhood education and development system. **Description:** The project had three main components: 1. Provision on integrated early childhood education and development services. These services were delivered through community-driven mechanisms in targeted poor communities. The program helped communities identify early childhood education and development service needs, prepare a proposal, and then implement this proposal. 2. Ideation of a sustainable system to ensure quality in early childhood education and development services. This includes the generation and implementation of standards and quality-assurance systems and the institutionalization of early childhood education and development at the district and provincial levels. 3. Program management, monitoring, and evaluation. **Cost:** n/a	**Authors:** Hasan and others (2013) **Type:** RCT **Location:** Indonesia **Follow-up:** 20 months later **Sample:** More than 6,000 children in two age cohorts (10 to 46 months), living in 310 poor villages. **Term used:** Social and emotional development	**Academic/cognitive related:** Enrollment (+)***; receptive language skills (+)**; communication and general knowledge for children in poorest families (+)*; social competence for children in poorest communities (+)**; language and cognitive development for children in poorest families (+)*; executive function in children of poor families (+)* **Note:** Most results were in the correct direction but not statistically significantly. When looking at the younger cohort, the results are mixed. No effects on parenting practices.
Abecedarian program	**Beneficiaries:** Economically disadvantaged children up to age 5 **Objective:** Improve children's school readiness by social-cognitive and linguistic development.	**Authors:** Barnett and Masse (2007); Campbell and others (2002); Heckman and Kautz (2013) **Type:** RCT **Location:** United States: North Carolina **Follow-up:** 20 years	**Health related:** Mortality rates (–)**; likelihood of halting work because of illness (–)**; smoking (–)** **Behavior related:** Arrests (–)***; externalizing behavior (+)**; engaging in risky behavior (–)***

table continues next page

Table A.2 Before-School Programs—Child Care Centers *(continued)*

Program		*Evaluation*	
Name	*Description*	*Author/description*	*Results*
	Description: Program provides full day (10 hours/day) child care, nutrition, and transportation year-round, from infancy to kindergarten (approximately 250 days per year). Teacher–child ratios ranged from 1:3 for infants and toddlers to 1:6 for older children. **Cost:** US$67,000 for the five years of attendance ($11,000 in year 1; US$16,000 in each of years 2 and 3; US$12,000 in each of years 4 and 5)	**Sample:** 112 children, mostly African American, born between 1972 and 1977, who were believed to be at risk of retarded intellectual and social development (51 in control group and 53 in treatment); 104 children in follow-up for 20 years **Terms used:** Social development; social adjustment; noncognitive skills	**Academic/cognitive related:** IQ until age 1 (+)** then faded; grade repetition (–)**; assigned to special education (–)**; high school graduation by age 19 (+)**; college attendance (+) **; educational attainment at age 40 (+)*** **Economic related:** Earnings (+)***; homeownership (+)** *Note:* Annual social rates of return: 7%–16% (US$9–US$13 for every US$1 invested).
Montessori	**Beneficiaries:** 3- to 5-year-old children **Objective:** Foster a child's natural inclination to learn. **Description:** Montessori schooling is a 100-year-old system that naturally incorporates practices that align with mindfulness and are suited to very young children. Montessori education is characterized by multiage classrooms, a special set of educational materials, long periods spent in student-chosen activities, collaboration, the absence of grades and tests, and individual and small-group instruction in both academic and social skills. **Cost:** Because all Montessori schools are operated independently, tuitions vary widely. According to a 2009–10 NAMTA survey of North American Montessori schools, tuitions range from a low of less than US$999 per year to a high of more than US$14,000 per year.	**Authors:** Lillard and Else-Quest (2006) **Type:** RCT **Location:** United States: Milwaukee, Wisconsin **Follow-up:** 2 years **Sample:** 25 control children attending public inner-city schools and suburban public, private, or charter schools; and 30 Montessori 5-year-old children **Term used:** Social skills	**Behavior related:** Social problem solving through fairness (+)***; positive peer play (+)**; rough play ambiguous in intent, like wrestling without smiling (–)**; false belief (+)** **Academic/cognitive related:** Letter/word identification (+)**; phonological decoding ability (+)**; applied problems/math skills (+)**; executive function (+)** *Note:* No difference found on basic vocabulary, a test of children's ability to delay gratification.

table continues next page

Table A.2 Before-School Programs—Child Care Centers *(continued)*

Program		*Evaluation*	
Name	*Description*	*Author/description*	*Results*
Early Child Development Program	**Beneficiaries:** Children born in three regions (13 provinces) of the Philippines **Objective:** Improve survival and developmental potential of children, particularly the most vulnerable and disadvantaged. **Description:** Children participated in interdepartmental programs on nutrition, health, early education, and social services programs with the following components: (a) minimizing the health risks to very young children, (b) contributing to the knowledge of parents and the community about child development and encouraging their active involvement, (c) advocating for child-friendly policies and legislation, (d) improving the ability and attitude of child-related service providers, and (e) mobilizing resources and establishing viable financing mechanisms for ECD projects. **Cost:** n/a	**Authors:** Armecin and others (2006) **Type:** Intent to treat difference in propensity score matching **Location:** The Philippines **Follow-up:** 3 years **Sample:** 6,693 children ages 0 to 4 years **Term used:** Social-emotional skills	**Health related:** Weight for height (+)**; proportion wasted (–)**; anemia (+)**; hemoglobin (+)** **Behavior related:** Social-emotional skills (+)**; self-help (+)**; social development (+)** **Academic/cognitive related**: Cognitive development (+)**; expressive language (+)**; gross motor skills (+)**; fine motor skills (+)**; receptive language (+)**
Proyecto Integral de Desarrollo Infantil (PIDI)	**Beneficiaries:** Poor children ages 6 to 72 months in urban areas **Objectives:** Improve child nutrition and provide environments that are conducive to learning. **Description:** Day care, nutrition, and educational services are provided to children who live in poor, predominantly urban areas. Under the program, children are cared for in groups of 15 in homes in their own neighborhood. The community selects local women to become home day care mothers. These nonformal, home-based day care centers, with two to three caregivers, provide integrated child development services (play, nutrition, growth screening, and health referrals). The women receive child development training before becoming educators but are usually not highly trained. **Cost:** US$516 yearly per beneficiary	**Authors:** Behrman, Cheng, and Todd (2004) **Type:** Propensity score matching **Location:** Bolivia **Follow-up:** n/a. They compare children in the program for short (<2 months) and longer durations **Sample:** 1,227 children for round 1; 2,420 children for round 2; and 364 children for both rounds as controls. **Term used:** Psychosocial development	**Health related:** Height for children up to 36 months (+); weight for children younger than 36 months (–) **Behavior related:** Psychosocial skills for those ages 37 to 54 months (+)* **Academic/cognitive related:** Bulk motor skills, fine motor skills, language skills for those ages 37 to 54 months (+)* **Economic related:** Earnings (+); earning benefits/cost: 1.7–3.7

table continues next page

Table A.2 Before-School Programs—Child Care Centers *(continued)*

Program		*Evaluation*	
Name	*Description*	*Author/description*	*Results*
Turkish Early Enrichment Project (TEEP)	**Beneficiaries:** 4- to 6-year-old children from deprived backgrounds. These children were at risk for low educational achievement and failure to develop to their full potential because of poverty and their families' low educational level. **Objective:** Improve overall child development. **Description:** Under TEEP, children were sorted into one of three environments: (a) an educational day care center (educational group), (b) a custodial day care center (custodial group), or (c) a home (home group). Randomization of children within each environment happened only if there was excess demand for that particular service. Mothers of approximately half of the children in each care environment were randomly assigned to receive maternal training emphasizing educational activities with the child plus support for the mother through group meetings and guided discussions. **Cost:** n/a	**Authors:** Kagitcibasi, Sunar, and Bekman (2001); Kagitcibasi and others (2009) **Location:** Istanbul, Turkey **Follow-up:** 22 years later. Intervention carried out in 1983–85. **Sample:** 255 participants divided into the following groups: (a) 27 received mother training and educational day care, (b) 40 received mother training and custodial day care, (c) 23 received mother training in a home care environment, (d) 37 did not receive mother training while in educational day care, (e) 65 did not receive mother training while attending a custodial day care center, and (f) 63 did not receive mother training while in a home care environment. The 22-year follow-up gathered information on 131 of the 255 participants (39% attrition). **Term used:** Personality and social development	**Behavior related:** For children with trained mothers, immediate postprogram positive self-concept (+)*; aggression (–)*; school adjustment for children with mother training (+)**; emotional problems for children in the home environment immediately postintervention (+)***; child self-confidence six years later for mother-trained children (+)**; child self-confidence six years later for children in the custodial group (–)** **Academic/cognitive related:** IQ scores for children with mother training postintervention (+)***; IQ scores for children who were in educational or home environment postintervention (+)*; achievement test scores postintervention (+)**; school grades for the children in the educational environment at age 3 (+)**; school grades for the children with mother training at age 5 (+)* [no effect of mother training in grades after primary school]; school enrollment seven years after the program for those with mother training (+)***; failed years in middle school for the custodial group (+)**; college attendance for those with mother training (+)*

table continues next page

Table A.2 Before-School Programs—Child Care Centers *(continued)*

Program		*Evaluation*	
Name	*Description*	*Author/description*	*Results*
			Economic related: Ownership of a credit card for those with mother training (+)**; occupational status of those who attended an educational day care center (+)**; ownership of a computer for those who attended an educational day care center (+)* **Other:** Indicators of integration into modern urban life, such as owning a computer. For children with trained mothers, immediately postprogram: mother's attentiveness to and direct interaction with the child (+); involvement with children in cognitive-oriented activities (+); educational aspirations and expectations for the child (+); positive disciplinary strategies and praise (+)
Early Childhood Parenting Programme in Rural Bangladesh	**Beneficiaries:** Poor children under age 3 and their mothers **Objective:** Promote physical and mental development of children **Description:** In this program, 90-minute weekly education sessions are offered by trained women, known as facilitators, to groups of about 20 mothers. The topics include common diseases and oral rehydration solutions, hygiene, sanitation, breastfeeding, weaning foods, micronutrient deficiencies, stages of cognitive and language development, how parents can help children learn, how to encourage language development, positive discipline, gender equality, and child rights. The facilitators had some secondary education; to deliver the program, they received 17 additional days of basic training with a manual of 40 topics, four days a month of supervision, and monthly refresher courses. **Cost:** n/a	**Author:** Aboud (2011) **Type:** Intervention-control posttest design **Location:** Poor rural communities in Bangladesh **Follow-up:** 2 months **Sample:** 170 mothers attended a year of educational sessions; 159 mothers and children from neighboring villages that did not receive the program served as controls **Term used:** Psychosocial stimulation	**Health related:** Weight for height (+)**; preventive health (+)*** **Behavior related:** Knowledge of mother (+)***; amount and quality of stimulation and support provided to a child in the family setting—home inventory (+)***; stimulation (+)*** *Note:* The parenting mothers did not communicate differently with their children while doing a picture-talking task, and children did not show benefits in nutritional status or language comprehension.

table continues next page

Table A.2 Before-School Programs—Child Care Centers *(continued)*

Program		*Evaluation*	
Name	*Description*	*Author/description*	*Results*
ECD intervention in Mozambique	**Beneficiaries:** Families with children ages 36 to 59 months **Objectives:** Improve children's cognitive, social, emotional, and physical development. Specifically, the project aims to (a) deliver quality early stimulation, psychosocial support, and emergent literacy and numeracy instruction; (b) strengthen positive parenting practices and decrease harmful ones; and (c) facilitate children's transition to primary school. **Description:** In a center-based community-driven preschool model, young children "learn by doing" under the care of supportive adults. Thirty-five children per classroom receive three hours of care. Parents participate in monthly meetings. Teachers are selected by the community and then receive a five-day component, refresher training sessions, and hands-on mentoring and supervision. **Cost:** US$29.74 per child, average estimated cost for a 12-month program	**Authors:** Martinez, Nadeau, and Pereira (2012) **Type:** RCT **Location:** Gaza Province in Mozambique **Follow-up:** 2 years **Sample:** 76 communities **Term used:** Socioemotional and behavioral outcomes	**Behavior related:** Socioemotional indicator (ASQ) (+)**; caregivers' belief that physical punishment is appropriate (–); daily routines between parents and children (+)***; self-sufficiency activities between parents and children (+)** **Academic/cognitive related:** Primary school enrollment rates (+)***; enrollment at appropriate age in primary school (+)**; hours spent on schooling and homework-related activities (+)***; cognitive and problem-solving abilities (+)**; fine motor skills (+)*; school attendance of older siblings of beneficiary children (+)*** **Economic related:** Caregivers working in the 30 days before the interview (+)* **Other:** Caregivers report a significant increase in satisfaction with their children's preparation for future school. *Note:* Some of the principal measures of communication and language development are not significantly different between groups and remain alarmingly low. No differences are noted in rates of stunting and wasting, which was expected since a child's growth potential is largely determined by age 3. The study finds mixed impacts in children's health (less diarrhea and fewer skin problems, more illnesses).

table continues next page

Table A.2 Before-School Programs—Child Care Centers *(continued)*

Program		*Evaluation*	
Name	*Description*	*Author/description*	*Results*
Promoting Alternative Thinking Strategies (PATHS) curriculum	**Beneficiaries:** Preschool-age children in Head Start **Objectives:** Improve children's social competence and reduce problem behavior **Description:** The PATHS program uses a universal, teacher-taught social-emotional curriculum. Thirty lessons that were delivered once a week included the topics of compliments, basic and advanced feelings, a self-control strategy, and problem solving. In addition to the lessons, teachers generalized the concepts of the curriculum through detailed extension activities (such as group games, art projects, and books) that were integrated into the existing typical preschool programs (such as language arts, music, and art). **Cost:** n/a	**Authors:** Domitrovich, Cortes, and Greenberg (2007) **Type:** RCT **Location:** United States: Pennsylvania **Follow-up:** 9 months **Sample:** 20 classrooms with 246 children **Term used:** Socioemotional	**Behavior related:** Anger attribution bias (–)***; emotion knowledge skills (+)*; social competence (+)***; internalizing behavior (+)**; anxiety (–)***; socially withdrawn (–)**; parental perceptions of children as socially and emotionally competent (+)*** *Note:* No significant differences in inhibitory control, attention, or problem solving.

Note: ASQ = Ages and Stages Questionnaire; ECD = early childhood development; IQ = intelligence quotient; NAMTA = North American Montessori Teachers' Association; PEF = Peace Education Foundation; PPVT = Peabody Picture Vocabulary Test; RCT = randomized control trial; n/a = not available. Significance levels of results, positive (+) or negative (–), are reported at 1 percent (*), 5 percent (**), and 10 percent (***).

References

Aboud, Frances E. 2011. "Evaluation of an Early Childhood Parenting Programme in Rural Bangladesh." *Journal of Health, Population and Nutrition* 25 (1): 3–13.

Armecin, Graeme, Jere R. Behrman, Paulita Duazo, Sharon Ghuman, Socorro Gultiano, Elizabeth M. King, and Nanette Lee. 2006. "Early Childhood Development through an Integrated Program: Evidence from the Philippines." Policy Research Working Paper 3922, World Bank, Washington, DC.

Attanasio, Orazio P., Camila Fernández, Emla O. A. Fitzsimons, Sally M. Grantham-McGregor, Costas Meghir, and Marta Rubio-Codina. 2014. "Using the Infrastructure of a Conditional Cash Transfer Program to Deliver a Scalable Integrated Early Child Development Program in Colombia: Cluster Randomized Controlled Trial." *BMJ* 349: g5785.

Baker, Amy J. L., Chaya S. Piotrkowski, and Jeanne Brooks-Gunn. 1999. "The Home Instruction Program for Preschool Youngsters (HIPPY)." *Future of Children* 9 (1): 116–33.

Barnett, W. Steven, Kwanghee Jung, Donald J. Yarosz, Jessica Thomas, Amy Hornbeck, Robert Stechuk, and Susan Burns. 2008. "Educational Effects of the Tools of the Mind Curriculum: A Randomized Trial." *Early Childhood Research Quarterly* 23 (3): 299–313.

Barnett, W. Steven, and Leonard N. Masse. 2007. "Comparative Benefit–Cost Analysis of the Abecedarian Program and Its Policy Implications." *Economics of Education Review* 26 (1): 113–25.

Behrman, Jere R., Yingmei Cheng, and Petra E. Todd. 2004. "Evaluating Preschool Programs When Length of Exposure to the Program Varies: A Nonparametric Approach." *Review of Economics and Statistics* 86 (1): 108–32.

Bick, J., and M. Dozier. 2013. "The Effectiveness of an Attachment-Based Intervention in Promoting Foster Mothers' Sensitivity toward Foster Infants." *Infant Mental Health Journal* 34 (2): 95–103.

Bouguen, Adrien, Deon Filmer, Karen Macours, and Sophie Naudeau. 2014. "Preschools and Early Childhood Development in a Second Best World: Evidence from a Scaled-Up Experiment in Cambodia." CEPR Discussion Paper 10170, Center for Economic Policy Research, Washington, DC.

Bradley, Robert H., and Barbara Gilkey. 2002. "The Impact of the Home Instructional Program for Preschool Youngsters (HIPPY) on School Performance in 3rd and 6th Grades." *Early Education and Development* 13 (3): 301–12.

Caldera, Debra, Lori Burrell, Kira Rodriguez, Sarah Shea Crowne, Charles Rohde, and Anne Duggan. 2007. "Impact of a Statewide Home Visiting Program on Parenting and on Child Health and Development." *Child Abuse and Neglect* 31 (8): 829–52.

Campbell, Frances A., Craig T. Ramey, Elizabeth Pungello, Joseph Sparling, and Shari Miller–Johnson. 2002. "Early Childhood Education: Young Adult Outcomes from the Abecedarian Project." *Applied Developmental Science* 6 (1): 42–57.

Chetty, Raj, John N. Friedman, Nathaniel Hilger, Emmanuel Saez, Diane Whitmore Schanzenbach, and Danny Yagan. 2010. "How Does Your Kindergarten Classroom Affect Your Earnings? Evidence from Project STAR." NBER Working Paper 16381, National Bureau of Economic Research, Cambridge, MA.

Diamond, Adele, W. Steven Barnett, Jessica Thomas, and Sarah Munro. 2007. "Preschool Program Improves Cognitive Control." *Science* 318 (5855): 1387–88.

http://dx.doi.org/10.1596/978-1-4648-0872-2

Dodge, Kenneth A., W. Benjamin Goodman, Robert A. Murphy, Karen O'Donnell, Jeannine Sato, and Susan Guptill. 2014. "Implementation and Randomized Controlled Trial Evaluation of Universal Postnatal Nurse Home Visiting." *American Journal of Public Health* 104 (Suppl. 1): S136–S143.

Domitrovich, Celene E., Rebecca C. Cortes, and Mark T. Greenberg. 2007. "Improving Young Children's Social and Emotional Competence: A Randomized Trial of the Preschool PATHS Curriculum." *Journal of Primary Prevention* 28 (2): 67–91.

Dozier, M., O. Lindhiem, E. Lewis, J. Bick, K. Bernard, and E. Peloso. 2009. "Effects of a Foster Parent Training Program on Young Children's Attachment Behaviors: Preliminary Evidence from a Randomized Clinical Trial." *Child and Adolescent Social Work Journal* 26 (4): 321–32.

Duggan, Anne, Debra Caldera, Kira Rodriguez, Lori Burrell, Charles Rohde, and Sarah Shea Crowne. 2007. "Impact of a Statewide Home Visiting Program to Prevent Child Abuse." *Child Abuse and Neglect* 31 (8): 801–27.

DuMont, Kimberly, Kristen Kirkland, Susan Mitchell-Herzfeld, Susan Ehrhard-Dietzel, Monica Rodriguez, Eunju Lee, China Layne and Rose Greene. 2010. "A Randomized Trial of Healthy Families New York (HFNY): Does Home Visiting Prevent Child Maltreatment." National Institute of Justice, Washington, DC. https://www.ncjrs.gov/pdffiles1/nij/grants/232945.pdf.

DuMont, Kimberly A., Susan Mitchell-Herzfeld, Rose Greene, Eunju Lee, Ann Lowenfels, and Monica Rodriguez. 2006. "Healthy Families New York (HFNY) Randomized Trial: Impacts on Parenting after the First Two Years." OCFS Working Paper No. 1, New York State Office of Children and Family Services, Albany, NY.

DuMont, Kimberly, Susan Mitchell-Herzfeld, Rose Greene, Eunju Lee, Ann Lowenfels, Monica Rodriguez, and Vajeera Dorabawila. 2008. "Healthy Families New York (HFNY) Randomized Trial: Effects on Early Child Abuse and Neglect." *Child Abuse and Neglect* 32 (3): 295–315.

Eckenrode, John, Mary Campa, Dennis W. Luckey, Charles R. Henderson, Robert Cole, Harriet J. Kitzman, Elizabeth Anson, Kimberly Sidora-Arcoleo, and David L. Olds. 2010. "Long-Term Effects of Prenatal and Infancy Nurse Home Visitation on the Life Course of Youths: 19-Year Follow-Up of a Randomized Trial." *Journal of the American Medical Association* 164 (1): 9–15.

Epstein, Ann S. 1993. *Training for Quality: Improving Early Childhood Programs through Systematic In-Service Training.* Ypsilanti, MI: HighScope Press.

Gertler, Paul, James Heckman, Rodrigo Pinto, Arianna Zanolini, Christel Vermeerch, Susan Walker, Susan Chang-Lopez, and Sally Grantham-McGregor. 2013. "Labor Market Returns to Early Childhood Stimulation: A 20-Year Follow-Up to an Experimental Intervention in Jamaica." Policy Research Working Paper 6529, World Bank, Washington, DC.

Hasan, Amer, Marilou Hyson, and Mae Chu Chang. 2013. *Early Childhood Education and Development in Poor Villages of Indonesia: Strong Foundations, Later Success.* Directions in Development. Washington, DC: World Bank.

Heckman, James J., and Tim Kautz. 2013. "Fostering and Measuring Skills: Programs That Improve Character and Cognition." NBER Working Paper 19656, National Bureau of Economic Research, Cambridge, MA.

Heckman, James J., Seong Hyeok Moon, Rodrigo Pinto, Peter A. Savelyev, and Adam Q. Yavitz. 2010. "The Rate of Return to the HighScope Perry Preschool Program." *Journal of Public Economics* 94 (1–2): 114–28.

Kagitcibasi, Cigdem, Diane Sunar, and Sevda Bekman. 2001. "Long-Term Effects of Early Intervention: Turkish Low-Income Mothers and Children." *Journal of Applied Developmental Psychology* 22 (4): 333–61.

Kagitcibasi, Cigdem, Diane Sunar, Sevda Bekman, Nazli Baydar, and Zeynep Cemalcilar. 2009. "Continuing Effects of Early Enrichment in Adult Life: The Turkish Early Enrichment Project 22 Years Later." *Journal of Applied Developmental Psychology* 30 (6): 764–79.

Kitzman, Harriet J., David L. Olds, Robert E. Cole, Carole A. Hanks, Elizabeth A. Anson, Kimberly J. Arcoleo, Dennis W. Luckey, Michael D. Knudtson, Charles R. Henderson Jr., and John R. Holmberg. 2010. "Enduring Effects of Prenatal and Infancy Home Visiting by Nurses on Children: Follow-Up of a Randomized Trial among Children at Age 12 Years." *Archives of Pediatrics and Adolescent Medicine* 164 (5): 412–18.

Krueger, Alan B., and Diane M. Whitmore. 2001. "The Effect of Attending a Small Class in the Early Grades on College-Test Taking and Middle School Test Results: Evidence from Project STAR." *Economic Journal* 111 (468): 1–28.

Landry, Susan H., Karen E. Smith, and Paul R. Swank. 2006. "Responsive Parenting: Establishing Early Foundations for Social, Communication, and Independent Problem-Solving Skills." *Developmental Psychology* 42 (4): 627–42.

Landry, Susan H., Karen E. Smith, Paul R. Swank, and Cathy Guttentag. 2008. "A Responsive Parenting Intervention: The Optimal Timing across Early Childhood for Impacting Maternal Behaviors and Child Outcomes." *Developmental Psychology* 44 (5): 1335–53.

Letourneau, Nicole, Jane Drummond, Darcy Fleming, Gerard Kysela, Linda McDonald, and Miriam Stewart. 2001. "Supporting Parents: Can Intervention Improve Parent-Child Relationships?" *Journal of Family Nursing,* 7 (2): 159–87.

Levenstein, Phyllis, Susan Levenstein, James A. Shiminski, and Judith E. Stolzberg. 1998. "Long-Term Impact of a Verbal Interaction Program for At-Risk Toddlers: An Exploratory Study of High School Outcomes in a Replication of the Mother–Child Home Program." *Journal of Applied Developmental Psychology* 19 (2): 267–85.

Lieberman, A. F., C. G. Ippen, and P. Van Horn. 2006. "Child-Parent Psychotherapy: 6-month Follow-up of a Randomized Controlled Trial." *Journal of the American Academy of Child & Adolescent Psychiatry* 45 (8): 913–18.

Lillard, Angeline, and Nicole Else-Quest. 2006. "The Early Years: Evaluating Montessori." *Science* 313 (5795): 1893–94.

Luckey, Dennis W., David L. Olds, Weiming Zhang, Charles R. Henderson Jr., John Eckenrode, Harriet J. Kitzman, Robert Cole, and Lisa Pettitt. 2008. "Revised Analysis of 15-Year Outcomes in the Elmira Trial of the Nurse-Family Partnership." Prevention Research Center for Family and Child Health, University of Colorado Department of Pediatrics, Aurora.

Martinez, Sebastian, Sophie Nadeau, and Vitor Pereira. 2012. "The Promise of Preschool in Africa: A Randomized Impact Evaluation of Early Childhood Development in Rural Mozambique." enGender Impact: the World Bank's Gender Impact Evaluation Database, World Bank, Washington, DC.

Muennig, Peter, Lawrence Schweinhart, Jeanne Montie, and Matthew Neidell. 2009. "Effects of a Prekindergarten Educational Intervention on Adult Health: 37-Year Follow-Up Results of a Randomized Controlled Trial." *American Journal of Public Health* 99 (8): 1431–37.

http://dx.doi.org/10.1596/978-1-4648-0872-2

Olds, David L., John Eckenrode, Charles R. Henderson Jr., Harriet J. Kitzman, Jane Powers, Robert Cole, Kimberly Sidora, Pamela Morris, Lisa M. Pettitt, and Dennis W. Luckey. 1997. "Long-Term Effects of Home Visitation on Maternal Life Course and Child Abuse and Neglect: Fifteen-Year Follow-Up of a Randomized Trial." *Journal of the American Medical Association* 278 (8): 637–43.

Olds, David L., Charles R. Henderson Jr., Robert Chamberlin, and Robert Tatelbaum. 1986. "Preventing Child Abuse and Neglect: A Randomized Trial of Nurse Home Visitation." *Pediatrics* 78 (1): 65–78.

Olds, David L., Charles R. Henderson Jr., Robert Cole, John Eckenrode, Harriet J. Kitzman, Dennis W. Luckey, and Jane Powers. 1998. "Long-Term Effects of Nurse Home Visitation on Children's Criminal and Antisocial Behavior: 15-Year Follow-Up of a Randomized Controlled Trial." *Journal of the American Medical Association* 280 (14): 1238–44.

Olds, David L., Charles R. Henderson Jr., and Harriet J. Kitzman. 1994. "Does Prenatal and Infancy Nurse Home Visitation Have Enduring Effects on Qualities of Parental Caregiving and Child Health at 25 to 50 Months of Life?" *Pediatrics* 93 (1): 89–98.

Olds, David L., Charles R. Henderson Jr., Robert Tatelbaum, and Robert Chamberlin. 1988. "Improving the Life-Course Development of Socially Disadvantaged Mothers: A Randomized Trial of Nurse Home Visitation." *American Journal of Public Health* 78 (11): 1436–45.

Olds, David L., John R. Holmberg, Nancy Donelan-McCall, Dennis W. Luckey, Michael D. Knudtson, and JoAnn Robinson. 2014. "Effects of Home Visits by Paraprofessionals and by Nurses on Children: Follow-Up of a Randomized Trial at Ages 6 and 9 Years." *JAMA Pediatrics* 168 (2): 114–21.

Olds, David L., Harriet J. Kitzman, Robert Cole, Carole Hanks, Kimberly Arcoleo, Elizabeth Anson, Dennis W. Luckey, Michael D. Knudtson, Charles R. Henderson Jr., Jessica Bondy, and Amanda J. Stevenson. 2010. "Enduring Effects of Prenatal and Infancy Home Visiting by Nurses on Maternal Life Course and Government Spending: Follow-Up of a Randomized Trial among Children at Age 12 Years." *Journal of the American Medical Association* 164 (5): 419–24.

Olds, David L., Harriet J. Kitzman, Carole Hanks, Robert Cole, Elizabeth Anson, Kimberly Sidora-Arcoleo, and Jessica Bondy. 2007. "Effects of Nurse Home Visiting on Maternal and Child Functioning: Age-9 Follow-Up of a Randomized Trial." *Pediatrics* 120 (4): e832–e845.

Pickens, Jeffrey. 2009. "Socio-Emotional Programme Promotes Positive Behavior in Preschoolers." *Child Care in Practice* 15 (4): 261–78.

Pierre, R. G. S., J. I. Layzer, B. D. Goodson, and L. S. Berstein. 1997. "National Impact Evaluation of the Comprehensive Child Development Program." Abt Associates, Cambridge, MA.

Pierre, R. G. S, and J. I Layzer, 1989. "Using Home Visits for Multiple Purposes: The Comprehensive Child Development Program." Future of Children 9 (1): 134–51.

Raine, Adrian, Kjetil Mellingen, Jianghong Liu, Peter Venables, and Sarnoff A. Mednick. 2003. "Effects of Environmental Enrichment at Ages 3–5 Years on Schizotypal Personality and Antisocial Behavior at Ages 17 and 23 Years." *American Journal of Psychiatry* 160 (9): 1627–35.

Raine, Adrian, Peter Venables, Cyril Dalais, Kjetil Mellingen, Chandra Reynolds, and Sarnoff A. Mednick. 2001. "Early Educational and Health Enrichment at Age 3–5 Years

http://dx.doi.org/10.1596/978-1-4648-0872-2

Is Associated with Increased Autonomic and Central Nervous System Arousal and Orienting at Age 11 Years: Evidence from the Mauritius Child Health Project." *Psychophysiology* 38 (2): 254–66.

Reynolds, Arthur J., Judy A. Temple, Dylan L. Robertson, and Emily A. Mann. 2001. "Long-Term Effects of an Early Childhood Intervention of Educational Achievement and Juvenile Arrest: A 15-Year Follow-Up of Low-Income Children in Public Schools." *Journal of the American Medical Association* 285 (18): 2339–46.

Schweinhart, Lawrence J., Jeanne Montie, Zongping Xiang, W. Steven Barnett, Clive R. Belfield, and Milagros Nores. 2005. "The High/Scope Perry Preschool Study Through Age 40: Summary, Conclusions, and Frequently Asked Questions." HighScope Press, Ypsilanti, MI.

Venables, Peter. 1978. "Psychophysiology and Psychometrics." *Psychophysiology* 15 (4): 302–15.

Wagner, Mary M., and Serena L. Clayton. 1999. "The Parents as Teachers Program: Results from Two Demonstrations." *Future of Children* 9 (1): 91–115.

Wagner, Mary M., Donna Spiker, and Margaret Inman Linn. 2002. "The Effectiveness of the Parents as Teachers Program with Low-Income Parents and Children." *Topics in Early Childhood Special Education* 22 (2): 67–81.

Westat. 2010. "Head Start Impact Study: Final Report." U.S. Department of Health and Human Services, Washington, DC.

WHO (World Health Organization). 1968. "Neurophysiological and Behavioral Research in Psychiatry." Technical Report No. 381, WHO, Geneva.

———. 1975. "Working Group on Primary Prevention of Schizophrenia in High Risk Groups: Summary Report." WHO, Geneva.

Zielinski, David S., John Eckenrode, and David L. Olds. 2009. "Nurse Home Visitation and the Prevention of Child Maltreatment: Impact on the Timing of Official Reports." *Development and Psychopathology* 21 (2): 441–53.

http://dx.doi.org/10.1596/978-1-4648-0872-2

APPENDIX B

School-Based Program Descriptions

Table B.1 School-Based Program Descriptions

Program		Evaluation	
Name	*Description*	*Author/description*	*Results*
4Rs Program	**Beneficiaries:** Students from kindergarten to grade 5 **Objective:** Develop social and emotional skills related to understanding and managing feelings, listening and developing empathy, being assertive, solving conflict creatively and nonviolently, honoring diversity, and standing up to teasing and bullying. **Description:** The 4Rs Program is a universal school-based preventive intervention in literacy development, conflict resolution, and intergroup understanding that trains and supports teachers from kindergarten through grade 5 on how to integrate the teaching of social and emotional skills into the language arts curriculum and to achieve positive rules and norms, as well as safe and secure environments. The program has three primary components: (a) a comprehensive seven-unit, 21–35 lesson, literacy-based curriculum in conflict resolution and social-emotional learning (provided to teachers in a standardized, grade-specific teaching guide); (b) 25 hours of training followed by ongoing coaching of teachers to support them in teaching the 4Rs curriculum with a minimum of 12 contacts in one school year; and (c) a parent component (4Rs Family Connections) that consists of activities for children to do with their parents at home. **Cost:** US$90 per child per year (2011 dollars)	**Authors:** Brown and others (2010); Jones, Brown, and Aber (2011); Jones and others (2010) **Type:** RCT **Location:** United States: New York, New York **Follow-up:** 2 years **Sample:** 82 third-grade teachers and 82 classrooms in 18 New York City public elementary schools: (a) 45 classrooms (690 children) received the intervention, and (b) 37 classrooms (554 children) served as controls **Term used:** Socioemotional	**Behavior related:** Hostile attribution bias 1.5 years later (–)**; depressive symptoms 1.5 years later (–)**; aggressive interpersonal negotiation 1.5 years later (–)***; for those with the highest level of aggression, 1 year after the program aggressive fantasies (–)*; attention/hyperactivity symptoms (–)*** [especially for those with higher levels of initial aggression]; hyperactivity (–)*; social competence (+)** [especially for those with higher levels of initial aggression]; prosocial behavior (+)**; aggression (–)** [especially for those with higher levels of initial aggression] **Academic/cognitive related:** Teacher's report of academic skills for those with the highest level of initial aggression 1 and 1.5 years after (+)*; attendance for those with the highest level of initial aggression (+)*; standardized reading achievement for those with the highest level of initial aggression (+)*; math 1.5 years later for those with the highest level of initial aggression (+)**; classroom quality (+)**; teacher's emotional ability (+)**; classroom's emotional support (+)*; classroom's instructional support (+)** *Note:* No effect on children's literacy, attention problems, social competence, academic achievement.

table continues next page

Table B.1 School-Based Program Descriptions *(continued)*

Program		*Evaluation*	
Name	*Description*	*Author/description*	*Results*
Al's Pals: Kids Making Healthy Choices	**Beneficiaries:** Prekindergarten to second-grade students (3- to 8-year-old children) **Objectives:** (a) Increase the protective factor of social-emotional competence in young children, and (b) decrease the risk factor of early and persistent antisocial or aggressive behavior by preventing the development of increased aggression and antisocial behaviors in young children over the course of a typical school year. In particular, Al's Pals lessons are designed to help young children develop specific skills related to the following four components of resiliency: (a) social competence, (b) problem solving, (c) autonomy, and (d) a sense of purpose and belief in a bright future. **Description:** Al's Pals is a universal early childhood prevention initiative that involves teacher training, a yearlong classroom curriculum, and a companion parent education program. Specifically, it involves a 46-lesson resiliency-based prevention curriculum implemented over 23 weeks (15–20 minutes/lesson) by trained teachers in a variety of settings, including preschools, child care centers, other early childhood classrooms, and after-school programs. It also involves materials and music, including 14 parent letters that explain what the curriculum is teaching and that offer activities for parents to do at home. **Cost:** Over five years, implementing the program costs approximately US$9–US$15 per child, depending on the number of children in the classroom. Start-up costs include training on the intervention (core, refresher, and advanced online training cost about US$495) and the purchase of materials (each curriculum kit costs US$685).	**Authors:** Lynch, Geller, and Schmidt (2004) **Type:** RCT **Location:** United States: Virginia (1994/95); Virginia (1995/96); Lansing, Michigan (1996/97) **Follow-up:** 7 months **Sample:** 173 intervention and 48 comparison children in 1994/95 Virginia group; 230 intervention and 103 comparison children in the 1995/96 Virginia group; 218 intervention and 181 comparison children in the 1996/97 Michigan group. Thirty-seven classrooms were selected randomly. Seventeen classrooms (218 children) were randomly assigned to the intervention group and 16 classrooms (181 children) were randomly assigned to the control group. **Term used:** Socioemotional competence	**Health related:** Anxiety, somatic problems (–)*** **Behavior related:** For the 1994/95 and 1995/96 Virginia and the 1996/97 Michigan programs, Child Behavior Rating Scale (+)***; in the 1994/95 Virginia pilot, positive coping strategies (+)***, negative coping strategies (–)**; for the 1996/97 Michigan group, problem behavior (–)**; self-centered, explosive/attention problems/antisocial, aggressive/social withdrawal (–)**; positive coping (+)*; distract/avoid (+)* *Note:* The children in the Michigan trial did not experience any changes in the problem behavior scale.

table continues next page

Table B.1 School-Based Program Descriptions *(continued)*

Program		*Evaluation*	
Name	*Description*	*Author/description*	*Results*
Project CARE Child Development Project	**Beneficiaries:** Students from kindergarten to grade 6 **Objective:** Promote the growth of the whole child through character, social, ethical, and academic development. The program aimed to enhance prosocial characteristics by affecting participants' attitudes, motives, and behaviors. **Description:** This character education program promotes academic and social growth in teachers and students through the following components: (a) School Wide Activities—cooperative activities that encouraged students working together to solve problems and build relationships and create caring classroom communities; (b) Developmental Discipline—an approach to classroom management that fosters respectful and caring relationships among students and teachers; (c) Making Meaning—a literature-based language arts/reading component that explicitly integrates ethical and moral conversation into the curriculum by using a diverse set of reading materials with various cultures, issues, and themes; (d) KidzLit—after-school enrichment activities to support reading; and (e) parent activities—Second Step training provided to parents to support prosocial parenting skills. (The impact evaluation analyzes the effect of components a–c). **Cost:** n/a	**Authors:** Chang and Muñoz (2006) **Type:** Quasi-experiment **Location:** United States: Louisville, Kentucky **Follow-up:** 1 year **Sample:** From 87 eligible elementary schools, 8 schools were chosen for treatment and 8 for control. Participants included 390 teachers across 16 schools (190 in control group and 200 in treatment group) and 3,908 students from grades 3, 4, and 5 (2,025 control group; 1,883 in the treatment group) across the 16 schools. **Term used:** Character	**Behavior related:** Student autonomy and influence in the classroom scale (+)***; classroom supportiveness scale (+)*** **Academic/cognitive related:** Reading for high-quality treatment schools (+)**; number of referrals (–)** **Other:** Principal supportiveness (+)*; faculty collegiality (+)***; trust in students (+)*** *Note:* No significant differences between control and treatment in academic outcomes, attendance, or suspension.
		Authors: Battistich, Schaps, and Wilson (2004) **Type:** Quasi-experiment **Location:** Six school districts across the United States **Follow-up:** 4 years	**Behavior related:** Global self-esteem (+)*; victimization at school (–)*; misconduct at school (–)*; involvement in positive youth activities (+)***; gets along well with others, is sought out by his/her fellow students, and has many friends (+)*

table continues next page

Table B.1 School-Based Program Descriptions *(continued)*

Program		*Evaluation*	
Name	*Description*	*Author/description*	*Results*
		Sample: 700 beneficiaries and 546 controls belonging to six elementary schools, serving at-risk students **Term used:** Social behavior	In high implementation subsample: sense of efficacy (+)**; delinquent behaviors (–)**; friends' drug use (+)*; friends' delinquent behaviors (+)**; friends' positive involvement in school (+)**; gets along well with others, is sought out by his/her fellow students, and has many friends (+)**; does not hesitate to state opinions, even when others disagree with his/her views (+)*; is engaged in class—participates in discussions, stays on the topic, and generally takes an active part in whatever the class is doing (+)**; appears to be socially awkward and inept—tends to say the "wrong thing" and to be rebuffed or ridiculed by other students (+)**; considers others' feelings, treats them with respect, and offers and gives help to those who need it (+)* **Academic/cognitive related:** Sense of efficacy (+)***. In high-implementation subsample: trust in and respect for teachers (+)**; positive teacher–student relations (+)***; educational aspirations (+)***; educational expectations (+)*; GPA (+)***; achievement test scores (+)**; comes to class and completes assignments on time, tries to learn the material, and does the best work he/she can (+)*; task orientation toward learning (+)* **Other:** Sense of school (+)*; positive teacher–student relations (+)**; liking for school (+)**; attendance at religious services (+)* *Note:* No significant differences between control and treatment in academic outcomes, attendance, or suspension.

table continues next page

Table B.1 School-Based Program Descriptions *(continued)*

Program		*Evaluation*	
Name	*Description*	*Author/description*	*Results*
I Can Problem Solve	**Beneficiaries:** Kindergarten and first-grade students **Objectives:** Increase prosocial behavior and reduce aggressive behavior in children in kindergarten and first grade in a large, ethnically diverse, urban school district. **Description:** The Interpersonal Cognitive Problem-Solving curriculum (also known as I Can Problem Solve) is a school-based universal/primary prevention program that focuses on children's cognitive processes and problem-solving skills. It uses various techniques, including games, stories, puppets, and role playing. It consists of 83 20-minute lessons delivered by trained teachers. The lessons include a stated purpose of the lesson, a list of suggested materials, and a teacher's script that explains the basic steps in conducting the lessons. I Can Problem Solve is optimally taught three to five times per week. Lessons focus on training children to (a) generate a variety of solutions to interpersonal problems; (b) think through the consequences of each potential solution; and (c) identify thoughts, feelings, and motives that can generate problem situations. Teachers are highly trained (they receive a manual and subsequent booster training, as well as follow-up training when needed). **Cost:** n/a	**Authors:** Boyle and Hassett-Walker (2008) **Type:** RCT **Location:** United States **Follow-up:** 2 years **Sample:** 226 students were randomly assigned in three groups: (a) 96 students received instruction for two consecutive years; (b) 106 students received only one year of program instruction, either in kindergarten or first grade; and (c) 24 students were assigned to the control group for two consecutive years. **Term used:** Prosocial behaviors	**Behavior related:** Preschool Social Behavior Scale for those with two years of instruction (+)***; Hahnemann behavior rating scale for those with one or two years of instruction (+)***; rational aggression for those with two years of instruction (–)**; overt aggression of those with two years of instruction (–)****; prosocial behavior for those with two years of instruction (+)***; passivity for those receiving two years of instruction (+)**; prosocial behavior for those who received either one or two years of instruction (+)*** *Note:* There is a modest additive effect of the program, with students who received two years of instruction becoming more prosocial and less aggressive than students who received one year of instruction.
Project SAFE (Strategies Aimed at Family Empowerment)	**Beneficiaries:** Students from kindergarten to grade 5 **Objectives:** Prevent substance abuse. In particular, the I Can Problem Solve program (ICPS) is directed at enhancing problem-solving and critical thinking skills. The Strengthening Families (SF) program was originally designed for children of drug abusers.	**Authors:** Kumpfer and others (2002) **Type:** RCT **Location:** United States **Follow-up:** 9 months **Sample:** 655 first-grade students from 12 rural schools randomly divided into the following groups: (a) 256 received the	**Behavior related:** Parenting skills for the group receiving ICPS+SF1 (+)***; family relationships for ICPS+SF1 (+)**; social competency for ICPS+SF1 (+)** and ICPS+SF2 (+)***; behavioral self-regulation for all groups (+)*** **Academic/cognitive related:** School bonding for all programs except for ICPS+SF2 (+)***

table continues next page

Table B.1 School-Based Program Descriptions *(continued)*

Program		*Evaluation*	
Name	*Description*	*Author/description*	*Results*
	Description: The I Can Problem Solve program is described above. The SF program is a 14-session family skills training program that consists of three courses: (a) parent skills training, (b) children skills training, and (c) family life skills training. To maintain the intervention's gains, it has booster sessions at 6 and 12 months. Four trainers (two parent and two children cotrainers) conduct the programs at the schools in weekly scheduled sessions. **Incredible Cost:** n/a	ICPS, (b) 56 received the ICPS combined with the SF program (referred to as ICPS+SF1), (c) 21 received the ICPS and the parenting training of the SF program (referred to as ICPS+SF2), and (d) 322 were in the control group. **Term used:** Social skills	*Note:* The variables measured are associated with the risk for substance abuse.
Incredible Years	**Beneficiaries:** Children from prekindergarten to grade 5 **Objective:** Promote children's social skills, self-regulation, and classroom behavior. **Description:** The Incredible Years Child Training Curriculum (Dinosaur School) consisted of 30 classroom lessons per year (at least 2 per week, lasting 35–40 minutes each), with preschool and primary grade versions. The content is broken into seven units: (a) learning school rules; (b) how to be successful in school; (c) emotional literacy, empathy, and perspective taking; (d) interpersonal problem solving; (e) anger management; (f) social skills; and (g) communication skills. Materials include over 300 small-group activities, over 100 videotaped models of children demonstrating social skills and conflict management strategies, life-size puppets, Dinosaur homework activities, picture cue cards, and games. Teachers were trained for four days (28 hours) spread out in monthly workshops. The training involved explanations of how to deliver the Dinosaur School curriculum, as well how to use effective classroom management strategies.	**Authors:** Webster-Stratton, Reid, and Stoolmiller (2008) **Type:** RCT **Location:** United States: Seattle, Washington **Follow-up:** 2 years **Sample:** 120 classrooms from Seattle-area Head Starts and 14 elementary schools were involved in the project. These schools were matched on variables such as size, geographic location, and demographics of the children. The sample consisted of 1,746 kindergarten or first-grade students who were nested in 160 classrooms, which in turn were nested under 119 teachers (40 teachers had 2 or more classrooms). Classrooms were in culturally diverse schools with high rates of poverty. **Term used:** Social emotional and self-control skills	**Behavior related:** School readiness and conduct problems (–)**; social competence; child disengagement (–)**; number of positive feelings identified by children (+)***; emotional self-regulation; conduct problems (–)** **Academic/cognitive related:** Effective discipline by Head Start teachers (+)**; positive classroom management strategies **Other:** Involvement with parents (+)** *Note:* Overall, children who were initially most at risk benefited most from the intervention. Furthermore, all of the student behavioral outcomes showed strong teacher-level effects (the teacher played an important role in the effects).

table continues next page

Table B.1 School-Based Program Descriptions *(continued)*

Program		*Evaluation*	
Name	*Description*	*Author/description*	*Results*
	Cost: US$2,506 for a group with 12 children (2007 dollars) (Edwards and others 2007)		
Michigan Model for Health (MMH)	**Beneficiaries:** Students from kindergarten to 12th grade **Objective:** Help young people live happier and healthier lives. **Description:** The MMH uses a universal prevention approach to facilitate skills-based learning through 20- to 50-minute lessons that incorporate a variety of teaching and learning techniques, skills development and practice, and approaches for building positive lifestyle behaviors in students and families. The fourth-grade curriculum consisted of 25 lessons on social and emotional health; alcohol, tobacco, and other drugs; safety; and nutrition and physical activity. In fifth grade, 28 lessons were taught across the same health topics. The intervention was implemented in classrooms over 12 weeks in grade 4 and 14 weeks in grade 5 during a normal class period of 40–50 minutes by the classroom or health teacher, who received a 12-hour curriculum training course with follow-up support provided as needed. **Cost:** n/a	**Authors:** O'Neill, Clark, and Jones (2011) **Type:** RCT **Location:** United States: Michigan and Indiana **Follow-up:** 2 years **Sample:** 2,512 students in 52 schools, who were randomly assigned to: (a) 1,847 children in 29 schools received the intervention in fourth grade and (b) 29 schools and 1,536 were the control in fourth grade. The size of the groups changed for fifth grade: (a) on the treatment group, 3 schools closed and 1 declined, therefore, 1,345 children in 25 schools received the intervention in fifth grade and (b) 2 of the control schools closed, therefore, 27 schools and 1,167 students were the control in fifth grade. **Terms used:** Social and emotional health, self-management, interpersonal communication	**Health related:** Intentions to smoke cigarettes (–)***; intentions to drink alcohol (–)*** **Behavior related:** Social and emotional skills (+)***; interpersonal skills (+)***; drug refusal skills (+)***; self-management skills (+)*; aggressive behavior (–)**
MindUp: Mindfulness Education Program	**Beneficiaries:** Students from grades 4 to 7 **Objective:** Foster children's positive emotions, self-regulation, and goal setting **Description:** MindUp is a classroom-based universal preventive intervention that focuses on facilitating the development of social and emotional competence and positive emotions. In the curriculum, the mindful attention training exercises are practiced three times a day (three	**Authors:** Schonert-Reichl and Lawlor (2010) **Type:** Quasi-experimental design **Location:** Canada **Follow-up:** 9 weeks **Sample:** 139 students in grades 4 to 7 participated in the program, and 107 students were in control classrooms. **Term used:** Social and emotional competence	**Behavior related:** Optimism (+)**; positive affect (+)*; aggressive behaviors (–)***; oppositional behavior/dysregulation (–)***; attention and concentration (+)***; social-emotional competence (+)*** *Note:* The program demonstrated more positive benefits for preadolescents than for early adolescents.

table continues next page

Table B.1 School-Based Program Descriptions *(continued)*

Program		*Evaluation*	
Name	*Description*	*Author/description*	*Results*
	minutes per practice), along with affirmations and visualizations. **Cost:** n/a		
Open Circle	**Beneficiaries:** Students from kindergarten to grade 8 **Objective:** Enhance social skills of elementary school children **Description:** Twice a week, children and their teachers come together to work on 1 of 35 lessons. Verbal cues encouraging class members to speak up, calm down, and adopt the "school listening look" come out of discussions of concepts and behaviors drawn from the children's own experiences; students also develop agreed-upon nonverbal signals that emphasize respectful communication. **Cost:** n/a	**Author:** Hennessey (2007) **Type:** Quasi-experimental design **Location:** United States **Follow-up:** Approximately 10 months **Sample:** 154 fourth graders in eight classrooms in four schools (two in middle- to upper-middle-class suburban areas and two that served more diverse populations) were sampled. A group of students participated in classrooms headed by teachers well versed in the Open Circle curriculum. The rest of the students participated in classes that were not implementing a social competence program. **Term used:** Social skills	**Behavior related:** Social skills (+)***; problem behaviors (–)*** *Note:* No statistical difference was found in student-reported measures or on academic performance.
Fast Track PATHS (Promoting Alternative Thinking Strategies)	**Beneficiaries:** Students from prekindergarten to grade 6 **Objectives:** Promote emotional and social competencies and reduce aggression and behavior problems **Description:** The Fast Track program integrated the provision of universal services (all children) and selective services (children at some risk) into a comprehensive model that involved the child, school, family, and community. Children demonstrating the greatest degree of early conduct problems were selected for a series of programs that included weekly parenting support classes, small-group social skills programs,	**Authors:** CPPRG (2010) **Type:** Clustered RCT **Location:** United States: Nashville, Tennessee; Seattle, Washington; central Pennsylvania **Follow-up:** 3 years **Sample:** 2,937 children of multiple ethnicities from grades 1, 2, and 3 in elementary schools located in high-risk neighborhoods (high delinquency and juvenile arrests) **Term used:** Emotional and social competences	**Behavior related:** Authority acceptance (+)***; problem levels (–)***; aggression in boys (–)***; hyperactivity in boys (–)**; prosocial behavior in boys (+)* **Academic/cognitive related:** Cognitive concentration (+)***; academic engagement (+) *Note:* Most intervention effects were moderated by school environment, with effects stronger in less disadvantaged schools. Effects on aggression were greater in students who showed higher baseline levels of aggression.

table continues next page

Table B.1 School-Based Program Descriptions *(continued)*

Program		*Evaluation*	
Name	*Description*	*Author/description*	*Results*
	academic tutoring, and home visits. The universal intervention was started in the classroom concurrent with the initiation. The PATHS curriculum model synthesizes the domains of self-control, emotional awareness and understanding, peer-related social skills, and social problem solving to focus on promoting social and emotional competence. Of these programs for the high-risk children and families, 2 to 3 lessons were presented on a regular basis throughout most of the school year, and daily activities were used to promote generalization (57 lessons in grade 1, 46 lessons in grade 2, and 48 lessons in grade 3). **Cost:** With 500 students participating, the cost per student is US$119.	**Authors:** Domitrovich, Cortes, and Greenberg (2007) **Type:** RCT **Location:** United States: Pennsylvania **Follow-up:** 1 year **Sample:** 292 three- to four-year-old children in 20 classrooms. Ten of the classrooms were treated with 30 weekly lessons and extension activities (such as group games, art projects, and books) for nine months. **Term used:** Emotional and social competences	**Behavior related:** Emotion knowledge skills (+) [Kusche Emotional Inventory—emotion vocabulary (+)***; assessment of children's emotions scales—emotion expression knowledge (+)** and anger bias (–)***; Denham Puppet Interview—affective perspective-taking skills (+)**]; teacher's report on social competence (+)***, social skills (+)***, social cooperation (+)***, social interaction (+)***, and social independence (+)***; social withdrawal (–)**; parents' report on social competence (+)***
Positive Action	**Beneficiaries:** Children in kindergarten to grade 12 **Objective:** Positively influence multiple behavioral domains, such as student academic achievement and substance use. **Description:** The curriculum has the following components: self-concept; social and emotional positive actions for managing oneself responsibly; and positive actions directed toward physical and mental health, honesty, getting along with others, and continually improving oneself. Each grade level includes 140 lessons (15–20 minutes each; kindergarten to grade 6) or 70 lessons (20 minutes each; grades 7 and up). The program also includes teacher, counselor, family, and community training, as well as activities directed toward school-wide climate development. **Cost:** Average cost per participant: US$510 (2013 dollars) (Belfield and others 2015)	**Authors:** Lewis and others (2013) **Type:** RCT **Location:** United States: Chicago, Illinois **Follow-up:** 6 years **Sample:** 624 children in 14 low-income, mostly minority, urban Chicago public schools were followed for six years (from grades 3 to 8). Attrition was high, and by eighth grade, only 363 students remained in the study. **Term used:** Socioemotional	**Behavior related:** Normative beliefs in support of aggression (–)***; bullying behaviors (–)***; disruptive behavior (–)***; parents' report of bullying(–)** **Academic/cognitive related:** Disciplinary referrals(–)***; suspensions (–)***

table continues next page

Table B.1 School-Based Program Descriptions *(continued)*

Program		*Evaluation*	
Name	*Description*	*Author/description*	*Results*
		Authors: Snyder and others (2013) **Type:** RCT **Location:** United States: Hawaii **Follow-up**: 3 years **Sample:** 1,784 elementary-age students who were followed from grades 1 and 2 to grade 5. These children attended 20 racially and ethnically diverse schools in Hawaii: 10 of the schools received the intervention for four to five years, and 10 schools served as control. **Term used:** Socioemotional and character development	**Health related:** Substance use (–)***; sexual activity (–)*** **Behavior related:** Violence (–)*** **Academic/cognitive related:** Academic behavior (+)***
Raising Healthy Children (RHC)	**Beneficiaries:** Students from kindergarten to grade 12 **Objective:** Reduce developmental expression of risk factors for problem behaviors while increasing protective factors. **Description:** A multicomponent, multiyear social development intervention is delivered to participants during grades 1 through 12. The school intervention strategies provided during elementary and middle school consisted of a series of teacher and staff development workshops. Student intervention strategies during the elementary school years consisted of social, emotional, and cognitive skill training infused into classroom and school-wide activities, after-school tutoring sessions and study clubs during grades 4 to 6, and student summer camps during the first four summers of the project.	**Authors:** Catalano and others (2003) **Type:** RCT **Location:** United States **Follow-up:** 1.5 years **Sample:** 938 elementary students from first or second grade who were enrolled in 10 high-risk (low income, low standardized achievement test scores, high absenteeism, and high mobility) schools in the Pacific Northwest and randomly divided into two groups: (a) 497 participated in schools with the RHC program, and (b) 441 participated in control schools **Term used:** Social skills	**Behavior related:** Social competence (+)***; antisocial behaviors (–)** **Academic/cognitive related:** Teacher reported academic performance (+)***; school commitment (+)**

table continues next page

Table B.1 School-Based Program Descriptions *(continued)*

Program		*Evaluation*	
Name	*Description*	*Author/description*	*Results*
	The family intervention strategies offered during the elementary school years consisted of universal and selected components. Multiple-session parenting workshops (for example, "Raising Healthy Children," "How to Help Your Child Succeed in School," and "Preparing for the Drug Free Years") were offered to all parents at intervention schools. For families of students identified as high risk because of academic or behavioral problems, in-home services tailored to the specific risk factors of these children were provided to reinforce curricula covered in the parenting workshops. **Cost:** n/a		
Resolving Conflict Creatively	**Beneficiaries:** Children in grades 1 through 6 **Objective:** Change the mental processes and interpersonal behavioral strategies that lead children to engage in aggression and violence by teaching them constructive conflict resolution strategies and promoting positive intergroup relations **Description:** The universal, school-based intervention involves violence prevention and intergroup understanding. The intervention has two major components: (a) training and coaching of teachers to support them in implementing a curriculum in conflict resolution and intergroup understanding (teacher training and coaching), and (b) the delivery of that curriculum through classroom instruction for children provided by the trained teachers (classroom instruction). Additional features of the program include peer mediation, principals' training, and parent training. **Cost:** n/a	**Authors:** Aber, Brown, and Jones (2003) **Type:** Quasi-experimental design **Location:** United States: New York, New York **Follow-up:** 2 years **Sample:** 11,160 public elementary students, from first to sixth grade in 15 schools in New York City. **Term used:** Socioemotional development	**Health related:** Depressive symptoms (–)*** **Behavior related:** Hostile attribution bias (–)***; aggressive interpersonal negotiation strategies (–)***; competent interpersonal negotiation strategies (–)***; conduct problems (–)***; aggressive fantasies (–)***; prosocial behavior (+)***

table continues next page

Table B.1 School-Based Program Descriptions *(continued)*

Program		*Evaluation*	
Name	*Description*	*Author/description*	*Results*
Responsive Classroom	**Beneficiaries:** Students from kindergarten to sixth grade **Objectives:** Integrate social and academic learning and bolster classroom social support. **Description:** The social and emotional learning intervention provides professional development for elementary teachers in the use of 10 specific classroom practices: Morning Meeting, Rule Creation, Interactive Modeling, Teacher Language, Logical Consequences, Academic Choice, Classroom Organization, Guided Discovery, Collaborative Problem Solving, and Working with Families. **Cost:** US$900 (2013 dollars); calculated for schools with high implementation fidelity (Belfield and others 2015)	**Authors:** Brock and others (2008); Curby, Rimm-Kaufman, and Abry (2013); Rimm-Kaufman and others (2014) **Type:** RCT **Location:** United States **Follow-up:** 3 years **Sample:** 24 schools: 13 were randomized into the intervention and 11 were assigned to a wait list. Brock and others (2008) used a sample of 520 children and 51 teachers in grades 3 to 5. **Term used:** Socioemotional	**Behavior related:** Teacher-rated social skills (+)**; child perceptions (+)**; emotional support (+); teacher's emotional support (+)*** **Academic/cognitive related:** Teacher-rated academics (+)**; standardized reading (+)**; math for children with low levels (+)***; reading (+)** **Other:** Classroom organization (+)**
RULER program	**Beneficiaries:** Students from kindergarten to eighth grade **Objective:** Modify the quality of classroom social interactions so that the climate becomes more supportive, empowering, and engaging. **Description:** The program provides comprehensive professional development with a literacy-based, skill-building, and social and emotional learning program for students. It is applied universally and includes professional development for school leaders, teachers, and staff, as well as classroom instruction protocols to enhance skill-building opportunities and characteristics of the learning environment. Training program: schoolteachers attended a day and a half of training on RULER at the beginning of the academic year. **Cost:** n/a	**Authors:** Rivers and others (2013) **Type:** RCT **Location:** United States: Brooklyn and Queens, New York **Follow-up:** 15 months **Sample:** 155 fifth- and sixth-grade classrooms in 62 schools randomized into receiving either the RULER curriculum or the English Language Arts curriculum **Term used:** Social and emotional	**Behavior related:** Emotional support domain (+)**; positive climate (+)***; regard for student perspectives (+)**; emotion-focused interactions (+)** **Academic/cognitive related:** Classroom emotional climate (+)

table continues next page

Table B.1 School-Based Program Descriptions *(continued)*

Program		*Evaluation*	
Name	*Description*	*Author/description*	*Results*
Second Step (Student Success through Prevention)	**Beneficiaries:** Students from preschool to 11th grade **Objective:** Help students stay engaged in school; make good choices; set goals; and avoid bullying, cyberbullying, and peer pressure. **Description:** Second Step is a universal curricular classroom intervention, which for sixth grade involves 15 weekly lessons (50 minutes each) focused on socioemotional learning skills, including empathy, communication, bullying prevention, and problem-solving skills. Lessons are highly interactive, incorporating small group discussions and activities, dyadic exercises, whole-class instruction, and individual work. Lessons are structured and supported through an accompanying DVD that contains rich media content, including topic-focused interviews with students and video demonstrations of skills. **Cost:** US$440 per student (2013 dollars) (Belfield and others 2015)	**Authors:** Espelage and others (2013) **Type:** RCT **Location:** United States: Illinois and Kansas **Follow-up:** 3 years **Sample:** 3,616 sixth-grade students within 36 middle schools randomly assigned: (a) 18 schools and 1,940 students in the experimental group, and (b) 18 schools and 1,676 students in the control group **Term used:** Socioemotional learning skills	**Behavior related:** Physical aggression (–)** *Note:* No significant intervention effects for perpetration of or victimization by bullying, homophobic teasing, and sexual violence.
Steps to Respect	**Beneficiaries:** Upper elementary school years (grades 3 to 6) **Objective:** Decrease school bullying problems by (a) increasing adult monitoring and intervention in bullying incidents, (b) improving systemic supports for socially responsible behavior, (c) changing student normative beliefs that support bullying, and (d) addressing student socioemotional skills that counter bullying and support social competence. **Description:** The multilevel program coordinates a school-wide environmental intervention, three sequential classroom curricula, and a selected	**Authors:** Frey and others (2009) **Type:** RCT **Location:** United States: Pacific Northwest **Follow-up:** 2 years **Sample:** 624 elementary school students in grades 3 through 5 were surveyed, and 360 students were observed on the playground. **Term used:** Social emotional skills	**Behavior related:** Bullying (–)***; victimization by bullying (–)***; destructive bystander behavior (–)***; aggression (–)***; argumentative students (–)***; self-reports of victimization (–)**; self-reports of direct aggression (+)***; peer interaction skills for fourth-grade teachers (+)**; acceptance of bullying (–)* *Note:* Agreeable interactions did not increase. Acceptance of bullying/aggression did not change.

table continues next page

Table B.1 School-Based Program Descriptions *(continued)*

Program		*Evaluation*	
Name	*Description*	*Author/description*	*Results*
	intervention for students involved in bullying. The program includes manuals, written material, and audiovisual presentations for school administration, staff training, classroom curricula, and parent outreach. In the school-wide environmental intervention, school administrators and staff establish school-wide bullying policies and procedures that protect reporting students, stop problems before they escalate, follow up cases, dispel myths regarding bullying, and so on. The classroom curricula include 10 weeks of biweekly basic lessons followed by 8 to 10 literature-based lessons. The individual intervention consists of brief individual coaching sessions with each participant in bullying incidents, intended to provide solution-oriented responses to immediate and long-term student needs and assess effectiveness. **Cost:** n/a		
Unique Minds	**Beneficiaries:** Students from kindergarten to fifth grade **Objectives:** Promote cognitive-social-emotional (CSE) skills, including student self-efficacy, problem solving, socioemotional competence, and a positive classroom climate, with the dual goals of preventing youth behavioral problems and promoting academic learning. **Description:** A classroom package of concepts, activities, tools, and strategies is designed to involve multiple agents (students, peers, teachers and other school staff, and parents) across different settings (classrooms, cafeterias, playgrounds, and the home). The intervention targets student proximal CSE competencies	**Authors:** Linares and others (2005) **Type:** Quasi-experimental design **Location:** United States: New York **Follow-up:** 2 years **Sample:** 119 students (57 in intervention school and 62 in comparison school) from 13 fourth-grade classrooms (6 in intervention and 7 in comparison) in urban public schools **Term used:** Socioemotional skills	**Behavior related:** Student self-efficacy (+)***; socioemotional competencies (+)**; attention and concentration (+)***; social and emotional competence (+)***; authority and compliance problems (–)***; aggression (+)*** **Academic/cognitive related:** Problem-solving skills (+)**; math grades (+)** *Note:* No significant effect for classroom climate, standardized reading, or math test.

table continues next page

Table B.1 School-Based Program Descriptions *(continued)*

Program		*Evaluation*	
Name	*Description*	*Author/description*	*Results*
	(self-efficacy, problem solving, and socioemotional functioning) and distal academic learning (grades and achievement). **Cost:** n/a		
Family Check-Up (FCU)	**Beneficiaries:** Children ages 2 to 17 **Objective:** Reduce children's problem behavior through changing parent–child interactions. **Setting:** Public middle schools **Description:** In this school-based, family-centered intervention, a family resource center is established at the school site. The resource center provides general informational and consultation services (such as brochures, parenting materials, parenting topics nights, community resources, and feedback to parents on their student's behavior). Additionally, using LifeSkills Training, it provides six in-class lessons to students on the following topics: (a) school success, (b) health decisions, (c) building positive peer groups, (d) the cycle of respect, (e) coping with stress and anger, and (f) solving problems peacefully. Furthermore, the FCU model identifies students with early signs of risk in emotional, behavioral, or academic domains and treats them with more intensive family support services (three family-centered intervention sessions that assess family strengths and weaknesses and motivate parents to improve their parenting practices and engage in intervention services that address the specific needs of their family). Families that participate have the opportunity to select intervention options that are tailored to the unique needs of each family and that are grounded in empirically validated family management strategies and	**Authors:** Caruthers, Van Ryzin, and Dishion (2014); Connell and Dishion (2008); Connell, Klostermann, and Dishion (2012); Dishion and others (2002); Stormshak, Connell, and Dishion (2009); Van Ryzin, Stormshak, and Dishion (2012) **Type:** RCT **Location:** United States: midsize urban city in the Pacific Northwest **Follow-up:** From ages 12 to 23 **Sample:** 998 sixth-grade adolescents and their families: 498 assigned to control and 500 assigned to treatment. 80% in follow-up.	**Health related:** Depression (–)**; substance use (–); high-risk sexual behavior in adulthood (–) **Behavior related:** Arrests (–)**; antisocial behavior at age 19 (–)**; family relationship (+); involvement in deviant peer friendship (–) **Academic/cognitive related:** School absences during middle school and into high school (–)**; GPA (+)**

table continues next page

Table B.1 School-Based Program Descriptions *(continued)*

Program		*Evaluation*	
Name	*Description*	*Author/description*	*Results*
	school and community resources that can support family change. The intervention was delivered by highly trained personnel who were continuously trained during the study. **Cost:** n/a		
		Authors: Stormshak and others 2011; Van Ryzin, Stormshak, and Dishion (2012) **Type:** RCT **Location:** United States: midsized urban city in the Pacific Northwest **Follow-up:** 3 years **Sample:** 593 adolescents in sixth grade that belonged to ethnic minorities: 386 families assigned to intervention (students at risk and not at risk were invited to participate) and 207 to control. 86% retained across three years.	**Health related:** Cigarette, alcohol, and marijuana use (–)** **Behavior related:** Effortful control/self-regulation (+)**; antisocial behavior [lying to parents, skipping school, damaging property, fighting] (–)**; spending time with deviant peers [peers who smoke, get in trouble, steal, fight, use alcohol or drugs] (–)***; family conflict (–)*
Aerobic Running	**Beneficiaries:** Fourth, fifth, and sixth graders **Objectives:** Compare the effects of running with a normal physical education program. **Setting:** Public middle schools. It is a school-based, family-centered intervention. **Description:** Those assigned to running had to do three 30-minute sessions per week for 12 weeks in lieu of attending regular physical education classes. **Cost:** n/a	**Authors:** Tuckman and Hinkle (1986) **Type:** RCT **Location:** United States **Follow-up:** 6 months **Sample:** 154 children in grades 4, 5, and 6	**Health related:** Pulse rates (–)*** **Academic/cognitive related:** Creativity (+)*** *Note:* No significant differences in classroom behavior, self-concept, and Bender-Gestalt or Maze test scores.
Leadership Education Through Athletic Development (LEAD) curriculum	**Beneficiaries:** Children from kindergarten to grade 5 **Objectives:** Examine the impact of school-based tae kwon do training on self-regulatory abilities. **Setting:** Private lower school **Description:** A high-level martial arts teacher (with a black belt and close to 10 years of instruction experience) gave two to three martial art classes	**Authors:** Lakes and Hoyt (2004) **Type:** RCT **Location:** United States: private lower school in a midsize midwestern city **Follow-up:** 3 months	**Behavior related:** Cognitive, affective, and physical self-regulation (+)*; prosocial behavior (+)*; classroom conduct for girls (+)* **Academic/cognitive related:** Performance on a mental math test (+)*

table continues next page

Table B.1 School-Based Program Descriptions *(continued)*

Program		*Evaluation*	
Name	*Description*	*Author/description*	*Results*
	per week to treated children in an environment characterized by respect, discipline, and self-control. All classes started with a short meditation session. Children in control group participated in a standard physical education curriculum that included stretching, running, and sports. **Cost:** n/a	**Sample:** 193 children from kindergarten through grade 5, randomly assigned to treatment (martial arts) or control (traditional physical education)	*Note:* No effect on freedom from distractibility, self-esteem.
Mindful Awareness Practices (MAPs)	**Beneficiaries:** Second- and third-grade children ages 7 to 9 **Objective:** Improve executive functions. **Setting:** On-campus university elementary school **Description:** Thirty minutes of exercises generate a state of heightened and receptive attention to moment-by-moment experience, twice per week, for eight weeks. The program is modeled after classical mindfulness training for adults and uses secular and age-appropriate exercises and games to promote (a) awareness of self through sensory awareness, attentional regulation, and awareness of thoughts and feelings; (b) awareness of others; and (c) awareness of the environment. **Cost:** n/a	**Authors:** Flook and others (2010) **Type:** RCT **Location:** United States: Los Angeles, California **Follow-up:** 3 months **Sample:** 64 children ages 7 to 9 from second- and third-grade classrooms	**Behavior related:** Behavioral regulation (+)**; global executive control (+)*** **Academic/cognitive related:** Metacognition (+)** *Note:* No effect on freedom from distractibility, self-esteem.
Attention Academy Program (AAP)	**Beneficiaries:** Elementary school children (grades 1 to 3) of nine classrooms within two elementary schools **Objectives:** Help students learn to (a) increase their attention to the present experience, (b) approach each experience without judgment, and (c) view each experience as novel and new with a "beginner's eye." **Setting:** Elementary schools **Description:** A 24-week training program employed a series of exercises, including breath work, body	**Authors:** Napoli, Krech, and Holley (2005) **Type:** RCT **Location:** United States: a southwestern city **Follow-up:** 3 months **Sample:** 194 children in grades 1 to 3 in nine classrooms within two elementary schools: 97 receiving treatment (mindfulness program) and 97 in control (reading or quiet activities)	**Health related:** Anxiety (+)* **Behavior related:** Social skills (+)*** **Academic/cognitive related:** Selective attention (+)*** *Note:* No improvement on sustained attention.

table continues next page

Table B.1 School-Based Program Descriptions *(continued)*

	Program	*Evaluation*	
Name	*Description*	*Author/description*	*Results*
	scan, movement, and sensorimotor awareness activities. The classes met for 45 minutes bimonthly during students' regular physical education class. Instructors were highly trained and experienced in mindfulness meditation. **Cost:** n/a		
Montessori	**Beneficiaries:** Children from preschool to grade 12 (Montessori) **Objectives:** Generate the optimal development in children. **Description:** Montessori schooling is a 100-year-old system that naturally incorporates practices that align with mindfulness and are suited to very young children. Montessori education is characterized by multiage classrooms, a special set of educational materials, and student-chosen work in large time blocks; collaboration and the absence of grades and tests; and individual and small-group instruction in both academic and social skills. **Cost:** n/a	**Authors:** Lillard and Else-Quest (2006) **Type:** RCT **Location:** United States: Milwaukee, Wisconsin **Follow-up:** 6 years **Sample:** 57 12-year-old children attending a public inner-city school and suburban public, private, or charter school: (a) 28 control and (b) 29 attending a Montessori school	**Behavior related:** Positive, direct strategy to social problem solving (+)***; greater sense of community (+)** **Academic/cognitive related** Creativity of narrative (+)**; sentence sophistication in narrative (+)** *Note:* No difference found on spelling, grammar, and punctuation or on Woodcock-Johnson tests.
Social and Emotional Aspects of Learning (SEAL)	**Beneficiaries:** Children from kindergarten to grade 5 **Objective:** Promote the social and emotional skills that underpin effective learning, positive behavior, regular attendance, staff effectiveness, and the emotional health and well-being of all who learn and work in schools. **Description:** SEAL is a loose enabling framework for school improvement. Schools are encouraged to explore different implementation approaches to tailor the program to their specific needs. At the school level, SEAL is characterized by the following principles: (a) SEAL implementation is underpinned by clear planning focused on	**Authors:** Humphrey, Lendrum, and Wigelsworth (2010) **Type:** Quasi-experimental **Location:** United Kingdom **Follow-up:** 2 years **Sample:** 8,630 children in grade 7 attending 22 SEAL schools and a matched group of 19 comparison schools **Term used:** Social and emotional skills	*Note*: SEAL failed to significantly affect pupils' social and emotional skills, general mental health difficulties, prosocial behavior, or behavior problems.

table continues next page

Table B.1 School-Based Program Descriptions *(continued)*

Program		*Evaluation*	
Name	*Description*	*Author/description*	*Results*
	improving standards, behavior, and attendance; (b) building a school ethos provides a climate and conditions to promote social and emotional skills; (c) all children are provided with planned opportunities to develop and enhance social and emotional skills; (d) adults are provided with opportunities to enhance their own social and emotional skills; (e) staff members recognize the significance of social and emotional skills to effective learning and to the well-being of pupils; (f) pupils who would benefit from additional support have access to small-group work; (g) there is a strong commitment to involving pupils in all aspects of school life; (h) there is a strong commitment to working positively with parents and careers; and (i) the school engages well with other schools, the local community, wider services, and local agencies. **Cost:** n/a		
Drama in Finland	**Beneficiaries:** Children in grades 4 and 5 **Objectives:** Improve social relationships and social and emotional well-being in the classroom and reduce bullying. **Description:** Universal school-based drama program aims to enhance social relationships and to decrease bullying at school. The drama program included classroom drama sessions, follow-up activities at home, and three parents' evenings concerning issues of social well-being. The program was delivered by regular teachers or a teacher and a school nurse as a dyad. The implemented drama program included four to nine classroom drama sessions, one to four follow-up home activities, and three parents' evenings. **Cost:** n/a	**Authors:** Joronen and others (2011) **Type:** Quasi-experimental longitudinal design **Location:** Finland **Follow-up:** 8 months later **Sample:** 190 primary school students (response rate 71%) in grades 4 and 5: 78 were treated and 56 acted as controls. **Term used:** Social relationships	**Behavior related:** Social relationships (+)*

table continues next page

Table B.1 School-Based Program Descriptions *(continued)*

Program		*Evaluation*	
Name	*Description*	*Author/description*	*Results*
School-based programs in Colombia	**Beneficiaries:** First- and second-grade students in public schools **Objective:** Reduce aggressive and antisocial behavior by first- and second-grade students in a resource-poor setting. **Description:** The study tested two school-based programs. The first was a teacher-only intervention that consisted of teacher training that focused on standard classroom management techniques (arranging the physical environment to reduce opportunities for conflict, establishing and consistently enforcing clear rules, and instituting routines and procedures) and strategies for shaping children's behaviors (modeling and reinforcing appropriate behavior consistently in the classroom's daily activities and interactions). Teachers received 10 four-hour weekly workshops, a manual, and weekly written and verbal feedback. The second program was a teacher/parent combined intervention that included the same teacher training as well as parenting intervention that covered almost the same topics as the teacher training (the session on redesigning the classroom was replaced by one of prosocial behavior). This session lasted one hour, once a week for 10 weeks. **Cost:** n/a	**Authors:** Klevens and others (2009) **Type:** RCT with pre- and postassessments **Location:** Pereira, Colombia **Follow-up:** 6 months after the program starts (just after it finishes) **Sample:** 2,491 children in 12 public schools: (a) 5 schools with 40 first- and second-grade classrooms and 881 students participated in the teacher-only intervention group, (b) 4 schools with 39 first- and second-grade classrooms and 787 students were assigned to the teacher/parent combined intervention group, and (c) 3 schools with 41 classrooms and 823 students were assigned to a wait-list control group. **Term used:** Antisocial/prosocial behavior	**Behavior related:** Aggressive behavior (–)***; antisocial behavior for the teacher-only intervention (–)***

table continues next page

Table B.1 School-Based Program Descriptions *(continued)*

Program		*Evaluation*	
Name	*Description*	*Author/description*	*Results*
Mato-Oput5	**Beneficiaries:** Children ages 9 to 18 **Objectives:** Reduce negative attitudes toward conflict and violence, and reduce injury and violence rates. **Description:** Mato-Oput5 is a value-based, formalized curriculum taught by specifically trained teachers. Its learning areas include conflict, conscience, violence, nonviolence, impulse control, anger management, kindness, forgiveness, empathy, and reconciliation. At least two 40-minute weekly lessons are taught in class. **Cost:** n/a	**Authors:** Mutto and others (2009) **Type:** Cluster randomized control design **Location:** Northern Uganda **Follow-up:** 3 months **Sample:** Six schools: three assigned to control and three assigned to treatment **Term used:** Social development	**Behavior related:** Attitude toward forgiving a bully (+)**; attitude toward forgiving a friend who returns a book he/she had stolen (+)**; not fighting a friend who lies about one (+)**; self-reporting verbally abusing others (–)** *Note:* Statistically significant behavioral effects were not detected, although a downward trend was seen in the intervention group.
Linking the Interests of Families and Teachers (LIFT)	**Beneficiaries:** All first- and fifth-grade elementary school boys and girls and their families living in at-risk neighborhoods characterized by high rates of juvenile delinquency **Objective:** Affect a set of interrelated antecedents of the conduct disorders of children in high-risk neighborhoods. **Description:** Universal preventive intervention consists of (a) parent training aimed at teaching parents how to create a home environment that is most conducive to the ongoing practice of good discipline and supervision (parents met in groups of 10 to 15 families once each week for six weeks, free child care was provided, and a prize was raffled at the end of every session); (b) a classroom-based social skills program consisting of 20 one-hour sessions that included classroom instruction and discussion on specific social and problem-solving skills, skill practice in small and large groups, free play in the context of a group cooperation game, and review and presentation of daily rewards; (c) a playground behavioral program; and (d) systematic communication between teachers and parents. **Cost:** n/a	**Authors:** Reid and others (1999) **Type:** RCT **Location:** United States **Follow-up:** 1 year later **Sample:** 671 first and fifth graders and their families, from 12 elementary schools: 382 attended the intervention schools and 289 attended the control schools. **Term used:** Social skills	**Behavior related:** Teacher rating of peer-preferred behavior (+)**; child physical aggression on the playground (–)*** *Note:* Those mothers in the LIFT program exhibiting the highest preintervention levels of aversive behaviors showed the largest immediate reductions in mother-aversive behavior.

table continues next page

Table B.1 School-Based Program Descriptions *(continued)*

Program		*Evaluation*	
Name	*Description*	*Author/description*	*Results*
		Authors: DeGarmo and others (2009) **Type:** RCT **Location:** United States **Follow-up:** 1 year **Sample:** 351 youths in fifth grade within 17 different classrooms in six randomized schools. **Term used:** Social skills	**Health related:** Risk in initiation of tobacco use (–)***; risk in initiation of alcohol use (–)**; risk in initiation of illicit drug use (–)*; use of tobacco (–)**; use of alcohol (–)***; use of illicit drugs (–)** **Behavior related:** Playground aggression (–)**; effective family problem solving (+)**
Becoming a Man	**Beneficiaries:** Children attending grades 9 and 10, referred by school staff **Objective:** Provide both academic and nonacademic remediation for disadvantaged youths who are falling behind and at great risk of dropping out. **Description:** The socioemotional intervention called Becoming a Man includes school programming that exposes youths to prosocial adults and provides youths with social-cognitive skills training using principles of cognitive behavioral therapy. Youths have the chance to participate in up to 27 one-hour, weekly group sessions during the school day over the school year (the program lasts for three-quarters of an academic year). The intervention is delivered in groups of fewer than 15 youths. Students skip an academic class in order to participate in the program. The program can be delivered by college-educated people without specialized training in psychology or social work. The curriculum also includes efforts to develop specific social or social cognitive skills, such as generating new solutions to problems, learning new ways of behaving, considering another's perspective, thinking ahead, and evaluating consequences ahead of time.	**Authors:** Cook and others (2014) **Type:** RCT **Location:** United States: Chicago, Illinois **Follow-up:** 1 year **Sample:** 106 disadvantaged males in grades 9 and 10 in public high schools (95% are black and 99% are eligible for free or reduced-price lunch) divided into three groups: (a) 24 children received just the nonacademic intervention, (b) 48 received both the nonacademic intervention and the academic intervention, (c) 34 received status quo services. **Term used:** Social-cognitive skills	**Academic/cognitive related:** Math test cores (+)**; math grades (+)*; nonmath courses failed (–)**; expected graduation rates (+)**; absence without an excuse (–)* *Note:* The confidence levels are too wide to say anything about which of the two intervention arms is more effective. Additionally, there was contamination among the different groups and spillover.

table continues next page

Table B.1 School-Based Program Descriptions *(continued)*

Program		*Evaluation*	
Name	*Description*	*Author/description*	*Results*
	The academic intervention is delivered by intensive, individualized two-on-one math tutoring provided for one hour per day every day by well-educated, committed people without formal teacher training. **Cost:** Approximately US$4,400 per participant (ranging from US$3,000 to US$6,000)		
Social and Emotional Training (SET)	**Beneficiaries:** Children in grades 1 through 9 in Swedish schools **Objectives:** Train students to improve self-control, social competence, empathy, motivation, and self-awareness. **Description:** SET is a classroom-based intervention that focuses on developing the following five functions in students: self-awareness, emotional management, empathy, motivation, and social competence. The program was delivered by regular classroom teachers during scheduled hours: to grades 1 through 5 twice a week in two 45-minute sessions, and to grades 6 through 9 in one 45-minute session per week over the school year. The program is guided by detailed manuals for the teacher, one volume for each grade. It also includes a student workbook for each grade. Altogether, the program consists of 399 concrete exercises, some of which are inspired by similar programs in the United States. Teachers are instructed and supervised monthly. Interaction between school and parents is emphasized. **Cost:** US$540 per student (or US$140 excluding the teacher instruction time) for the five years of intervention (2013 dollars) (Belfield and others 2015)	**Authors:** Kimber, Sandell, and Bremberg (2008) **Type:** Quasi-experimental longitudinal design **Location:** Sweden **Follow-up:** 5 years **Sample:** Children in grades 1 through 9 in four schools: (a) 41 classes and 52 teachers in two schools received the treatment; (b) 14 classes did not receive the treatment **Term used:** Socioemotional	**Health related:** Alcohol use (–)**; narcotic drug use (–)* **Behavior related:** Self-image (+)**; well-being (+)**; relations with others (+)**; aggressiveness (–)**; anxiety (–)***; assertiveness (+)*; bullying (–)**; attention seeking (–)*** *Note:* No differential effect on social skills.

table continues next page

Table B.1 School-Based Program Descriptions *(continued)*

Program		*Evaluation*	
Name	*Description*	*Author/description*	*Results*
Teen Outreach	**Beneficiaries:** High school students in grades 9 through 12 **Objectives:** Prevent adolescent problem behaviors by enhancing normative processes of social development in high school students; prevent teen pregnancy and academic failure. In addition, the program was designed to empower students, as they would be "help givers" rather than "help receivers." **Description:** The program consists of three interrelated elements: (a) a minimum of 20 hours per year of supervised volunteer community service (activities were selected by students and varied substantially in their nature and in the amount of commitment required from participants), (b) classroom-based discussions of service experiences (discussions were designed to engage students through structured discussions, group exercises, role play, guest speakers, and informational presentations), and (c) classroom-based discussions and activities related to key social-developmental tasks of adolescence (classroom discussions were led by trained facilitators and met at least once weekly during a full academic year). **Costs:** US$500–US$700 per student per year, for a class of 18–25 students (these figures include the cost for facilitators and site-level coordinator time)	**Authors:** Allen and others (1997) **Type:** RCT **Location:** United States **Follow-up:** 9 months later (at program exit) **Sample:** 695 high school students at 25 sites nationwide, who were randomly assigned to either a Teen Outreach or control group. **Term used:** Life skills	**Health related:** Pregnancy rates (–)* **Academic/cognitive related:** Failing courses (–)***; academic suspension (–)***

table continues next page

Table B.1 School-Based Program Descriptions *(continued)*

Program		*Evaluation*	
Name	*Description*	*Author/description*	*Results*
Learn and Serve America	**Beneficiaries:** Students in grades 6 through 12 **Objectives:** Help young people (a) develop as responsible citizens, improve their academic skills, and develop as individuals, while helping to meet the unmet needs in the public safety nets of the United States; (b) promote the integration of service learning in schools and academic curriculum; and (c) promote the delivery of needed services in the community. **Description:** The program helps young people develop as responsible citizens, improve their academic skills, and develop as individuals through involvement in meaningful service linked to structured learning activities. **Costs:** Approximately US$149.12 per participant (1995–96 dollars)	**Author:** Melchior (1998) **Type:** Quasi-experimental **Location:** United States **Follow-up:** 1 year **Sample:** 1,052 participants in grades 6 through 12 attending 17 middle school and high school sites across the country **Term used:** Life skills	**Health related:** Ever pregnant or made someone pregnant (–)* **Behavior related:** Cultural diversity (+)**; service leadership (degree to which students feel they are aware of the needs in a community, are able to develop and implement a service project, and are committed to service now and later in life) (+)***; total civic attitudes (+)***; volunteered for a community organization or got involved in other community service in the last six months (+)***; hours or support to community service initiatives in the last six months (+)*** **Academic/cognitive related:** Engagement in school (+)***; math grades (+)**; science grades (+)*; core GPA (+)* *Note:* Results are greater for specific subgroups. For example, the impact was statistically significant for the educationally disadvantaged students on English, math, and science grades; overall and core GPA; and a number of at-risk behaviors. For the economically disadvantaged students, impacts were significant for school engagement, days absent, and aggressive behaviors (fighting, hurting someone, or using weapons). For females, the program had statistically significant effects on the use of illegal drugs in the past 30 days, aggressive behavior, and the number of at-risk behaviors. Further, the program had effects on English, math, and social studies grades; GPA; and course failures of minority students.

table continues next page

Table B.1 School-Based Program Descriptions *(continued)*

Program		*Evaluation*	
Name	*Description*	*Author/description*	*Results*
Bal Sabha (Girls' Parliament)	**Beneficiaries:** Girls from grades 6, 7, and 8 in the poorest districts of Rajasthan, India **Objective:** Create soft skills in girls and their communities. **Description:** The program consists of democratic elections (by both boys and girls) of 13 girls from grades 6, 7, and 8 to meet after school several times per month to participate in life skills games that stimulate growth and development and build confidence, leadership, and self-esteem. They practice setting goals for their school or community and are told to pass on the life skills games to other students. **Cost:** n/a	**Authors:** Delavallade, Griffith, and Thornton (2015) **Type:** RCT **Location:** Rajasthan, India **Follow-up:** 1 year **Sample:** 30 schools randomly assigned as follows: (a) 10 received the standard program, (b) 10 received a modified program in which girls were randomly selected rather than elected, and (c) 10 were controls and did not receive the program **Terms used:** Soft skills, life skills	**Behavior related:** Expectations of democratically elected girls about age at marriage (+); expectations about career prospects (–); educational expectations and aspirations for nonelected girls in democratically elected program (–); partition of friendship groups between those who are randomly selected and those who are not (+) *Note:* Main effects on the standard program where girls are elected.
Iowa Strengthening Families Program (ISFP) and Preparing for the Drug Free Years (PDFY) program	**Beneficiaries:** Sixth graders **Objective:** Strengthen parent and child skills that have been found to delay the onset or reduce the use of substances. **Description:** The ISFP consists of seven sets of sessions that are conducted once per week for seven consecutive weeks and are held on weekday evenings in participating schools. The ISFP includes separate, concurrent one-hour training sessions for parents and children, followed by a joint one-hour family session. The PDFY program is delivered in five two-hour training sessions held on weekday evenings once per week for five consecutive weeks (four sessions are for parents only, and another session on peer-resistance skills is for parents and children). **Cost:** n/a	**Authors:** Spoth, Randall, and Shin (2004) **Type:** RCT **Location:** United States: Iowa **Follow-up:** 6 years **Sample:** 667 families of sixth-grade students enrolled in 33 rural public schools were randomly assigned to the ISFP (11 schools and 238 families), the PDFY program (11 schools and 221 families), or a minimal-contact control condition (11 schools or 208 families). **Term used:** prosocial behavior	**Behavior related:** Alcohol use (–) *; lifetime drunkenness (–)*; lifetime cigarette use (–)* *Note:* The PDFY program had no significant effects.

table continues next page

Table B.1 School-Based Program Descriptions *(continued)*

Program		*Evaluation*	
Name	*Description*	*Author/description*	*Results*
Chicago Child-Parent Center Program	**Beneficiaries:** Disadvantaged, African American, inner-city, 3- and 4-year-old children **Objectives:** Promote academic success by providing a school-stable learning environment during the preschool and primary grade years and actively involve parents in their children's education. **Description:** Comprehensive education, family, and health services, including half-day preschool at ages 3 to 4, half- or full-day kindergarten, and school-age services in linked elementary schools at ages 6 to 9. Child-to-teacher ratios of 17:2 in preschool and 25:2 in kindergarten. Parental participation includes interaction with other parents in workshops, reading groups, crafts projects, classroom volunteering, school events, and field trips, and completing high school. The program also includes health and nutrition services, such as screening, speech therapy, and nursing **Cost:** Mean per-child expenditures in 1996 for one year of preschool and one year of school-age participation are US$4,350 and US$1,500, respectively.	**Authors:** Reynolds and others (2001) **Type:** Matching **Location:** United States: Chicago, Illinois **Follow-up:** 15 years **Sample:** 1,539 low-income, mostly African American children born in 1980: 989 attending the Chicago program; 550 children participating in full-day kindergarten **Term used:** Social outcomes	**Behavior related:** Juvenile arrest (–)**; violent arrests (–)** **Academic/cognitive related:** High school completion at age 20 (+)***; years of education (+)**; school dropout (–) **. For those with extended program participation from preschool to second and third grade: grade retention (–)***; special education (–)**.

table continues next page

Table B.1 School-Based Program Descriptions *(continued)*

Program		*Evaluation*	
Name	*Description*	*Author/description*	*Results*
Project Student/ Teacher Achievement Ratio (STAR)	**Beneficiaries:** Students in Tennessee **Objective:** Analyze the effects of class size, teacher quality, and peers on student's results. **Description:** Students in 79 Tennessee schools were randomly assigned to small classes (15 students) or large classes (22 students on average). **Cost:** The average cost per child of reducing class size by 33% for 2.14 years (the mean treatment duration for STAR students) is US$9,355 (2009 dollars).	**Authors:** Chetty and others (2010); Krueger and Whitmore (2001) **Type:** RCT **Location:** United States: Tennessee **Follow-up:** 27 years later **Sample:** 11,571 students from kindergarten through third grade were randomly assigned to a small class (13–17 students), regular-size class (22–25 students), or regular-size class with a teacher's aide. **Term used:** Noncognitive	**Behavior related**: Effort, initiative, lack of disruptive behavior in grades 4 and 8 (+)**; arrests for crime (–) **Academic/cognitive related**: Standardized tests (+)**; finish high school (+); college attendance at age 20 (+)* **Economic related:** Home ownership (+); retirement savings (+); earnings (+) ** *Note:* No significant differences in earnings at age 27. No significant difference in student's self-concept and motivation.
HighScope Perry Preschool Program	**Beneficiaries:** High-risk African American children. Risk is defined as parents with low educational attainment (high school or less); low occupational status (unemployed or unskilled); low socioeconomic status; low IQ scores (between 70 and 85) with no organic deficiencies; and at high risk of failing school. **Objective:** Support long-term cognitive and educational benefits in children from disadvantaged backgrounds. **Description:** From ages 3 to 5, participants received a 2.5-hour preschool program on weekdays during the school year (approximately 180 days), and weekly home visits by the teachers. The curriculum fostered active learning (children were encouraged to plan, carry out, and reflect on their own activities). Teachers were certified to teach in elementary, early childhood, and special education. There were four teachers for 20 to 25 children (in Perry Preschool) and two teachers for 16 children in HighScope preschool. Seems to work with 2 adults and up to 20 children (Epstein 1993). **Cost**: US$17,759 per student per year (undiscounted 2006 dollars)	**Authors:** Heckman and others (2010); Muennig and others (2009); Schweinhart and others (2005) **Type:** Quasi-experimental **Location:** United States: Michigan **Follow-up**: 37 years later **Sample:** 123 disadvantaged African American children between ages 3 and 5: 58 were assigned to treatment (high-quality preschool) and 65 to control (no preschool) **Terms used**: Behavioral skills; socioemotional development; personal and social dispositions	**Health related:** Mortality rates (–)**; likelihood of halting work because of illness (–)**; smoking (–)** **Behavior related:** Arrests (–)***; externalizing behavior (+)**; engaging in risky behavior (–)*** **Academic/cognitive related:** IQ until age 1 (+)** then faded; grade repetition (–)**; assigned to special education (–)**; high school graduation by age 19 (+)**; college attendance (+)**; educational attainment at age 40 (+)*** **Economic related:** Earnings (+)***; homeownership (+)** *Note:* Annual social rates of return: 7%–16% (US$9–US$13 for every US$1 invested).

table continues next page

Table B.1 School-Based Program Descriptions *(continued)*

Program		*Evaluation*	
Name	*Description*	*Author/description*	*Results*
Head Start	**Beneficiaries:** Children ages 3 to 5 **Objective:** Guarantee school readiness by (a) improving the child's health and physical abilities; (b) improving the family's attitude toward future health care and physical abilities; (c) encouraging self-confidence, spontaneity, curiosity, and self-discipline, which will assist in the development of the child's social and emotional health; (d) enhancing the child's mental processes and skills with particular attention to conceptual and communications skills; (e) establishing patterns and expectations of success for the child, which will create a climate of confidence for present and future learning efforts and overall development; (f) increasing the ability of the child and the family to relate to each other and to others; and (g) enhancing the sense of dignity and self-worth within the child and his/her family. **Description:** Comprehensive services include preschool education; medical, dental, and mental health care; nutrition services; efforts to help parents foster their child's development **Cost:** US$7,000 per child on average	**Authors:** Westat (2010) **Type:** RCT **Location:** United States **Follow-up:** 3 years **Sample:** 378 centers, 2,783 Head Start children (some newly entering 3- and 4-year-olds) and 1,884 control children **Term used:** Social-emotional development	**Health related:** Child insurance coverage (+)*; health status for 3-year-olds (+)* **Behavior related:** Closer and more positive relationship of 3-year-old children to parents(+)*; hyperactivity in 3-year-olds (–)*; total problem behavior in 3-year-olds (–)*; social skills in 3-year-olds (+)*; positive approaches to learning for 3-year-olds (+)* **Academic/cognitive related:** PPVT vocabulary for 4-year-olds (+)*; Woodcock Johnson III oral comprehension for 3-year-olds (+)*

table continues next page

Table B.1 School-Based Program Descriptions *(continued)*

Program		*Evaluation*	
Name	*Description*	*Author/description*	*Results*
Tools of the Mind	**Beneficiaries**: 3- and 4-year-old children attending a state-financed, full-day "Abbott" preschool education program located in high-poverty school districts **Objective:** Build strong foundations for school success by promoting intentional and self-regulated learning in preschool- and kindergarten-age children. **Description:** A child care program with a curriculum is focused on self-regulation, while teaching literacy and math. During pretend play, children must inhibit acting out of character, remember their own and others' roles, and flexibly adjust as their friends improvise. **Cost:** According to What Works Clearinghouse, the first year costs about US$3,000 per classroom. Curriculum guides cost an additional US$100. The second year costs about US$1,500 per classroom.	**Authors:** Barnett and others (2008) **Type:** RCT **Location**: United States: New Jersey, One school with a high proportion of children from low-income and non-English-speaking families **Follow-up:** 8 months later **Sample:** 274 children ages 3 and 4: (a) 106 received Tools of the Mind; (b) 168 received the district's curriculum **Term used:** Social development	**Behavior related:** Problem Behaviors Scale of the Social Skills Rating System (–)** **Academic/cognitive related:** Cognitive outcomes as measured by the IDEA Oral Language Proficiency Test (+)* **Other:** Curriculum for language and reasoning (+)***; activities in the curriculum (+)**; interactions in the curriculum (+)*; positive classroom climate, teacher sensitivity, behavior management techniques, and productivity (+)*
		Authors: Diamond and others (2007) **Type:** RCT **Location**: United States: 18 classrooms in a low-income, urban school with state-financed Abbott full-day preschool education **Follow-up:** 2 years **Sample:** 147 preschoolers who received two years of program: 62 in district's version of balanced literacy curriculum and 85 in Tools of the Mind **Term used:** Inhibitory control (resisting habits, temptations, or distractions)	**Academic/cognitive related:** Performance on demanding tasks for executive functions (+)**

table continues next page

Table B.1 School-Based Program Descriptions *(continued)*

Program		*Evaluation*	
Name	*Description*	*Author/description*	*Results*
Child Health Project	**Beneficiaries:** Children ages 3 to 5 selected for the study on the basis of electrodermal functioning (amplitude, frequency, and half-recovery data) at age 3 **Objective**: Originally, this study had the goal of bringing psychiatrically at-risk children together in nursery schools where "drugs could be used to bring their autonomic functions within normal range" (WHO 1968, 381). Ethical considerations precluded the use of drugs to change autonomic functioning (WHO 1975, 39), and instead of drugs, the research team developed nursery schools to provide an enriched, stimulating experience for an experimental versus matched control group containing psychiatrically unselected children drawn from the community (Venables 1978). **Description:** The two-year intervention consisted of preschool education, nutrition (education on nutrition and meals), physical exercise, health screening and referral, parental involvement, remediation of behavioral and learning problems, and home visits to the family. With regard to cognitive-behavioral and socialization, an important feature of the experimental schools was the use of time-out in place of the more traditional physical punishments for misbehavior, and the provision of one-to-one explanations for why behavior was inappropriate. Particular efforts were made to ensure that individual children were never left on their own or socially isolated. Conversation sessions included the discussions of emotion concepts, such as sadness and love.	**Author:** Raine and others (2001); Raine and others (2003) **Type:** RCT **Location:** Two randomly selected communities in Mauritius **Follow-up:** At ages 11, 17, and 23 **Sample:** 200 children: 100 assigned to an enriched nursery school intervention, of which 93 were followed at age 11; and 100 assigned to the control group receiving a normal educational experience, of which 95 were followed at age 11. This normal experience consisted of preschool with untrained childminders, in units of poor educational quality that provided traditional and very rudimentary education with a teacher-to-pupil ratio of 1:30. **Term used:** Social and emotional development	**Behavior related:** Improved psychophysiological arousal and orienting at age 11. This is seen through: skin conductance amplitudes (+) ***; skin conductance rise times (+) ***; skin conductance recovery times (+) **; slow-wave electroencephalogram measure during rest (–) ***; electroencephalogram measure during continuous performance task conditions (–) ***. Behavioral problems at age 17 (–) ***, which included conduct disorder (–)***; psychotic behavior (–)**; motor excess (–)**; schizotypal personality at age 23 for those who received enrichment and were not malnourished (–)**; criminal offending (–)**

table continues next page

Table B.1 School-Based Program Descriptions *(continued)*

Program		*Evaluation*	
Name	*Description*	*Author/description*	*Results*
	Drama and puppet sessions were used to enhance the child's emotional sensitivity. Game sessions were used to help the children understand the importance of following rules. These sessions were also used to illustrate life problems and how they may be successfully resolved. Requiring children to wear identical clothing (uniforms were provided to the parents) was done in an attempt to reduce social divisions among the children. Staff was highly trained, and the teacher-to-pupil ratio ranged from 1:5.5 to 1:10. **Cost:** n/a		
Preschool program in Cambodia	**Beneficiaries**: 3- to 5-year-old children living in 138 villages situated in disadvantaged rural areas **Objective:** Provide preschool education to vulnerable children, which was integrated into a primary school rehabilitation effort. **Description:** The preschool curriculum was composed of singing, drawing (mixing colors, reproducing signs/geographic figures on a board or with small sticks), physical activities (such as gymnastics and games), some vocabulary (listing words), and counting. It was designed for the 3- to 5-year age group and does not explicitly include writing or reading. Teachers often organized social games in which children had to recall the names of other students and add or subtract them from a group of pupils. **Cost**: n/a	**Authors:** Bouguen and others (2014) **Type**: RCT **Location:** Cambodia **Follow-up:** 17–20 months later **Sample:** 26 villages received preschool and 19 villages served as controls; 1,731 children living in these villages were interviewed. Take-up of preschools was small (only 36% of the children in treatment villages attended preschool). **Term used:** Noncognitive	**Academic/cognitive related:** Preschool attendance (+); primary school attendance (–); ASQ gross motor scale (+)*; ASQ problem-solving subscale (–)*; overall development index for 5-year-old children (–)*; cognitive development index (–)*** *Note:* No impacts on receptive vocabulary, communication, fine motor skills, emotion, conduct, hyperactivity, peer, prosocial behavior, height or weight for age, overall development index, cognitive development index, motor development index, anthropometrics index, noncognitive index. The low impacts can be attributed to implementation constraints, low take-up rates, and a short duration of program exposure for participating children. The negative impact of preschool participation on the cognitive development of 5-year-old children may derive from two facts: (a) some children were attending primary school before and switched to preschool, or (b) some other children who were attending primary school left the formal school system when the official age of primary school was enforced.

table continues next page

Table B.1 School-Based Program Descriptions *(continued)*

Program		*Evaluation*	
Name	*Description*	*Author/description*	*Results*
Peace Works	**Beneficiaries:** Preschool children ages 4 to 5 years **Objectives:** Promote preschoolers' social skills and reduce behavior problems **Description:** The program instructs teachers and parents in how to use activities and "I-Care Rules and Language" to encourage empathy and fair play, express feelings, avoid conflict, manage anger, and interact more positively with others. The curriculum models conflict resolution, anger management, and communication skills to promote children's positive interactions, cooperation, and emotional self-regulation. **Cost:** n/a	**Author:** Pickens (2009) **Type:** RCT **Location:** United States: Miami, Florida **Follow-up:** 1 school year **Sample:** 246 preschool children in the PEF treatment classrooms; 50 evaluated from nontreatment schools **Term used:** Socioemotional	**Behavior related:** Social cooperation (+)***; positive interaction quality (+)***; social independence (+)***; external and internal problem behaviors (–)***

Note: CARE = character actualization requires education; 4Rs = reading, writing, respect, and resolution; GPA = grade point average; RCT = randomized control trial; n/a = not available. Significance levels of results, positive (+) or negative (–), are reported at 1 percent (*), 5 percent (**), and 10 percent (***).

Table B.2 School-Based Programs by Component

	Program components			
Program	*Teacher training*	*Class curriculum*	*Household activities*	*Extracurricular*
4Rs	X	X	X	X
Raising Healthy Children	X	X	X	X
Bal Sabha	X	X		X
Teen Outreach	X	X		X
Resolving Conflict Creatively	X	X	X	
Al's Pals	X	X	X	
Project CARE Child Development Project	X	X	X	
I Can Problem Solve	X	X	X	
Project SAFE	X	X	X	
Incredible Years	X	X	X	
Drama in Finland	X	X	X	
LIFT	X	X	X	
Family Check-Up		X	X	
ISFP and PDFY	X		X	X
School-based programs in Colombia	X		X	
Michigan Model for Health	X	X		
MindUp	X	X		
Open Circle	X	X		
Fast Track PATHS	X	X		
Positive Action	X	X		
Responsive Classroom	X	X		
RULER program	X	X		
Second Step	X	X		
Steps to Respect	X	X		
Attention Academy	X	X		
Montessori	X	X		
SEAL	X	X		
Social and Emotional Training	X	X		
Mato-Oput5	X	X		
Learn and Serve America		X		
Unique Minds		X		
LEAD		X		
MAPs		X		
Becoming a Man		X		
	28	**32**	**13**	**5**

Note: Shading indicates that the program includes that particular component. 4Rs = reading, writing, respect and resolution; CARE = character actualization requires education; ISFP = Iowa Strengthening Families Program; LEAD = Leadership Education Through Athletic Development; LIFT = Linking the Interests of Families and Teachers; MAPs = Mindful Awareness Practices; PATHS = Promoting Alternative Thinking Strategies; PDFY = Preparing for the Drug Free Years; SAFE = Strategies Aimed at Family Empowerment; SEAL = Social and Emotional Aspects of Learning.

http://dx.doi.org/10.1596/978-1-4648-0872-2

References

Aber, J. Lawrence, Joshua L. Brown, and Stephanie M. Jones. 2003. "Developmental Trajectories toward Violence in Middle Childhood: Course, Demographic Differences, and Response to School-Based Intervention." *Developmental Psychology* 39 (2): 324–48.

Allen, Joseph P., Susan Philliber, Scott Herrling, and Gabriel P. Kuperminc. 1997. "Preventing Teen Pregnancy and Academic Failure: Experimental Evaluation of a Developmentally Based Approach." *Child Development* 68 (4): 729–42.

Battistich, Victor, Eric Schaps, and Nance Wilson. 2004. "Effects of an Elementary School Intervention on Students' 'Connectedness' to School and Social Adjustment during Middle School." *Journal of Primary Prevention* 24 (3): 243–62.

Belfield, Clive, Brooks Bowden, Alli Klapp, Henry Levin, Robert Shand, and Sabine Zander. 2015. "The Economic Value of Social and Emotional Learning." Center for Benefit-Cost Studies in Education, Teachers College, Columbia University, New York.

Boyle, Douglas, and Connie Hassett-Walker. 2008. "Reducing Overt and Relational Aggression among Young Children: The Results from a Two-Year Outcome Study." *Journal of School Violence* 7 (1): 27–42.

Brock, Laura L., Tracy K. Nishida, Cynthia Chiong, Kevin J. Grimm, and Sara E. Rimm-Kaurman. 2008. "Children's Perceptions of the Classroom Environment and Social and Academic Performance: A Longitudinal Analysis of the Contribution of the Responsive Classroom Approach." *Journal of School Psychology* 46 (2): 129–49.

Brown, Joshua L., Stephanie M. Jones, Maria D. LaRusso, and J. Lawrence Aber. 2010. "Improving Classroom Quality: Teacher Influences and Experimental Impacts of the 4Rs Program." *Journal of Educational Psychology* 102 (1): 153–67.

Caruthers, Allison S., Mark J. Van Ryzin, and Thomas J. Dishion. 2014. "Preventing High-Risk Sexual Behavior in Early Adulthood with Family Interventions in Adolescence: Outcomes and Developmental Processes." *Prevention Science* 15 (1): 59–69.

Catalano, Richard F., James J. Mazza, Tracy W. Harachi, Robert D. Abbott, Kevin P. Haggerty, and Charles B. Fleming. 2003. "Raising Healthy Children through Enhancing Social Development in Elementary School: Results after 1.5 Years." *Journal of School Psychology* 41 (2): 143–64.

Chang, Florence, and Marco A. Muñoz. 2006. "School Personnel Educating the Whole Child: Impact of Character Education on Teachers' Self-Assessment and Student Development." *Journal of Personality Evaluation in Education* 19: 35–49.

Connell, Arin M., and Thomas J. Dishion. 2008. "Reducing Depression among At-Risk Early Adolescents: Three-Year Effects of a Family-Centered Intervention Embedded within Schools." *Journal of Family Psychology* 22 (4): 574–85.

Connell, Arin M., Susan Klostermann, and Thomas J. Dishion. 2012. "Family Checkup Effects on Adolescent Arrest Trajectories: Variation by Developmental Subtype." *Journal of Research on Adolescence* 22 (2): 367–80.

Cook, Philip J., Kenneth Dodge, George Farkas, Roland G. Fryer Jr., Jonathan Guryan, Jens Ludwig, Susan Mayer, Harold Pollack, and Laurence Steinberg. 2014. "The (Surprising) Efficacy of Academic and Behavioral Intervention with Disadvantaged Youth: Results from a Randomized Experiment in Chicago." NBER Working Paper 19862, National Bureau of Economic Research, Cambridge, MA.

http://dx.doi.org/10.1596/978-1-4648-0872-2

CPPRG (Conduct Problems Prevention Research Group). 2010. "The Effects of a Multiyear Universal Socio-Emotional Learning Program: The Role of Student and School Characteristics." *Journal of Consulting and Clinical Psychology* 78 (2): 156–68.

Curby, Timothy W., Sara E. Rimm-Kaufman, and Tashia Abry. 2013. "Do Emotional Support and Classroom Organization Earlier in the Year Set the Stage for Higher Quality Instruction?" *Journal of School Psychology* 51 (5): 557–69.

DeGarmo, David S., J. Mark Eddy, John B. Reid, and Rebecca A. Fetrow. 2009. "Evaluating Mediators of the Impact of the Linking the Interests of Families and Teachers (LIFT) Multimodal Preventive Intervention on Substance Use Initiation and Growth across Adolescence." *Prevention Science* 10 (3): 208–20.

Delavallade, Clara, Alan Griffith, and Rebecca Thornton. 2015. "Girls' Education, Aspirations, and Social Networks: Evidence from a Randomized Trial in Rural Rajasthan." Paper presented at the Ninth Annual PopPov Conference on Population, Reproductive Health, and Economic Development, Addis Ababa, Ethiopia, June 25.

Dishion, Thomas J., Kathryn Kavanagh, Alison Schneiger, Sarah Nelson, and Noah K. Kaufman. 2002. "Preventing Early Adolescent Substance Use: A Family-Centered Strategy for the Public Middle School." *Prevention Science* 3 (3): 191–201.

Domitrovich, Celene E., Rebecca C. Cortes, and Mark T. Greenberg. 2007. "Improving Young Children's Social and Emotional Competence: A Randomized Trial of the Preschool PATHS Curriculum." *Journal of Primary Prevention* 28 (2): 67–91.

Edwards, Rhiannon T., Alan Céilleachair, Tracey Bywater, Dyfrig Hughes, and Judy Hutchings. 2007. "Parenting Programme for Parents of Children at Risk of Developing Conduct Disorder: Cost Effectiveness Analysis." *BMJ* 334 (7595): 682–85.

Espelage, Dorothy L., Sabina Low, Joshua R. Polanin, and Eric C. Brown. 2013. "The Impact of a Middle School Program to Reduce Aggression, Victimization, and Sexual Violence." *Journal of Adolescent Health* 53 (2): 180–86.

Flook, Lisa, Susan L. Smalley, M. Jennifer Kitil, Brian M. Galla, Susan Kaiser-Greenland, Jill Locke, Eric Ishijima, and Connie Kasari. 2010. "Effects of Mindful Awareness Practices on Executive Functions in Elementary School Children." *Journal of Applied School Psychology* 26 (1): 70–95.

Frey, Karin S., Miriam K. Hirschstein, Leihua Van Schoiack Edstrom, and Jennie L Snell. 2009. "Observed Reductions in School Bullying, Non-Bullying Aggression, and Destructive Bystander Behavior: A Longitudinal Evaluation." *Journal of Educational Psychology* 101: 466–81.

Hennessey, Beth A. 2007. "Promoting Social Competence in School-Aged Children: The Effects of the Open Circle Program." *Journal of School Psychology* 45 (3): 349–60.

Humphrey, Neal, Ann Lendrum, and Michael Wigelsworth. 2010. "Social and Emotional Aspects of Learning (SEAL) Programme in Secondary Schools: National Evaluation." Research Report DFE-RR049. Department for Education, London.

Jones, Stephanie M., Joshua L. Brown, and J. Lawrence Aber. 2011. "Two-Year Impacts of a Universal School-Based Social-Emotional and Literacy Intervention: An Experiment in Translational Developmental Research." *Child Development* 82: 533–54.

Jones, Stephanie M., Joshua L. Brown, Wendy Hoglund, and J. Lawrence Aber. 2010. "A School-Randomized Clinical Trial of an Integrated Social-Emotional Learning and Literacy Intervention: Impacts after One School Year." *Journal of Consulting and Clinical Psychology* 78 (6): 829–42.

http://dx.doi.org/10.1596/978-1-4648-0872-2

Joronen, Katja, Anne Konu, H. Sally Rankin, and Päivi Åstedt-Kurki. 2011. "An Evaluation of a Drama Program to Enhance Social Relationships and Anti-Bullying at Elementary School: A Controlled Study." *Health Promotion International* 27 (1): 5–14.

Kimber, Birgitta, Rolf Sandell, and Sven Bremberg. 2008. "Social and Emotional Training in Swedish Classrooms for the Promotion of Mental Health: Results from an Effectiveness Study in Sweden." *Health Promotion International* 23 (2): 134–43.

Klevens, Joanne, José William Martínez, Brenda Le, Carlos Rojas, Adriana Duque, and Rafael Tovar. 2009. "Evaluation of Two Interventions to Reduce Aggressive and Antisocial Behavior in First and Second Graders in a Resource-Poor Setting." *International Journal of Educational Research* 48 (5): 307–19.

Kumpfer, Karol L., Rose Alvarado, Connie Tait, and Charles Turner. 2002. "Effectiveness of School-Based Family and Children's Skills Training for Substance Abuse Prevention among 6–8-Year-Old Rural Children." *Psychology of Addictive Behaviors* 16 (45): S65–S71.

Lakes, Kimberley D., and William T. Hoyt. 2004. "Promoting Self-Regulation through School-Based Martial Arts Training." *Journal of Applied Developmental Psychology* 25 (3): 283–302.

Lewis, Kendra M., Marc B. Schure, Niloofar Bavarian, David L. Dubois, Joseph Day, Peter Ji, Naida Silverthorn, Alan Acock, Samuel Vuchinich, and Brian R. Flay. 2013. "Problem Behavior and Urban, Low-Income Youth: A Randomized Controlled Trial of Positive Action in Chicago." *American Journal of Preventive Medicine* 4 (6): 622–30.

Lillard, Angeline, and Nicole Else-Quest. 2006. "The Early Years: Evaluating Montessori." *Science* 313 (5795): 1893–94.

Linares, L. Oriana, Nicole Rosbruch, Marcia B. Stern, Martha E. Edwards, Gillian Walker, Howard B. Abikoff, and Jose M. Alvir. 2005. "Developing Cognitive-Social-Emotional Competencies to Enhance Academic Learning." *Psychology in the Schools* 42 (4): 405–17.

Lynch, Kathleen Bodisch, Susan R. Geller, and Melinda G. Schmidt. 2004. "Multi-Year Evaluation of the Effectiveness of a Resilience-Based Prevention Program for Young Children." *Journal of Primary Prevention* 24 (3): 335–53.

Melchior, Alan. 1998. "National Evaluation of Learn and Serve America School and Community-Based Programs: Final Report." Brandeis University, Center for Human Resources, Waltham, MA.

Mutto, Milton, Kathleen Kahn, Ronald Lett, and Stephen Lawoko. 2009. "Piloting an Educational Response to Violence in Uganda: Prospects for a New Curriculum." *African Safety Promotion* 7 (2): 37–46.

Napoli, Maria, Paul Rock Krech, and Lynn C. Holley. 2005. "Mindfulness Training for Elementary School Students: The Attention Academy." *Journal of Applied School Psychology* 21 (1): 99–125.

O'Neill, James M., Jeffrey K. Clark, and James A. Jones. 2011. "Promoting Mental Health and Preventing Substance Abuse and Violence in Elementary Students: A Randomized Control Study of the Michigan Model for Health." *Journal of School Health* 81 (6): 320–30.

Reid, John B., J. Mark Eddy, Rebecca Ann Fetrow, and Mike Stoolmiller. 1999. "Description and Immediate Impacts of a Preventive Intervention for Conduct Problems." *American Journal of Community Psychology* 27 (4): 483–518.

Rimm-Kaufman, Sara E., Ross A. A. Larsen, Alison E. Baroody, Timothy W. Curby, Michelle Ko, Julia B. Thomas, Eileen G. Merritt, Tashia Abry, and Jamie DeCoster.

http://dx.doi.org/10.1596/978-1-4648-0872-2

2014. "Efficacy of the Responsive Classroom Approach: Results from a 3-Year, Longitudinal Randomized Controlled Trial." *American Educational Research Journal* 51 (3): 567–603.

Rivers, Susan E., Marc A. Brackett, Maria R. Reyes, Nicole A. Elbertson, and Peter Salovey. 2013. "Improving the Social and Emotional Climate of Classrooms: A Clustered Randomized Controlled Trial Testing the RULER Approach." *Prevention Science* 14 (1): 77–87.

Schonert-Reichl, Kimberly A., and Molly S. Lawlor. 2010. "The Effects of a Mindfulness-Based Education Program on Pre- and Early Adolescents' Well-Being and Social and Emotional Competence." *Mindfulness* 1 (3): 137–51.

Snyder, Frank J., Alan Acock, Sam Vuchinich, Michael W. Beets, Isaac J. Washburn, and Brian R. Flay. 2013. "Preventing Negative Behaviors among Elementary-School Students through Enhancing Students' Social-Emotional and Character Development." *American Journal of Health Promotion* 28 (1): 50–58.

Spoth, R., Redmond, C., Shin, C. and Azevedo, K., 2004. "Brief Family Intervention Effects on Adolescent Substance Initiation: School-Level Growth Curve Analyses 6 years Following Baseline." *Journal of Consulting and Clinical Psychology* 72 (3), 535.

Spoth, Richard L., G. K. Randall, and Chungyeol Shin. 2008. "Increasing School Success through Partnership-Based Family Competency Training: Experimental Study of Long-Term Outcomes." *School Psychology Quarterly* 23 (1): 70–89.

Stormshak, Elizabeth A., Arin M. Connell, and Thomas J. Dishion. 2009. "An Adaptive Approach to Family-Centered Intervention in Schools: Linking Intervention Engagement to Academic Outcomes in Middle and High School." *Prevention Science* 10 (3): 221–35.

Stormshak, Elizabeth A., Arin M. Connell, Marie Hélène Véronneau, Michael W. Myers, Thomas J. Dishion, Kathryn Kavanagh, and Allison S. Caruthers. 2011. "An Ecological Approach to Promoting Early Adolescent Mental Health and Social Adaptation: Family-Centered Intervention in Public Middle Schools." *Child Development* 82 (1): 209–25.

Tuckman, Bruce W., and J. Scott Hinkle. 1986. "An Experimental Study of the Physical and Psychological Effects of Aerobic Exercise on Schoolchildren." *Health Psychology* 5 (3): 197–207.

Van Ryzin, Mark. J., Elizabeth A. Stormshak, and Thomas J. Dishion. 2012. "Engaging Parents in the Family Check-Up in Middle School: Longitudinal Effects on Family Conflict and Problem Behavior through the High School Transition." *Journal of Adolescent Health* 50 (6): 627–33.

Webster-Stratton, Carolyn, M. Jamila Reid, and Mike Stoolmiller. 2008. "Preventing Conduct Problems and Improving School Readiness: Evaluation of the Incredible Years Teacher and Child Training Programs in High-Risk Schools." *Journal of Child Psychology and Psychiatry* 49 (5): 471–88.

http://dx.doi.org/10.1596/978-1-4648-0872-2

APPENDIX C

Out-of-School Program Descriptions

http://dx.doi.org/10.1596/978-1-4648-0872-2

Table C.1 Out-of-School Program Descriptions

Program		Evaluation	
Name	*Description*	*Author/description*	*Results*
Work related			
Procajoven	**Beneficiaries:** Low-income unemployed 18- to 29-year-olds, and first-time job seekers with complete secondary education **Objective:** Improve prospects for jobless youths and disadvantaged groups. **Description:** The program has two modalities. The first, called the insertion modality, provides short-term training for low-income unemployed 18- to 29-year-olds. Classroom training has two parts, job readiness skills and technical training (120 and 150 hours, respectively), followed by 172 hours of internship in a firm. The second modality, called the transition modality, focuses on the transition of the first-time job seekers with complete secondary education, providing job readiness and a longer internship (344 hours). **Cost:** The insertion modality costs US$611. The transition modality costs US$375. Both cost calculations include a transfer to participants of US$255.	**Authors:** Ibarrarán and Rosas-Shady (2006) **Type:** Quasi-experiment **Location:** Panama: Panama City and other provinces **Follow-up:** 9 to 20 months after the program **Sample:** 766 individuals divided into three groups: (a) 295 controls, (b) 199 receiving the insertion modality, and (c) 272 receiving the transition modality **Term used:** Social capital	**Economic related:** Probability of employment for women in Panama City in both modalities (+)**; number of weekly hours worked by females (+)** in Panama (+)* in the insertion modality, and by females (+)** in provinces outside Panama City (+)* in the transition modality; labor earnings in the month of the survey for the insertion modality by females (+)* in Panama (+)** *Note:* No significant effect in the probability of employment at a national level. No significant effect on labor income.
Jóvenes en Acción	**Beneficiaries:** Young people between the ages of 18 and 25 in the two lowest socioeconomic strata of the population **Objectives:** Mitigate the effects of the economic crisis in vulnerable youths by improving their employability conditions and the job and social insertion of unemployed youths. **Description:** Classroom training is offered in technical and soft skills plus internship. Program provided three months of classroom training and three months of on-the-job training, along with a cash transfer of US$2–US$3 per day. Training was provided for almost	**Authors:** Attanasio, Kugler, and Meghir (2008, 2009, 2011); **Type:** RCT **Location:** Colombia **Follow-up:** 13 to 15 months after the program **Sample:** 4,350 individuals, randomly divided into two groups: 2,040 in treatment and 2,310 in control **Term used:** Soft skills	**Economic related:** Probability of employment for women (+)**; number of weekly hours worked by women (+)**; tenure for both genders (+)***; labor income for women (+)***; formal contracts for both genders (+)**; formal wages for both genders (+) ** *Note:* No significant effect when analyzing only treated men.

table continues next page

Table C.1 Out-of-School Program Descriptions *(continued)*

	Program	Evaluation	
Name	*Description*	*Author/description*	*Results*
	eight hours per day for diverse occupations, such as sales, secretarial work, and marketing, as well as such positions as seamstress, cooking assistant, information technology specialist, and data entry clerk. On-the-job training lasted an average of five hours per day. **Cost:** US$750 per person, including participants' stipends		
Juventud y Empleo	**Beneficiaries:** Youths between 16 and 29 years of age who did not complete high school **Objective:** Improve the labor market entry of youths. **Description:** Training is provided in technical and soft skills plus internship. Courses are 225 hours (four months) and are split into two parts: 75 hours of basic or life skills training and 150 hours of technical or vocational training. Training courses are broad, including administrative assistant, baker, hairstylist, clerk, auto mechanic, and bartender. Basic skills training seeks to strengthen trainees' self-esteem and work habits. Finally, training is followed by a two-month internship in a private sector firm. All trainees receive RD$70 per day of class participation. **Cost:** About US$330 per participant	**Authors:** Ibarrarán and others (2014) **Type:** RCT **Location:** Dominican Republic **Follow-up:** 18–24 months after the program **Sample:** 18–24 months after program implementation, 10,309 randomly assigned youths were evaluated. They were divided into two groups: (a) 5,914 in treatment (977 did not participate); (b) 4,395 in control (977 served as replacements and participated in the program). Six years after program implementation, four groups were compared: (a) 1,901 individuals who were selected for treatment and effectively participated, (b) 262 individuals who were selected as part of the program but dropped out, (c) 438 individuals who were not selected in the lottery but participated as replacements, and (d) 678 controls. **Terms used:** Socioemotional skills/ noncognitive skills; life-skills	**Health related:** Teenage pregnancy (–)**; considers having very good health (+)** **Behavior related:** Youth expectations regarding having a better educational level for women ages 16 to 24 (–)*; living in a better neighborhood for women (+)**; owning a business for women ages 16 to 19 (+)**; completing professional aspirations for women ages 16 to 19 (+)**; having a better life in 20 years for women ages 16 to 19 (+)***; having children with a better life for women ages 16 to 19 (+)**; wealth position in 10 years for women older than age 24 (+); leadership skills for men (+)**; self-esteem for men (+)**; conflict resolution (+)***; self-organization (+)***; persistency of effort for women (+)** **Economic related:** Monthly earnings for women and for those residing in Santo Domingo (+)**; employment with health insurance for men (+)*; employment with written contract for men (+)**; duration of employment for men (+)** *Note:* No significant effect on labor market participation or on probability of employment.

table continues next page

Table C.1 Out-of-School Program Descriptions *(continued)*

Program		*Evaluation*	
Name	*Description*	*Author/description*	*Results*
Galpão Aplauso	**Beneficiaries:** Disadvantaged *favela* youths (a) younger than age 29, (b) living in households with total monthly income below the minimum wage, and (c) not involved in drugs or gang activity **Objectives:** Improve the socioeconomic situation and employability of youths by teaching them basic skills, life skills, and vocational skills and provide placement services. **Description:** Galpão Aplauso (or the Sociocultural and Productive Integration of At-Risk Youth Project) is an innovative labor training program that uses expressive arts and theater as a pedagogical tool. The program consists of a combination of vocational, academic, and life skills training, delivered through a pedagogic method that uses arts and dance. Program duration is approximately six months, five hours a day, five days a week, delivered in three shifts—morning, afternoon, and evening. It comprises 300 hours of vocational training (mainly construction related, soldering, and woodshop); 180 hours of training in academic and basic skills, including remedial courses in both mathematics and Portuguese; and 120 hours in life skills (social harmony and socioemotional development). **Cost:** The average cost per youth is R$810 (US$385) a month, or R$4,680 (US$2,225) for the entire curriculum (2014 dollars).	**Authors:** Calero and others (2014) **Type:** RCT **Location:** Rio de Janeiro, Brazil **Follow-up:** 1–2 months for the first cohort; 4–5 months for the second cohort; and 2–3 months for the third cohort. **Sample:** 380 individuals: 162 in the treatment group, 195 in the control group, and 23 nonrandomly assigned treated youths (preselected because of high vulnerability and high achievement, high need, or because participating sibling enrolled). Attrition was 77%. **Term used:** Life skills/emotional skills	**Economic related:** Employment during final week after four to five months (+)**; employment in salaried job during final week (+)***; monthly labor income (+)*; saving as main expenditure (+)** *Note:* No impact on personality-related traits (measured through Grit and the social and personal competencies scales, which capture leadership, behavior in situations of conflict, self-esteem, abilities to relate to others, order, and empathy and communication skills). No impacts on social activities or risky behavior.

table continues next page

Table C.1 Out-of-School Program Descriptions *(continued)*

Program		*Evaluation*	
Name	*Description*	*Author/description*	*Results*
Apprenticeship Training for Vulnerable Youth in Malawi	**Beneficiaries:** HIV/AIDS-vulnerable youths (poor, orphans, or school dropouts) who have dropped out of school and are younger than age 24 **Objective:** Improve vulnerable youths' labor market outcomes and welfare. **Description:** Vocational training apprenticeship is combined with entrepreneurial support and life skills training. Participants received apprenticeship training in the selected occupations (bricklaying, car repair, tailoring, and hairstyling; carpentry and joinery, fabrication, and welding among others in master craftsperson's shops) and were encouraged to start their own business upon completing training. The duration and quality of training vary by trade and master craftsperson, as each trade has a different curriculum and length of training. Master craftsperson received one-day training programs. Additionally, half of those trained received an individual "pep talk" that transmitted confidence and positivity. **Cost:** n/a	**Authors:** Cho and others (2013) **Type:** RCT **Location:** Malawi **Follow-up:** On average, 4 months after training **Sample:** 1,900 vulnerable youths: two-thirds were assigned to treatment, and one-third were assigned to control. **Term used:** Life skills	**Health related:** HIV testing among women (+)*; delay in marriage and births among women (+)** **Behavior related:** Happy and satisfied with life (+)***; perception that life has improved during the past year (+)***; felt stressed or nervous in past month (–)* **Academic related:** Knowledge of trades (+)***; knowledge of how to calculate profits of a business (+)***; knowledge of how to start a business (+)***; time spent on learning and training (+)*** **Economic related:** Time spent on traveling to work opportunities (–)**; perception that being an entrepreneur is better than being an employee (+)***; perception that the individual is able to earn money outside farming (+)*** *Note:* Only limited impact was found on new business activities and increased earnings. A benign, short "pep-talk" is found to be effective in reinforcing some of the positive results, which could be easily replicated in other programs at low cost.
Ninaweza	**Beneficiaries:** Unemployed young women living in informal settlements around Nairobi, Kenya **Objective:** Improve the employability and earning capacity of young women living in the informal settlements of Nairobi. **Description:** Ninaweza is a youth employability program providing young women with technical training in information and communication technology (ICT),	**Authors:** Alvarez de Azevedo, Davis, and Charles (2013) **Type:** RCT **Location:** Kenya **Follow-up:** After training (8 weeks) and after the internship and job placement support (6 months) **Sample:** 1,510 youths randomly assigned into one of three groups: (a) 350 received	**Behavior related:** Confidence levels of those who previously were not confident (+)*** **Academic/cognitive related:** Knowledge of ICT (+)***; knowledge of life skills for treatment 1 (+)*** **Economic related:** Probability of obtaining a job for those with treatment 1 (+)**; weekly income (+)***

table continues next page

Table C.1 Out-of-School Program Descriptions *(continued)*

Program		Evaluation	
Name	*Description*	*Author/description*	*Results*
	training in life skills, work experience through internships, and job placement support. **Cost:** n/a	treatment 1, which consisted of ICT and life skills, along with on-the-job experience through internships and job placement support; (b) 350 received treatment 2, which included everything in treatment 1 except for the life skills training; and (c) 810 acted as a control group and received none of the program. **Term used:** Life skills training	*Note:* Although both treatment groups faced statistically significant impacts on knowledge of ICT and weekly income, treatment 1 had greater impacts with regard to ICT knowledge and smaller impacts on weekly income when compared with treatment 2.
Jordan New Opportunities for Women (Jordan NOW)	**Beneficiaries:** Women graduating from eight public community colleges **Objective:** Assist female community college graduates in finding employment. **Description:** The project tested two programs: (a) a subsidy paid to employers equivalent to the minimum wage for up to six months if they hired the graduate and (b) 45 hours of employability skills training. The training course was 45 hours over nine days (5 hours per day), with a maximum of 30 participants in each training group. The course covered effective communication and business writing skills (such as making presentations and writing business reports and different types of correspondence), team-building and teamwork skills (such as characteristics of a successful team, how to work in different roles within a team), time management, positive thinking and how to use it in business situations, excellence in providing customer service, and résumé and interviewing skills. **Cost:** The cost of the voucher was JD 150 each month, for six months. The cost of the soft skills training was US$400 per assigned graduate.	**Authors:** Groh and others (2012) **Type:** RCT **Location:** Jordan **Follow-up:** 6 and 14 months after the start of the programs **Sample:** 1,347 women graduates randomly divided into four groups: (a) 299 were given a voucher that would pay employers a subsidy equivalent to the minimum wage for up to six months if they hired the graduate, (b) 300 were invited to attend 45 hours of employability skills training designed to provide them with the soft skills employers say graduates often lack, (c) 299 were offered both programs, and (d) 449 formed the control group. **Term used:** Soft skills	**Behavior related:** For group with voucher or both, life ladder (+)***; mobility index (+)***; life ladder for the future for those assigned to training (+)**; mental health for those assigned to training (+)* **Economic related:** For job voucher group: employment (+)***; employed and registered for social security (+)**; ever employed (+)***; months employed since graduation (+)***; work income (+)***; hours worked in past week (+)***; soft skills training's effect on employment outside the capital (+) *Note:* The impacts on the number of hours worked during the previous week occurred mostly in the nonformal sector. The effect was smaller and not statistically significant four months after the voucher period. Finally, the impacts were stronger outside the capital city.

table continues next page

Table C.1 Out-of-School Program Descriptions *(continued)*

Program		Evaluation	
Name	*Description*	*Author/description*	*Results*
entra21	**Beneficiaries:** Unemployed youths (ages 18 to 30) who have finished high school and have a total family income below the poverty line **Objective:** Facilitate job placement for unemployed youth. **Description:** The program has several components: (a) 100 hours of in-class training for an *oficio* (job), which results from actual employers' demands; (b) 64 hours of training on ICTs and life skills; (c) 704 hours of internship; and (d) 16 hours that varied from basic skills to extra in-class technical training according to each type of course. **Cost:** About US$1,722 per participant	**Authors:** Alzúa, Cruces, and Lopez Erazo (2013) **Type:** RCT **Location:** Córdoba, Argentina **Follow-up:** 2 years **Sample:** 407 individuals: 220 randomly assigned to treatment (only 178 participated in the program) and 187 as controls **Term used:** Life skills	**Economic related:** Formal employment for men (+)*** and younger participants [18–24] (+)**; earnings (+)**; credit in good standing for men (+)*** and younger participants [18–24] (+)***; welfare dependency [Asignación Universal por Hijo] for women ages 18–24 (–)**
Economic Empowerment of Adolescent Girls and Young Women (EPAG) program	**Beneficiaries:** Young women who (a) were ages 16 to 27, (b) possessed basic literacy and numeracy skills, (c) were not enrolled in school within several months before program initiation, and (d) resided in one of nine target communities in and around Monrovia, Liberia. **Objective:** Increase employment and income of young Liberian women by providing livelihood and life skills training and facilitating their transition to productive work. **Description:** The program combined six months of classroom-based technical and life skills training, with a focus on skills with high market demand, followed by six months of follow-up support to acquire wage employment or start a business. Upon recruitment, the participants were assigned to a job skills (JS) track or a business development services (BDS) track. The JS track provided training in six areas: (a) hospitality, (b) professional cleaning/waste management, (c) office/computer skills, (d) professional house/office painting, (e) security guard services, and (f) professional driving. The BDS training taught young	**Authors:** Adoho and others (2014) **Type:** RCT **Location:** Liberia **Follow-up:** 6 months after the program **Sample:** 2,042 young women randomly assigned to one of two treatments: (a) 1,273 assigned to the first round of training and (b) 769 assigned to a control group (who would participate in the second round of training). **Term used:** Life skills	**Behavior related:** Self-confidence (+)***; anxiety about circumstances and the future (–)**; gender norms (+)*** **Economic related:** Participation in income-generating activities (+)*** [for JS trainees (+)**; for BDS trainees (+)***]; wage employment for JS trainees (+)***; self-employment for BDS trainees (+)***; intensive employment (+)***; earnings (+)*** [especially for BDS trainees]; access to money (+)***; food security (+); savings (+)*** *Note:* No impact on fertility or sexual behavior.

table continues next page

Table C.1 Out-of-School Program Descriptions *(continued)*

Program		Evaluation	
Name	*Description*	*Author/description*	*Results*
	women how to identify microenterprise opportunities on the basis of an assessment of market needs and how to grow and manage any existing businesses they already had. EPAG trainees were given incentives to participate and to make the most of their training: (a) they signed trainee commitment forms at the start of training, (b) they were paid small stipends and a completion bonus contingent upon attendance, (c) they were offered free child care at every training site, (d) they were assisted in opening a savings account at a local bank for their stipend money, and (e) they were formed into small groups or "EPAG teams," each with a coach or mentor, to foster support networks and boost attendance. **Cost:** The unit cost of training in round 1 was about US$1,200 for the BDS track and US$1,650 for the JS track.		
Questscope Non-Formal Education program	**Beneficiaries:** Out-of-school youth typically in low-income communities (13- to 18-year-old males and 13- to 21-year-old females). The program also enrolls large numbers of Iraqi refugees. **Objective:** Integrate school dropouts into society (education, job, and so forth). **Description:** Questscope Non-Formal Education is a two-year program that consists of three eight-month education cycles based on participatory methodology. At the end of the program, graduates receive a 10th-grade alternative certificate that enables them to participate in vocational training and receive government business loans. The program takes place five days a week outside traditional school hours and has two- to three-hour sessions.	**Authors:** Morton and Montgomery (2012) **Type:** RCT **Location:** Jordan **Follow-up:** 4 months after the program started (at the end of the first part of the program cycle) **Sample:** 127 Jordanian youths (male and female) with a mean age of 15.91 years, randomly assigned to (a) an empowerment-based nonformal education program (67 youths) or (b) a wait-list comparison (60 youths) **Term used:** Social skills	**Behavior related:** Conduct problems (–)**; prosocial behavior in high-quality implementation centers with males (+)**; local adult connectedness and hyperactivity in low-quality implementation centers with males (–)**; social support of friends for high-attendance youths (+)* *Note:* No significant effects found for developmental assets (self-efficacy or social skills).

table continues next page

Table C.1 Out-of-School Program Descriptions *(continued)*

Program		*Evaluation*	
Name	*Description*	*Author/description*	*Results*
	Participants need to attend at least two sessions per week in order to receive their certificate. Trained adult facilitators deliver sessions with the following content: educationally, each session includes dialogue-based learning activities (for example, related to literacy, math, science, religion, and English). **Cost:** n/a		
Job Corps	**Beneficiaries:** Disadvantaged youth. Applicants must meet 11 criteria to be eligible: (a) be 16 to 24 years of age; (b) be a legal U.S. resident; (c) be economically disadvantaged (receiving welfare or food stamps or having income less than 70% of Department of Labor's "lower living standards income level"); (d) live in an environment characterized by a disruptive home life, high crime rates, or limited job opportunities; (e) need additional education, training, or job skills; (f) be free of serious behavioral problems; (g) have a clean health history; (h) have an adequate child care plan (for those with children); (i) have registered with the Selective Service Board (if applicable); (j) have parental consent (for minors); and (k) be judged to have the capability and aspirations to participate in Job Corps. **Objective:** Help youths become more responsible, employable, and productive citizens. **Description:** Participants receive intensive vocational training (in more than 75 trades), academic education (which aims to alleviate deficits in reading, math, and writing skills and to provide a GED certificate) and a wide range of other services, including counseling, social skills training, and health education.	**Authors:** Schochet, Burghardt, and McConnell (2008) **Type:** RCT **Location:** United States (nationally representative study) **Follow-up:** Survey data collected 4 years after random assignment; tax information collected 9 years after random assignment **Sample:** Nearly 81,000 youth randomly assigned: (a) 9,409 receiving Job Corps training; (b) 5,977 in control group, not receiving Job Corps training but able to enroll in other available programs (about 70% of the controls enrolled in other training programs in the four-year period after random assignment); and (c) program nonresearch group **Term used:** Social skills training	**Health related:** Health insurance (+)* **Behavior related:** Arrests and conviction rates (–)* **Academic/cognitive related:** Percentage ever enrolled in an education or training program during the 48 months after random assignment (+)*; average hours ever in education or training (+)*; degrees, diplomas, and certificates received (+)*; GED certificate (+)*; high school diploma (–)*; vocational, technical, or trade certificate (+)* **Economic related:** Percentage employed in previous three months (+)*; hourly wage (+)*; paid vacation (+)*; retirement or pension benefits (+)*

table continues next page

Table C.1 Out-of-School Program Descriptions *(continued)*

Program		*Evaluation*	
Name	*Description*	*Author/description*	*Results*
	Most participants reside at a center while training and receive meals and health and dental care and can participate in student government and recreation activities. Job Corps provides placement services to help participants find jobs or pursue additional training. **Cost:** About US$16,500 per participant (1995 dollars)		
Empowerment and Livelihood for Adolescents (ELA) program	**Beneficiaries:** Adolescent girls ages 14 to 20 **Objective:** Empower Ugandan women along economic and reproductive dimensions. **Description:** The program provides (a) vocational skills to enable adolescent girls to start small-scale, income-generating activities, including hairdressing, tailoring, computing, agriculture, poultry rearing, and small trade operations; and (b) life skills, including sexual and reproductive health, menstruation and menstrual disorders, pregnancy, sexually transmitted infections, HIV/AIDS awareness, family planning, rape, management skills, negotiation and conflict resolution, leadership among adolescents, bride price, child marriage, and violence against women. In addition, the clubs also host popular recreational activities, such as reading, staging dramas, singing, dancing, and playing games. The intervention is delivered from designated "adolescent development clubs" (a fixed meeting place in each community) rather than in schools. Clubs are typically open five afternoons per week and timed so that girls enrolled full-time in school can attend. Club activities are led by a trained female mentor from the community. **Cost:** US$85 per participating adolescent girl (2008 dollars)	**Authors:** Bandiera and others (2014) **Type:** RCT **Location:** Uganda **Follow-up:** 2 years after program initiated **Sample:** 4,800 girls living in 100 communities: 50 communities assigned to control and 50 to treatment **Term used:** Life skills	**Health related:** Teenage pregnancy (–)**; adolescent girls reporting having sex unwillingly (–)**; knowledge about pregnancy (+)** and HIV (+)***; if sexually active, use of condom (+)*** **Behavior related:** Gender empowerment index (+)***; early entry into marriage/cohabitation (–)***; self-reported anxieties about finding a good job in adulthood (–)***; perception of suitable ages for marriage (+)***; preferred number of children (–)***; perception of suitable age for pregnancy (+)***; girls' expectations about their own daughters' age at marriage (+)*** **Academic/cognitive related:** Plan to start/return to school for girls who dropped out (+)*; number of hours spent on going to and attending school, homework, or study per week, for enrolled girls (+)* **Economic related:** Entrepreneurial ability (+) ***; engagement in income-generating activity (+)***; self-employed (+)***; monthly consumption expenditure (+)***

table continues next page

Table C.1 Out-of-School Program Descriptions *(continued)*

Program		*Evaluation*	
Name	*Description*	*Author/description*	*Results*
JOBS program	**Beneficiaries:** Individuals who had recently lost a job and were unemployed for no longer than 13 weeks **Objectives:** Prevent and reduce negative effects on mental health associated with unemployment and job-seeking stress, while promoting high-quality reemployment. **Description:** This job-search skill enhancement seminar is carried out in five four-hour sessions conducted in the morning for one week. The program teaches participants effective strategies for finding and obtaining suitable employment, as well as for anticipating and dealing with the inevitable setbacks they will encounter. The program also incorporates elements to increase participants' self-esteem, sense of control, and job search self-efficacy. **Cost:** n/a	**Authors:** Vinokur and others (2000) **Type:** RCT **Location:** United States **Follow-up:** 2 years **Sample:** 1,801 individuals who had recently lost a job and were unemployed for no longer than 13 weeks **Term used:** mental health	**Health related:** Depressive symptoms (–)*; likelihood of experiencing a major depressive episode in the past year (–)* **Behavior related:** Role and emotional functioning (+)* **Economic related:** Reemployment (+)**; hours working per week (+)**; months working more than 35 hours (+)*; monthly income (+) ** *Note:* No effect on quality of job as assessed by wage rate, stability, or fringe benefits.
National Guard Youth ChalleNGe Program	**Beneficiaries:** Young people between the ages of 16 and 18 who have dropped out of (or have been expelled from) school and are unemployed, drug free, and not heavily involved with the justice system **Objective:** Reclaim the lives of at-risk youth who have dropped out. **Description:** The 17-month program is divided into three phases: (a) pre-ChalleNGe, a two-week orientation and assessment period (candidates are introduced to the program's rules and expectations; learn military bearing, discipline, and teamwork; and begin physical fitness training); (b) a 20-week residential phase structured around leadership/followership, responsible citizenship, service to the community, life-coping skills, physical fitness, health and hygiene, job skills, and academic excellence; and	**Authors:** Bloom, Gardenhire-Crooks, and Mandsager (2009); Millenky, Bloom, and Dillon (2010); Millenky and others (2011); Perez-Arce and others (2012) **Type:** RCT **Location:** United States **Follow-up:** 3 years after **Sample:** 1,173 young people randomly assigned to intervention (722) or control (451) **Term used:** life-coping skills	**Health related:** Overweight 36 months after program completion (–)**; very good/excellent health 9 months after program completion (+)***; obesity 9 months after program completion (–)**; always uses birth control 36 months after program completion (–)**; ever used other illegal drugs 36 months after program completion (+)* **Behavior related:** Collective civic efficacy (+)**; conventional citizen scale (+)*; arrest, conviction, and incarceration rates 9 months after program completion (–)**; conviction and violent incidents 21 months after program completion (–)**; property incidents 21 months after program completion (–)***

table continues next page

Table C.1 Out-of-School Program Descriptions *(continued)*

Program		*Evaluation*	
Name	*Description*	*Author/description*	*Results*
	(c) a one-year postresidential phase featuring a mentoring program. During the first two phases, participants live at the program site, often on a military base. The environment is "quasi-military," though there are no requirements for military service. **Cost:** US$11,630 per admitted student		**Academic/cognitive related:** Earned GED certificate (+)***; earned college credits (+)***; vocational training after 21 and 36 months(+)**; currently taking college courses (+)**; involved in job training after 9 months (+)*; attending high school after 9 and 21 months (+)***; preparing for GED after 9 and 21 months (+)** **Economic related:** Employment 9 months after (+)***, 21 months after (+)*, 36 months after program completion (+)**; weekly earnings 21 months after (+)*** and 36 months after program completion (+)*; earnings over the past 12 months, 36 months after program completion (+)***; number of months employed 36 months after program completion(+)***; living at parents' home (–)*; living at own home or apartment (+)** *Note:* No impacts on self-reported arrests/convictions, self-reported delinquency 36 months after program completion. Some negative impacts on health outcomes. No impacts on leadership and life-coping skills. Little impact on civic engagements.
Year Up	**Beneficiaries:** Low-income young adults, ages 18 to 24 **Objective:** Prepare vulnerable adults for positions with good wages and career advancement opportunities in the information technology and investment operations fields. **Description:** The program provides (a) six months of technical skills training that is regularly updated to meet the needs of the program's corporate partners	**Authors:** Roder and Elliot (2011) **Type:** RCT **Location:** United States **Follow-up:** 24 to 30 months after random assignment **Sample:** 164 young adults randomly assigned for treatment (120) or control (44) **Term used:** Professional skills	**Economic related:** Earnings (+)*; full-time employment (+)*; working in targeted fields (+) *Note:* No effect on college attendance.

table continues next page

Table C.1 Out-of-School Program Descriptions *(continued)*

Program		*Evaluation*	
Name	*Description*	*Author/description*	*Results*
	(includes basic training on operating systems and word processing, spreadsheet, and presentation software, and so forth), (b) classes in business writing and communications, (c) instruction on professional skills through both classroom training and enforcement of a performance contract on the rules of professional behavior (students must maintain high attendance rates, be on time, and complete assignments; additional skills taught include how to present oneself [dress and body language], interact with coworkers, make small talk, engage in social networking, and manage conflict), (d) support and guidance for personal or programmatic issues, and (e) assistance with job search process and/or college enrollment upon completion. **Cost:** n/a		
Violence prevention programs			
Program H	**Beneficiaries:** Young men ages 14 to 25 in three low-income communities (*favelas*) **Objective:** Help young men question traditional gender norms and behavior, including violence against women. **Description:** The program includes educational activities and community campaigns. One intervention component was six months of interactive group education sessions for young men led by adult male facilitators. The other was a community-wide "lifestyle" social marketing campaign to promote condom use, using gender-equitable messages that also reinforced those promoted in the group education sessions. The education sessions took place weekly for about 2 hours each over approximately six months, for a total of about 28 hours. **Cost:** n/a	**Authors:** Pulerwitz and others (2006) **Type:** Quasi-experimental **Location:** Rio de Janeiro, Brazil **Follow-up:** 12 months after the end of the activities **Sample:** 780 men in low-income communities were divided into three groups: (a) 258 received the education intervention only, (b) 250 received education and the community lifestyle campaign, and (c) 272 received a delayed intervention after a control period. **Term used:** Attitudes and behaviors	**Health related:** Sexually transmitted infection symptoms (–)*** **Behavior related:** Support of inequitable norms (–)** *Note:* The effect was equally great in both intervention groups, suggesting group education was most important.

table continues next page

Table C.1 Out-of-School Program Descriptions *(continued)*

Program		*Evaluation*	
Name	*Description*	*Author/description*	*Results*
Involucrando Hombres Jóvenes en el Fin de la Violencia de Género	**Beneficiaries:** Young men between ages 15 and 19 **Objective:** Prevent violence through socioeducational workshops. **Description:** The school- and health-sector-based intervention included educational workshops held for young men (through the public health sector and in public schools) on the prevention of violence against women, alternatives to violence, and gender equality. School programs lasted from three to five months. **Cost:** n/a	**Authors:** Obach, Sadler, and Aguayo (2011) **Type:** Quasi-experimental design, pre- and posttest with control **Location:** Chile **Follow-up:** At the end of the workshop (3 to 5 months) **Sample:** The sample was divided into two groups: (a) intervention, which had 260 individuals in the pretest and 153 in the posttest; and (b) control, which had 250 pretest and 150 posttest participants. **Term used:** Social skills	**Behavior related:** Attitudes about gender equality (+)***; violence toward partner index (–)***; stalking others index (–)** *Note:* No impact on the use of contraceptive methods.
Coping with work			
Team Awareness	**Beneficiaries:** Individuals ages 18 to 55+ **Objective:** Decrease substance abuse resulting from stress at work. **Description:** The study examined two prevention programs for small business: 1. *Team Awareness-SB (Team)*, which is a shortened version (lasting four hours) of *Team Awareness*, which seeks to decrease substance abuse by addressing stress, the social use of alcohol by coworkers, and ways to get help for problems. The training was delivered to groups of 6 to 28 individuals and included information, games, role playing, and other activities on substance abuse prevention, as well as individual employee roles in prevention, risks, and strengths in the workplace; communication; and peer referral skills. 2. *Choices in Health Promotion (Choices)* is derived from *Healthy Workplace*, which emphasizes the benefits of decreasing substance use and healthy alternatives to substance use. *Choices* combines elements from	**Authors:** Patterson, Bennett, and Wiitala (2005) **Type:** RCT **Location:** United States: southwestern urban and suburban communities **Follow-up:** 2 weeks after the training **Sample:** 530 employees of small businesses (<500) in industries identified as high risk for alcohol and drug abuse (construction, small-aircraft pilot, maintenance, bus driver, materials moving, hotels, and other services) were randomly assigned to three groups: (a) 194 into *Team*, (b) 124 into *Choices*, and (c) 212 into control. **Term used:** Emotional and social health	**Health related:** Use of tobacco to unwind in women in *Choices* (+)*; use of over-the-counter drugs in women receiving *Choices* (–)**; use of over-the-counter drugs in women receiving *Team* (+)** **Behavior related:** Positive unwinding behaviors for *Team* (+)*** and *Choices* (+)** (especially in men) *Note:* Training did not significantly change substance unwinding.

table continues next page

Table C.1 Out-of-School Program Descriptions *(continued)*

Program		*Evaluation*	
Name	*Description*	*Author/description*	*Results*
	Healthy Workplace and *Team Awareness* and a program in time management and spiritual health into a customized program. Participants set personal goals based on the customized program (it starts with a one-hour face-to-face interview), which helps them create a sense of optimism and future-mindedness. The topics covered include stress management, tobacco, active lifestyle, healthy eating, parenting, time management and spiritual health, safety in the workplace, information on alcohol and moderate drinking, prescription drug use, and team awareness. Then, a four-hour program is developed and carried out with 6 to 39 individuals. Both programs promote social interaction, bonding, and shared positive experiences among training participants. **Cost:** n/a		
Returning children to school			
Kingston YMCA Youth Development Programme	**Beneficiaries:** At-risk, low-income, inner-city male adolescents ages 14 to 17 who are not attending school because of academic or social problems, typically aggressive and defiant behavior **Objective:** Provide at-risk, low-income males with intensive remedial education, social skills training, and personal development. **Description:** Participants attend the program daily (in lieu of regular school) until they have attained proficiency on the grade 9 achievement test and are returned to regular schools. The typical length of program participation is four years. Participants receive comprehensive services, including daily	**Authors:** Guerra and others (2010) **Type:** Post hoc analysis **Location:** Jamaica **Follow-up:** 6 months (RCT) and 5 years with matching **Sample:** Two samples: (a) 180 males, 125 of whom were currently enrolled in the program for at least 6 months and 55 of whom were in a wait-list control group; and (b) 116 males, including 56 program graduates and a matched sample of 60 community controls **Term used:** Social/life skills	**Behavior related:** Aggressive behavior (–)**; aggressive propensity (–)***

table continues next page

Table C.1 Out-of-School Program Descriptions *(continued)*

Program		*Evaluation*	
Name	*Description*	*Author/description*	*Results*
	supervision (from 9:00 a.m. to 4:00 p.m.), remedial education (20 students per teacher), vocational training, social/life skills instruction, recreation, and positive behavior management. Although no specific social skills curricula are used, the program relies heavily on counseling, guidance, and authoritative discipline (emphasizing rewards for positive behavior), and providing positive male and female role models. **Cost:** n/a		
Decrease sexual risk			
Joven Noble	**Beneficiaries:** Latino male youths ages 10 to 24 **Objectives:** Promote positive youth development, support, and leadership, while preventing a number of risk-related sexual behaviors within a cultural context **Description:** This 10-week curriculum aimed at promoting the character development of young men, while targeting the reduction and prevention of unwanted or unplanned pregnancies, substance abuse, and community violence, and increasing the ability of youths to act in a responsible and respectful way in reference to their relationship. **Cost:** n/a	**Authors:** Tello and others (2010) **Type:** Quasi-experimental **Location:** United States **Follow-up:** After the sessions **Sample:** 683 adolescent Latino males ages 13 to 17: 64% came from middle school and high school, whereas 36% were recruited from probation and community-based programs. These individuals were unemployed and looking for work. **Term used:** Character development	**Health related:** Sexual activity (+)**; alcohol or drug consumption before sexual intercourse (–)***; report on having sex for money, drugs, or other things (–)***; HIV risk knowledge (+)*** **Behavior related:** Attitudes toward abstinence (+)***; perceived risk (+)***; Children and Adolescent Prevention Scale (CAPS) talk (+)***; CAPS cool sex (+)***; cultural esteem (–)***. **Other:** Cultural knowledge and beliefs; cultural esteem

Note: AIDS = acquired immune deficiency syndrome; GED = General Educational Development; HIV = human immunodeficiency virus; RCT = randomized control trial; n/a = not available. Significance levels of results, positive (+) or negative (–), are reported at 1 percent (*), 5 percent (**), and 10 percent (***).

Table C.2 Out-of-School Programs by Component

Program	*Stipend/ subsidy*	*Classroom training*	*Counseling/ mentoring*	*On-the-job training/internship/ apprenticeship*
Apprenticeship Training for Vulnerable Youth in Malawi		X	X	X
Ninaweza		X	X	X
Jóvenes en Acción	X	X		X
Juventud y Empleo	X	X		X
Procajoven		X		X
entra21		X		X
Jordan NOW	X	X		
Galpão Aplauso		X	X	
EPAG program		X	X	
Job Corps		X	X	
National Guard Youth ChalleNGe Program		X	X	
Year Up		X	X	
Kingston YMCA Youth Development Programme		X	X	
Questscope Non-Formal Education program		X		
Empowerment and Livelihood for Adolescents (ELA) program		X		
JOBS program		X		
Program H		X		
Involucrando Hombres Jóvenes en el Fin de la Violencia de Género		X		
Team Awareness		X		
Joven Noble		X		
	3	20	8	6

Note: Shading indicates that the program includes that particular component EPAG = Economic Empowerment of Adolescent Girls and Young Women; NOW = New Opportunities for Women; YMCA = Young Men's Christian Association.

References

Adoho, Franck, Shubha Chakravarty, Dala T. Korkoyah, Mattias Lundberg, and Afia Tasneem. 2014. "The Impact of an Adolescent Girls Employment Program: The EPAG Project in Liberia." Policy Research Working Paper 6832, World Bank, Washington, DC.

Alvarez de Azevedo, Thomaz, Jeff Davis, and Munene Charles. 2013. "Testing What Works in Youth Employment: Evaluating Kenya's Ninaweza Program." Global Partnership for Youth Employment, Washington, DC.

Alzúa, María Laura, Guillermo Cruces, and Carolina Lopez Erazo. 2013. "Youth Training Programs beyond Employment: Evidence from a Randomized Controlled Trial." https://www2.unine.ch/files/content/sites/irene/files/shared/documents/seminaires/Alzua.pdf.

Attanasio, Orazio, Adriana Kugler, and Costas Meghir. 2008. "Training Disadvantaged Youth in Latin America: Evidence from a Randomized Trial." NBER Working Paper13931, National Bureau of Economic Research, Cambridge, MA.

———. 2009. "Subsidizing Vocational Training for Disadvantaged Youth in Developing Countries: Evidence from a Randomized Trial." IZA Discussion Paper 4251, Institute for the Study of Labor, Bonn.

———. 2011. "Subsidizing Vocational Training for Disadvantaged Youth in Colombia: Evidence from a Randomized Trial." *American Economic Journal: Applied Economics* 3 (3): 188–220.

Bandiera, Oriana, Niklas Buehren, Robin Burgess, Markus Goldstein, Selim Gulesci, Imran Rasul, and Munshi Sulaiman. 2014. "Women's Empowerment in Action: Evidence from a Randomized Control Trial in Africa." Suntory and Toyota International Centres for Economics and Related Disciplines, London School of Economics.

Bloom, Dan, Alissa Gardenhire-Crooks, and Conrad Mandsager. 2009. "Reengaging High School Dropouts: Early Results of the National Guard Youth ChalleNGe Program Evaluation." Report, MDRC, New York.

Calero, Carla, Carlos Henrique Corseuil, Veronica Gonzales, Jochen Kluve, and Yuri Soares. 2014. "Can Arts-Based Interventions Enhance Labor Market Outcomes among Youth? Evidence from a Randomized Trial in Rio de Janeiro." IZA Discussion Paper 8210, Institute for the Study of Labor, Bonn.

Cho, Yoonyoung, Davie Kalomba, Mushfiq Mobarak, and Victor Orozco. 2013. "Gender Differences in the Effects of Vocational Training: Constraints on Women and Drop-Out Behavior." Policy Research Working Paper 6545, World Bank, Washington, DC.

Groh, Matthew, Nandini Krishnan, David McKenzie, and Tara Vishwanath. 2012. "Soft Skills or Hard Cash? The Impact of Training and Wage Subsidy Programs on Female Youth Employment in Jordan." Policy Research Working Paper 6141, World Bank, Washington, DC.

Guerra, Nancy G., Kirk Williams, Julie Meeks-Gardner, and Ian Walker. 2010. "The Kingston YMCA Youth Development Programme: Impact on Violence among At-Risk Youth in Jamaica." Caribbean Child Development Centre, University of the West Indies, Kingston, Jamaica.

Ibarrarán, Pablo, Laura Ripani, Bibliana Taboada, Juan Miguel Villa, and Brigida Garcia. 2014. "Life Skills, Employability and Training for Disadvantaged Youth: Evidence from a Randomized Evaluation Design." *IZA Journal of Labor and Development* 3 (1): 1–24.

Ibarrarán, Pablo, and David Rosas-Shady. 2006. "Impact Evaluation of the Job Training Component (PROCAJOVEN) of the Assistance Program for the Building of a Training and Employment System in Panama (PN0125)." Report, Inter-American Development Bank, Washington, DC.

Millenky, Megan, Dan Bloom, and Colleen Dillon. 2010. "Making the Transition: Interim Results of the National Guard Youth ChalleNGe Evaluation." Report, MDRC, New York.

Millenky, Megan, Dan Bloom, Sara Muller-Ravett, and Joseph Broadus. 2011. "Staying on Course: Three-Year Results of the National Guard Youth ChalleNGe Evaluation." Report, MDRC, New York.

Morton, Matthew H., and Paul Montgomery. 2012. "Empowerment-Based Non-Formal Education for Arab Youth: A Pilot Randomized Trial." *Children and Youth Services Review* 34 (2): 417–25.

Obach, Alexandra, Michelle Sadler, and Francisco Aguayo. 2011. "Resultados del proyecto involucrando hombres jóvenes en el fin de la Violencia de Género: Intervención multipaís con evaluación de impacto—Caso Chileno." CulturaSalud/EME, Santiago, Chile.

Patterson, Camille R., Joel B. Bennett, and Wyndy Wiitala. 2005. "Healthy and Unhealthy Stress Unwinding: Promoting Health in Small Businesses." *Journal of Business and Psychology* 20 (2): 221–47.

Perez-Arce, Francisco, Louay Constant, David S. Loughran, and Lynn A. Karoly. 2012. "A Cost–Benefit Analysis of the National Guard Youth ChalleNGe Program." RAND Research Monograph TR1193, RAND Corporation, Santa Monica, CA.

Pulerwitz, Julie, Gary Barker, Márcio Segundo, and Marcos Nascimento. 2006. "Promoting More Gender-Equitable Norms and Behaviors among Young Men as an HIV/AIDS Prevention Strategy." Horizons final report, Population Council, Washington, DC.

Roder, Anne, and Mark Elliott. 2011. "A Promising Start: Year Up's Initial Impacts on Low-Income Young Adults' Careers." Economic Mobility Corporation, New York:

Schochet, Peter Z., John Burghardt, and Sheena McConnell. 2008. "Does Job Corps Work? Impact Findings from the National Job Corps Study." *American Economic Review* 98 (5): 1864–86.

Tello, Jerry, Richard C. Cervantes, David Cordova, and Susana M. Santos. 2010. "Joven Noble: Evaluation of a Culturally Focused Youth Development Program." *Journal of Community Psychology* 38 (6): 799–811.

Vinokur, Amiram D., Yaacov Schul, Jukka Vuori, and Richard H. Price. 2000. "Two Years after a Job Loss: Long-Term Impact of the JOBS Program on Reemployment and Mental Health." *Journal of Occupational Health Psychology* 5 (1): 32–47.

http://dx.doi.org/10.1596/978-1-4648-0872-2

Environmental Benefits Statement

The World Bank Group is committed to reducing its environmental footprint. In support of this commitment, the Publishing and Knowledge Division leverages electronic publishing options and print-on-demand technology, which is located in regional hubs worldwide. Together, these initiatives enable print runs to be lowered and shipping distances decreased, resulting in reduced paper consumption, chemical use, greenhouse gas emissions, and waste.

The Publishing and Knowledge Division follows the recommended standards for paper use set by the Green Press Initiative. The majority of our books are printed on Forest Stewardship Council (FSC)–certified paper, with nearly all containing 50–100 percent recycled content. The recycled fiber in our book paper is either unbleached or bleached using totally chlorine-free (TCF), processed chlorine-free (PCF), or enhanced elemental chlorine-free (EECF) processes.

More information about the Bank's environmental philosophy can be found at http://www.worldbank.org/corporateresponsibility.

http://dx.doi.org/10.1596/978-1-4648-0872-2

www.ingramcontent.com/pod-product-compliance
Lightning Source LLC
Chambersburg PA
CBHW080422270326
41929CB00018B/3126